Direct Social
Work Practice

 SOCIAL WORK IN THE NEW CENTURY

Richard K. Caputo, *Policy Analysis for Social Workers*

Michael Reisch, *Social Policy and Social Justice*

Lisa E. Cox, Carolyn Tice, and Dennis D. Long, *Introduction to Social Work: An Advocacy-Based Profession*

SAGE was founded in 1965 by Sara Miller McCune to support the dissemination of usable knowledge by publishing innovative and high-quality research and teaching content. Today, we publish more than 750 journals, including those of more than 300 learned societies, more than 800 new books per year, and a growing range of library products including archives, data, case studies, reports, conference highlights, and video. SAGE remains majority-owned by our founder, and after Sara's lifetime will become owned by a charitable trust that secures our continued independence.

Los Angeles | London | Washington DC | New Delhi | Singapore | Boston

Direct Social Work Practice

Theories and Skills for Becoming an Evidence-Based Practitioner

Mary C. Ruffolo
University of Michigan

Brian E. Perron
University of Michigan

Elizabeth Harbeck Voshel
University of Michigan

Los Angeles | London | New Delhi
Singapore | Washington DC | Boston

Los Angeles | London | New Delhi
Singapore | Washington DC | Boston

FOR INFORMATION:

SAGE Publications, Inc.
2455 Teller Road
Thousand Oaks, California 91320
E-mail: order@sagepub.com

SAGE Publications Ltd.
1 Oliver's Yard
55 City Road
London EC1Y 1SP
United Kingdom

SAGE Publications India Pvt. Ltd.
B 1/I 1 Mohan Cooperative Industrial Area
Mathura Road, New Delhi 110 044
India

SAGE Publications Asia-Pacific Pte. Ltd.
3 Church Street
#10-04 Samsung Hub
Singapore 049483

Printed in the United States of America

Cataloging-in-publication data is available for this title from the Library of Congress.

ISBN 978-1-4833-7924-1

Acquisitions Editor: Kassie Graves
Editorial Assistant: Carrie Montoya
Associate Digital Content Editor: Lucy Berbeo
Production Editor: Kelly DeRosa
Copy Editor: Erin Livingston
Typesetter: C&M Digitals (P) Ltd.
Proofreader: Annie Lubinsky
Indexer: Jennifer Pairan
Cover Designer: Glenn Vogel
Marketing Manager: Shari Countryman

This book is printed on acid-free paper.

15 16 17 18 19 10 9 8 7 6 5 4 3 2 1

Table of Contents

Acknowledgements   xi

Chapter 1: An Overview of the Book   1

What Is Generalist Social Work Practice?   2

Major Themes in Each Chapter   3

    Advocacy   3

    Social Justice   3

    Global Focus   3

    Ethics   4

    Theory   4

    Critical Thinking   4

How This Book Is Organized   5

Suggestions for the Social Work Student   7

    Theory and Concept Tools   7

    Generalizable Knowledge and Skills   7

    Rationales for Decisions   8

    Technology as a Friend (and Possibly a Foe)   8

Suggestions to the Social Work Instructor   9

Chapter 2: Integrative Themes That Guide Social Work

    Practice with Individuals, Families, and Small Groups   11

Definition of the Social Work Profession and Principles of the Profession   16

The Mission of Social Work   17

Social Justice Lens   18

Core Theoretical Perspectives   20

    Ecological Systems Perspective and the Life Model of Social Work

        Practice Perspective   20

    Empowerment Perspective   24

    Sociocultural Perspective   25

    Evidence-Informed (EI) Practice Perspective   29

Integrating Conceptual Perspectives   31

Chapter Review Questions 32

References 33

Chapter 3: From Evidence-Based Practice to Evidence-Informed Practice 35

Defining Evidence-Based Practice (EBP) 37

Assessment, Diagnosis, and Service/Intervention Planning 41

Decision Making 41

Interpersonal Expertise 42

Self-Reflection and Skill Acquisition 42

Evaluating and Using Research Evidence 42

Understanding Sources of Diversity 43

Seeking and Utilizing Available Resources 43

Establishing a Rationale for Decisions 43

The Challenges in Using the EBP Framework in Social Work 44

Steps in Applying the EBP Framework 46

Resources to Promote Evidence-Based Decisions 50

Moving from EBP to Evidence-Informed (EI) Practice 52

Chapter Review Questions 52

References 53

Chapter 4: Professional Values, Ethics, and Professional Use of Self 55

Professional Social Work Values, Purpose, and Practice Principles 58

NASW Code of Ethics Standards 63

Ethical Decision Making 66

A Closer Look at Self-Determination, Informed Consent and Confidentiality, Privileged Communication, and Technology/Social Media Use 68

Self-Determination 68

Informed Consent and Confidentiality 69

Privileged Communication 70

Technology/Social Media Use 71

Addressing Malpractice and Unethical Behavior 74

Professional Use of Self 75

Chapter Review Questions 75

References 76

Chapter 5: Engagement and Relationship-Building Skills 77

Core Values That Guide Engagement and Relationship-Building Efforts in Social Work Practice 80

Pathways to Services 82

Approaches That Positively Impact the Engagement Phase 85

Skill Building That Emphasizes Collaboration to
Improve Follow-Through 87
The Stages of Change Framework 92
Alliance Building 96
Chapter Review Questions 96
References 96

**Chapter 6: Assessment in Social Work With
Individuals and Families** **99**

Defining Assessment 102
Bio-Psycho-Social-Spiritual Perspective, the
Problem-Based Approach, and the Strengths-
Based/Resiliency Approach to the Assessment Process 104
Multidimensional Functioning (MDF) Assessment 105
Systemic and Strengths-Focused/Resiliency Approach 108
The Bio-Psycho-Social-Spiritual History 110
Key Screening Tools 112
Functioning and Wellness Screening Tools 112
Trauma Assessments and Mandated Reporting Responsibilities 119
Diagnostic and Statistical Manual of Mental Disorders (DSM-5),
Cultural Assessment Tools in the *DSM-5*, and International Statistical
Classification of Diseases and Related Health Problems (ICD-10) 122
Chapter Review Questions 124
References 124

Chapter 7: Change Planning **127**

What Is Change Planning? 129
Core Principles of Change Planning 129
Program-Driven Versus Tailored Change Plans 130
Change Plans Developed Collaboratively 131
Change Plans Informed by Comprehensive Assessment 132
Flexible Change Plans 133
Change Plans Understood by and
Personally Meaningful to the Client 133
Change Goals 134
Intermediary Goals Versus Ultimate Goals 134
Outcomes and Processes 136
Goal Selection 137
Safety 137
Importance to the Client 138
Highest Level of Generalizability 139
Most Impairing 139
Easiest to Address 139

Goal Specification: A SMART Approach 139
   Specific 140
   Measurable 140
   Attainable 141
   Relevant 141
   Time Bound 141
Intervention Selection 142
   Skill Focused 142
   Simple Versus Complex 143
   Generalizable 143
   Resource Sensitive 143
   Evidence Based 143
   Adaptable 144
   Active 144
The Written Change Plan 145
Chapter Review Questions 146
References 146

Chapter 8: Core Intervention Skills: Using Cognitive and Behavioral Approaches in Social Work Practice With Individuals, Families, and Groups 149
The Cognitive Aspect of CBT 151
   Belief Structure 151
Cognitive Restructuring 153
   Step 1. Identifying Thoughts and Interpretations 153
   Step 2. Looking at Thoughts Objectively 158
   Step 3. Restating Unrealistic or Inaccurate Thoughts 160
   Step 4. Adjusting Behavior 160
Behavioral Aspects of CBT 160
ABC from a Behavioral Standpoint 161
   Reinforcement 163
   Punishment 166
   Extinction 167
CBT as an Integrative Framework 168
Practice of CBT 168
   Major Treatment Tasks 169
Structural Features of CBT 169
   Functional Analysis 170
   Skills Training 171
Ongoing Professional Development 173
Chapter Review Questions 173
References 177

Chapter 9: Intervention Skills: Using Problem-Solving, Psychoeducational, and Multisystemic Intervention Approaches and Case/Care Management Skills in Working With Individuals and Families   **179**

Problem-Solving Approach   182
Psychoeducational Approach   187
The Substance Abuse and Mental Health Service
    Administration (SAMHSA) Evidence-Based Toolkit   189
Online Psychoeducational Modules   191
Multiple-Family Psychoeducation Program (MF-PEP)   191
Multisystem Intervention Approaches   193
Case/Care Management Approaches   198
Chapter Review Questions   200
References   200

Chapter 10: Additional Skills for Working With Families and Groups   **203**

Introducing the Core Skills Needed When Working
    With Families and Helping Families to Change   205
Social Work's Mission in Working With Families   205
A Multidimensional Ecosystemic Comparative Approach (MECAmaps)
    to Assess Cultural and Contextual Sociopolitical Contexts   207
Establishing a Relationship With Each Family Member   208
Models of Family Work   209
Special Note: Working With Couples   210
Introducing the Core Skills Needed When Working With Groups   211
Leading Groups and Understanding Group Development Stages   211
Chapter Review Questions   215
References   216

Chapter 11: Outcome Monitoring   **217**

Overview of Outcome Monitoring   219
    What Is the Purpose of Outcome Monitoring?   219
    Are There Any Other Benefits to Outcome Monitoring?   219
Is Outcome Monitoring Research?   220
    Is Outcome Monitoring a Type of Program Evaluation?   221
General Principles of Outcome Monitoring   221
    Systematic and Formal   221
    Repeated Measurements   222
    Quality Over Quantity   223
    Relevance to Change Goals   224
    Accuracy of Measurement Tools   224
Measurement Types and Data Collection   225

Measurement Types 225
Data Collection 230
Summarizing Data and Making Inferences 233
Common Measurement Questions 234
Do I Measure Everything? 234
If I Select an Outcome Measure and Find
That It Isn't Working Well, Can I Change It? 234
If I Find a Standardized Measure—That Is, a
Questionnaire or Inventory—That Already Exists,
Can I Change It to Fit My Needs? 234
How Do I Find Standardized Measures? 234
My Outcome Measures for a Client Involve
Self-Reports. I'm Not Sure If My Client
Is Being Truthful in Reporting. What Should I Do? 235
Chapter Review Questions 235
References 236

**Chapter 12: Lifelong Learning and Professional
Development Over the Life Course** **237**
Your Professional Identity 238
Defining Your Current Professional Identity 238
Defining Your Future Professional Identity 239
Identity Development and Lifelong Learning 240
Supervision and Mentorship 240
Supervision 241
Mentorship 244
Remaining Current With the Research 245
Open Access Journals 245
Really Simple Syndication (RSS) 246
Licensure 248
Continuing Education 249
Professional Social Networks 250
Conclusion 251
References 251

Index **253**

About the Authors **265**

Acknowledgements

The authors and SAGE Publications gratefully acknowledge the contributions of the following reviewers:

Eileen Klein, *Ramapo College of New Jersey*

Herbert P. Shon, *California State University, San Bernardino*

Veronika Ospina-Kammerer, *Saint Leo University*

Christina C. Gigler, MSW, LCSW, ACSW, *Marywood University*

Denise L. Bump, *Keystone College*

Guia Calicdan-Apostle, DSW, MSSW, *the Richard Stockton College of New Jersey*

Maya A. Lewis, *the Richard Stockton College of New Jersey*

Raquel Warley, PhD, LCSW, *California State University, Los Angeles*

Tonya E. Perry, *Alabama A&M University*

Bruce D. Hartsell, *California State University, Bakersfield*

Nancy Giunta, *Hunter College, City University of New York*

Curtis D. Proctor-Artz, *Western New Mexico University*

Karen Rich, *Marywood University*

Ericka Kimball, *Augsburg College*

Jeff Driskell, *Salem State University*

Melissa A. Hensley, *Augsburg College*

R. Maldonado Moore, *Tennessee State University*

*We dedicate this book to our families, who enrich our lives,
and to the social work students we have had the privilege of
seeing develop into competent and committed social work professionals.*

An Overview
of the Book

Preparing a textbook to guide students in their training to become highly skilled generalist social workers who primarily work with individuals, families, and small groups is no easy task. Many different definitions exist for *generalist social work practice.* And, in the absence of a common definition of what constitutes generalist social work practice, it becomes even more difficult to delineate the specific knowledge domains and skill sets of the generalist social worker. We believe that having a clear definition at the outset can be useful in understanding *why* we have given focus to certain content and topics at the expense of excluding others. We also believe that a clear definition can help you develop a framework to help work through the complex decisions that are required of social work practitioners. These may seem like lofty claims, but we don't think they are.

Before moving forward and outlining the content of this chapter and the ensuing chapters, we want to bring your attention to the use of the phrase, "We believe...." This phrase is purposefully used to help explicate certain philosophical positions in which we don't have objectively defined right and wrong answers. In other words, our *beliefs* are not *facts,* but we have rationales for all the content contained in this book as well as the content that has necessarily been excluded for purposes of brevity. At the outset, we believe that generalist practice social workers should be highly skilled in separating beliefs from facts and that every social work decision has a clearly explicated and defensible rationale.

In this introductory chapter, we first provide you with our definition of *generalist social work practice.* Then, we want to raise awareness of a few other beliefs that we consider to be important in our overall educational approach. Finally, we provide separate sections for social work students and social work instructors on how to use this book.

What Is Generalist Social Work Practice?

Generalist social work practice is what a generalist social work practitioner does. This hardly satisfies our insistence on a clear definition, but it provides a good starting point. More specifically, it is suggestive of various activities as well as knowledge and skills that ensure effectiveness and efficiency when engaged in practice-related activities. To help achieve clarity in our definition, we will contrast a generalist with a specialist.

In our view, the primary difference between generalist and specialist social work practice is a matter of breadth versus depth. This may seem like an oversimplification, but the general idea serves our need. That is, we can consider the differences in the types of problems that a social worker could address on any given day. Consider the example of a social worker employed as a case manager at a community mental health center or another health-focused agency. Social workers in these positions have a wide range of tasks and responsibilities. Common responsibilities for this social worker would involve providing individual supportive counseling and facilitating support groups. The social worker will likely have some administrative responsibilities, such as helping clients complete paperwork for benefits or other services, as well as supervising students. Some social workers in these positions might also be engaged in advocacy efforts within the community, reaching out to other community stakeholder groups to provide information on issues and services. Thus, the generalist actively draws upon many different bodies of research, theory, and personal and professional experiences while also considering the roles of social justice within the various systems (e.g., individual, family, community). This can be considered *breadth* of knowledge.

On the other hand, a social work specialist may have a clearly and narrowly defined set of practice-related activities, such as providing therapy to persons with substance use disorders or conducting forensic interviews with children who have been sexually abused. The social work specialist, much like the generalist, may draw upon different bodies of research, theory, and personal and professional experiences, and also consider the role of social justice. However, the scope of the problems encountered by the specialist is more narrowly defined. And, often times, the social work specialist tends to focus on the more difficult or significant problems within a focused area. Thus, their scope in activities and knowledge informing their work are more narrowly defined, and a deeper understanding is typically required.

Hopefully, our delineation does not suggest a preference for either generalist or specialist social work practice. The differences are really a matter of degree, and it is often the case that social workers have to have generalist knowledge and skills as well as a specialty area. We choose to focus on generalist social work practice because we believe that social work practice with individuals, families, and small groups requires a breadth of knowledge and skills. More importantly, the knowledge and skill set of a generalist social worker readily generalizes to the work environment and activities of the specialist social worker. In fact, we take the bold stance that strong generalist knowledge and skills are necessary—but not sufficient!—for all types of social work practice, including specialty practice.

Major Themes in Each Chapter

It would be useful to have a clearly defined list of skills and knowledge to guide your training in generalist social work practice. Unfortunately, this is not possible, but this book is organized around a number of major themes that we believe define *contemporary* social work practice. We also want to emphasize that we consider these to be contemporary themes of generalist social work practice and thus recognize the overall dynamic nature of social work practice. Twenty years ago, one would not have found a strong emphasis on evidence-based decision making or globally focused issues. And it is difficult to say with any degree of certainty what will make the list of essential themes twenty years from now, but envisioning such a list is no mere academic exercise. We believe it is important for social work students to be able to envision possibilities. The core themes we address throughout the book include advocacy, social justice, global focus, ethics, theory, and critical thinking.

Advocacy

Advocacy involves the act of giving support for a specific cause, which we regard as a central function of generalist social work practice. Advocacy can occur at all levels of social work practice (e.g., individuals, families, communities). As you work through the ensuing chapters, we encourage you to think about the different ways you can provide case advocacy for a particular individual or family or advocacy for at-risk or disenfranchised groups.

Social Justice

Social justice is grounded in the related concepts of human rights and equality. The specific rights relate not only to social rights but also to political and economic rights. As social workers, we work to promote these rights for all members of society. When you encounter social work problems, as well as the various scenarios presented in this book, we encourage you to view these problems and scenarios using a social work lens. We devote the next chapter of this text to helping you develop this critical lens.

Global Focus

This text has a strong global focus and includes the diversity of persons, ideas, belief systems, and experiences that one is likely to encounter in contemporary social work practice. A global focus also implies diversity, which is fundamental to the work we do and the values that we espouse as social workers. We encourage you to consider the global relevance of the various issues that are provided in this text. Think about the different mechanisms that give rise to diversity. And consider how your practice decisions might change with a simple change in context—for example, when working with an immigrant population, consider how your work might change based on your client's country of origin. Ultimately, you want to sharpen your thinking to identify the factors that matter most in the services you provide, and bringing a global focus to your work is essential.

Ethics

Social work ethics refers to a system of core values that help define the conduct of social workers. It is often the case that we will encounter difficult decisions and complex situations, and we look to the National Association of Social Workers (NASW) Code of Ethics to assist us in helping to determine and sometimes defend a professional judgment or a particular course of action.

Theory

A *theory* is an organized system of knowledge that helps us describe, explain, and predict social phenomena. Social work is built on many different theories. And as a student of social work, you may have discovered that not all social work professionals and educators agree which are the *best* theories. Of course, the theories presented in this book represent what we consider to be essential theories to inform social work practice. We encourage you to consider the practical utility of these theories, but keep in mind that these represent only a small set of the theories available to help guide your practice.

Critical Thinking

In this text, we attempt to assist you in building a variety of critical thinking skills. For example, we emphasize the importance of articulating rationales for various decisions that you make as a social worker as well as grounding your decisions in the evidence-based practice (EBP) framework. We also encourage integrative thinking—that is, how do we weave together and apply the various themes of the book when making a practice-related decision or taking a particular course of action? In what ways does each theme contribute to these decisions? An entire chapter of this book is devoted to the aspect of EBP and evidence-informed practice, but we hope you will appreciate and learn to apply critical thinking to all aspects of your training and practice.

Our core themes are linked to the 2008 Council on Social Work Education Educational Policy and Accreditation Standards (CSWE–EPAS). The CSWE–EPAS identifies 10 core competencies critical to effective social work practice. Each competency highlights the knowledge, values, and skills that are core to the competency as well as the practice behaviors that social workers need to demonstrate to become proficient in applying these core competencies. Table 1.1 provides the list of core

Table 1.1	10 Core Competencies: 2008 CSWE–EPAS*

1. Professional Identity: Identify as a professional social worker and conduct oneself accordingly.
2. Values and Ethics: Apply social work ethical principles to guide professional practice.
3. Critical Thinking: Apply critical thinking to inform and communicate professional judgments.
4. Diversity: Engage diversity and difference in practice.
5. Social and Economic Justice: Advance human rights and social and economic justice.
6. Research: Engage in research-informed practice and practice-informed research.
7. Human Behavior and Social Environment: Apply knowledge of human behavior and the social environment.
8. Social Policy: Engage in policy practice to advance social and economic well-being and to deliver effective social work services.
9. Organizational Context: Respond to contexts that shape practice.
10. Engagement, Assessment, Intervention, and Evaluation: Engage, assess, intervene, and evaluate with individuals, families, groups, organizations, and communities.

*Please note that the 2015 Draft 1 (October 2013) of the Educational Policy and Accreditation Standards (EPAS) has identified nine social work competencies. These competencies include (1) ethical and professional behavior, (2) diversity and difference, (3) social justice and human rights, (4) practice-informed research and research-informed practice, (5) policy practice, (6) engagement, (7) assessment, (8) intervention, and (9) evaluation (http://www.cswe.org/File.aspx?id=69943).

Source: Council on Social Work Education Educational Policy and Accreditation Standards (EPAS) 2008.

competencies. In each chapter, we will highlight the core competencies emphasized in that particular chapter. Remember, these competencies are considered core to generalist social work practice and need to be a part of every professional social worker's portfolio of knowledge, skills, and abilities. Each core competency has identified practice behaviors that you will need to demonstrate in order to effectively engage in social work practice. You can find the practice behaviors that are linked to each competency at the CSWE website.

How This Book Is Organized

We authored this book with maximum flexibility in mind. Each chapter is designed to stand alone—that is, it does not necessarily call for information or skills from earlier chapters, although we believe that the order of the chapters capitalizes on learning.

Within each chapter, we have developed a variety of features that we would like to take a moment to highlight and explain:

- Chapter Learning Objectives: At the beginning of each chapter, we present a set of learning objectives. Keep these objectives in mind as you read the chapter. These objectives are intended to assist you in identifying the specific knowledge to be acquired. Other learning objectives can also be considered as part of the focus of the chapters, but the expressed objectives are the ones we consider most relevant.
- CSWE Core Competencies: We have worked in earnest to link the chapter content to the required core competencies related to social work knowledge and skills as defined by the CSWE. These core competencies can be of value to students in helping them to identify their specific areas of professional growth and development. For instructors and administrators, these can be used as a way to identify opportunities that can assist in monitoring educational outcomes.
- Case Situations: The case situations describes an issue confronting a social worker. Given our focus on diversity of persons, contexts, and issues, the case situations may not represent your specific interests or the population with whom you work. However, the case situations are intended to serve as a context for discussion and promote critical thinking across a range of issues. You will benefit from working actively to make connections between the case situations and the content covered in the respective chapter as well as in other chapters.
- Reflective Learning Activities: Throughout each chapter, you will find reflective learning activities to help you refine and challenge your thinking. For the reflective learning activities, you will discover that most do not have a single right or wrong answer. We consider the process of applying critical thinking during the activity to be the most important feature. In particular, take time to consider the various sources of information and the manner in which you integrate those sources to inform your ideas and decisions. The companion website for this book (http://study.sagepub.com/ruffolo) contains videos and links that will help you with these activities.
- Chapter Review Questions: Each chapter concludes with review questions. Similar to the other features of the book, these questions are designed to encourage further use and application of the information, which are necessary conditions for deeper understanding and learning. These questions are certainly not comprehensive of the chapter content, and we encourage you to formulate your own questions and actively test yourself on your knowledge building as you use this book.

As noted earlier, each chapter contains a case situation or situations featuring a social worker in action. These case situations are intended to provide a context for the information and skills presented. The case situations are referenced regularly throughout the chapter, so you are encouraged to begin each chapter by carefully reading the case situations.

One additional note about the organization of the book: the skill chapters highlight core skills that cross service settings and client/consumer populations. These core skills have emerged from a review of the evidence-based and evidence-informed practices that have demonstrated positive outcomes for individuals and families. Some of the core skills emphasize working with individuals, some with families, and some are used primarily when working in small groups. You will not find separate chapters focused on working with children, adults, families, or small groups, since the core skills cross all these domains.

Suggestions for the Social Work Student

As we wrote this text, we continually found ourselves wanting to make various suggestions that we believe will enhance your understanding of the material in this book as well as impact your broader social work training. For your convenience, we are providing them here with the hope that they will enhance your understanding of the content of this book as well as help you to highlight your ongoing educational and training needs.

Theory and Concept Tools

It is common to hear social work students express their frustrations with having to learn many different theories, particularly those that may be considered highly abstract without any immediate utility to inform their practice. We recognize the validity of these frustrations. At the same time, we often find that students have a hard time understanding the role that theory plays in sound social work practice. As you work through this book, we encourage you to view theory and the related concepts as tools you can use in your social work practice. More specifically, theory should serve a purpose in helping you describe, explain, and predict social phenomena in your practice. The theories you study and the concepts subsumed by those theories are designed to assist you in dissecting complex problems, which will help you identify and develop avenues for possible solutions.

Unfortunately, applying theories and concepts is a skill that takes a while to develop, and one that we will try to facilitate throughout this book. Toward this end, consider each theoretical system as a lens for viewing problems and issues in your own specific or emerging areas of interest. Actively think about how the theories and concepts apply to problems you encounter, and seek out guidance from your instructor when you don't make strong connections between the context of the text and the work you are involved in during your field placement. We are confident you will acquire a deep appreciation of the importance of theory and that your learning will be enhanced when practice-based connections are made.

Generalizable Knowledge and Skills

Related to the preceding suggestion, we encourage you to consider the *generalizability* of the theories and concepts you acquire, along with their associated technical skills. This means considering how you can apply theory, concepts, and skills broadly to other populations, contexts, and problems. When you seek out new training opportunities, you can further apply this concept by considering the type of knowledge and skills you need to develop that may have a broader application. Establishing a broad-based foundation of knowledge and skills will not only enhance the effectiveness of your practice, it can also open up employment prospects. The diversity of social work practice is rapidly expanding, so the contemporary generalist social worker will need to have knowledge and a skill set that is responsive to the dynamics of the ever-changing environment.

As you work through the activities in this book, continually consider how the theories, concepts, and skills presented can apply to other practice domains. Build upon or change the conditions of each chapter's case situations and consider how the theories, concepts, and skills may or may not apply. And when you look for future training opportunities, identify those opportunities that will apply broadly to different populations, contexts, and problems.

Rationales for Decisions

The primary work that social workers are involved in requires making decisions. A *decision* is broadly defined to include any act that follows careful deliberation. And it is often the case that any given decision represents only one of many decisions involved in an ongoing process. We believe it is essential that social workers develop the capability of providing defensible rationales for all decisions they make while practicing. In other words, providing a rationale means giving a sound and thoughtful justification for your actions (and sometimes inaction). Doing so is important for helping to ensure that a high standard of care for your clients is maintained as well as for providing you with some degree of protection in the event of a resultant legal problem (e.g., malpractice suit). This is not to suggest that rationales will absolve social workers who may be involved in a legal dispute, but a strong rational decision-making process can help ensure a high standard of care and thus reduce the likelihood of legal dispute occurring in the first place.

As you work through the activities throughout this book, try to construct a rationale using and applying the major themes found in this book. For example, what is the existing theory and evidence to support your decision? How does your decision align with the values and principles of social work practice (ethics and social justice)? How did the characteristics of the client influence your decision (diversity)? We believe that a social work student can become more effective and efficient in establishing rationales for decisions by engaging in reflective thinking. Thus, take advantage of the reflective activities throughout this book, in addition to your broader training, to develop and refine this important skill.

Technology as a Friend (and Possibly a Foe)

As you already know, the world in which we live and the context of our social work practice is influenced, at least to some degree, by technology. In fact, we would go so far as to argue that contemporary social work practice is embedded in the world of technology, requiring social workers to have strong technology competencies. Most of our clients are connected to the Internet and use it on a daily basis to manage many different parts of their lives. Thus, it should not be a surprise that many of the problems and issues that arise in social work practice are associated, to some degree, with technology. Virtually all new evidence is communicated in electronic format. Similarly, almost all government programs and services are described and managed in an online environment. And our communications with other professionals are commonly facilitated by some type of technology.

This book is not designed to promote the development of a comprehensive technology skill set. In fact, given the rapid changes in the world of technology, any book on the role of technology in social work practice is likely to be outdated shortly after publication. However, at various points throughout the text, we actively consider the role of technology and how it may impact generalist social work practice. We believe that technology, broadly defined, can be a tool for helping solve problems and improve processes. At the same time, technology can introduce a myriad of unintended consequences. Similar to clearly articulating rationales for your decisions that affect the well-being of your clients, it is also important to have a clear rationale for your use of technology in social work practice.

As you work through this text, we encourage you to continually think about the relevance of technology. For example, learning to use advanced search features of various websites and databases can help you more effectively and efficiently obtain the best available evidence to inform your practice. You should have an awareness of the rapidly changing environment of social media, including developing a sound rationale about how you will use social media in your personal life in ways that will not negatively affect your professional social work practice and developing a professional identity as a social worker. Even if you are a limited user of social media, you should have sufficient knowledge of social media to understand how client problems may manifest in an Internet environment. For example, assume you are working with a teenager who is being harassed/bullied at school because he openly identifies himself as being gay. How might your approach be different if the harassment were also occurring through electronic means—text messages or Facebook? Again, this text does not contain the individual answers to problems such as this, but we strongly encourage you to consider ways of using this book to help you explore possible problems and solutions when faced with the challenges involving technology.

Suggestions to the Social Work Instructor

As previously stated, we have worked in earnest to ensure that this text provides you with what we believe to be the essential knowledge and skills necessary for the development of generalist social work practice. In our approach, we have attempted to promote a general fund of knowledge regarding generalist social work practice along with the identification of core technical skills. Throughout the text, we have created various reflective activities and ethical challenges, which we believe are essential for students' professional growth and development. However, these embedded activities and challenges alone will be beneficial only to the extent that the students are also actively making connections with the practice-based experiences they are involved in while in field placement. Therefore, as an instructor, we strongly encourage you to expand upon or adapt these activities as you see fit, particularly so these activities align with your local context/services.

2

Integrative Themes That Guide Social Work Practice with Individuals, Families, and Small Groups

What an exciting time to be entering the social work profession! This chapter will highlight for you the emerging integrative themes that are guiding social work practice with individuals, families, and small groups. We examine in this chapter how various social contexts influence social work practice. We use a social justice lens to explore guiding principles for social work practice and explore the mission and definition of social work practice.

CHAPTER LEARNING OBJECTIVES

By the end of this chapter, you should be able to

- articulate a working definition of the social work profession;

(Continued)

(Continued)

- apply a social justice lens to the core theoretical perspectives that guide social work practice (ecological systems theory, life model of social work practice, and the empowerment approach);
- apply the sociocultural framework as it relates to relationships among cultures, race/ethnicity, and system disparities in working with client systems;
- apply a meta-systems analysis when working with client systems; and
- integrate principles across the major perspectives that inform contemporary social work practice.

The Council on Social Work Education Educational Policy and Accreditation Standards (CSWE-EPAS) Competencies that are highlighted in more depth in this chapter include the following:

2.1.3 Apply critical thinking to inform and communicate professional judgments.

2.1.4 Engage diversity and difference in practice.

2.1.5 Advance human rights and social and economic justice.

2.1.6 Engage in research-informed practice and practice-informed research.

2.1.7 Apply knowledge of human behavior and the social environment.

2.1.9 Respond to contexts that shape practice.

2.1.10 (a–d) Engage, assess, intervene, and evaluate with individuals, families, groups, and organizations.

We begin this chapter by defining the social work profession and identifying the principles that inform social work practice. We then examine some of the core theoretical perspectives that have guided social work practice (ecological systems theory, life model of social work practice, and the empowerment approach). These perspectives provide us with a way to think about our professional work. We also add the sociocultural framework as an additional context that helps us to think about the relationships among cultures, race/ethnicity, and health disparities or other system disparities. The final perspective that we introduce in this chapter is the evidence-informed (EI) practice perspective, which assists us in selecting a course of action/intervention that works best for individuals and families and identifying under what conditions this action/intervention should occur so as to promote the best practices and outcomes. Chapter 3 will address this perspective in more detail. We conclude this chapter with a discussion of core integrative themes that emerge from these fundamental perspectives. The integrative themes include a meta-systems framework that involves a bio-psycho-social-spiritual perspective in working with individuals and families, a strength orientation, a core commitment to valuing diversity and cultural norms, an emphasis on informed practice that incorporates emerging evidence-supported practices, and an awareness of the various service sectors that influence service delivery within the health and behavioral health sector. These include the justice sector, the child protection sector, the welfare sector, the aging sector, and other relevant service sectors.

In this chapter, we will use the following case situations to help illustrate the core integrative themes:

CASE SITUATION A: SEAN AND BRENNA

Sean and Brenna are in their late 20s, have been married for three years, and have a six-year-old son named Trevor, who is in first grade. Sean and Brenna identify as Caucasian and grew up in rural areas, where their families lived in poverty conditions. They are renting a mobile home that sits on the property of a large cherry farm in a rural community. The farm hosts migrants who arrive during crop harvesting time in May each year. Sean works odd maintenance jobs for the farm owner and has a part-time bartending job. Brenna has a day care license and cares for 2–4 other children while their parents work. Two of these children attend the same school as Trevor. She is assisted after school by a teenage helper named Marisol, who is from one of the migrant families.

Sean comes home many nights from his bartending job intoxicated and in a foul mood. He and Brenna have been fighting nonstop about his drinking, parenting techniques, finances, and his "redneck" attitude toward the migrants (and, in particular, the teenage helper). When Sean's anger escalates, he verbally and physically abuses Brenna. They agree to separate after the police are called, and Sean moves into town to live with a friend. Brenna is reluctant to file charges.

Two weeks after he moves out, Brenna gets a call from Trevor's principal, requesting a meeting. During the meeting, Brenna is told that Trevor is on the brink of being suspended due to fighting on the playground and in the classroom and for physically picking on kids smaller than he. He also has been using inappropriate language and his grades are slipping. Brenna is also paid a visit by the teenage helper's father, who is threatening to call the police and take action if Sean doesn't stop harassing Marisol and his family.

You are a social worker employed by the local Family Service agency. Brenna has sought services at your agency in order to help Trevor. She is worried about how Trevor is coping.

CASE SITUATION B: FRANK AND HELEN

Frank, a 90-year-old Italian immigrant to the United States, and Helen, an 88-year-old Caucasian woman, have been married 68 years. Frank and Helen moved to Florida when Frank retired at the age of 65. Their four adult children and all the grandchildren live up

(Continued)

(Continued)

north. The family has remained close over the years through annual visits at the parents' home in Florida and at the adult children's homes up north.

Frank is a retired plant superintendent and Helen was a large chain store manager. The couple has many friends in the community where they live. They have been extremely active throughout their lives, playing golf and tennis, and are very social, having many lifelong friendships. They belong to the community club and regularly meet friends for happy hour, dinner, and cards.

Soon after Frank turned 90, his oldest daughter, Susan, received a call from a neighbor in Florida expressing concern about how the couple is managing. They had been in two minor car accidents and Frank, on several occasions lately, appeared disoriented and unkempt, and looked as though he had lost a lot of weight. The neighbor indicated that several of the other members of their club have been doing what they can to assist Helen, but they are concerned and worried about Helen's declining patience and increasing frustration related to caring for Frank. They have heard her being verbally abusive to Frank and intolerant of his diminishing capacity to assist with household chores. When he attends the community club, he enjoys his cocktails and eats very little.

Susan has contacted your organization, which works with the elderly in the Florida community where her parents live. She is visiting with her parents this week and would like assistance in assessing what to do to help her parents. She wants her parents to move back up north, where she and her siblings can help them. Frank and Helen do not want to leave their home in Florida and resent that Susan is asking them to move.

CASE SITUATION C: DAIVON AND MONAE

An African American/Hispanic teenage boy named Daivon has been caught, with a gang of other teens, breaking and entering into private homes and stealing electronics, jewelry, and money. Daivon was placed by the courts in the Juvenile Detention Center. As the social worker at the Juvenile Detention Center, you have contacted his family to engage in family work with the goal of having Daivon return home and to school and not engage in illegal activities.

Daivon's mother, Monae, is a 32-year-old Hispanic single mom who works as a cashier in a major grocery store. Daivon usually only sees his biological father on or near his birthday. He has a fairly good relationship with his maternal mother's extended family, including his grandparents, who live in the same town.

Daivon has been on the wild side most of his life, missing a fair amount of school (more as he has gotten older), has been suspended from school several times, and spends most of his free time on his computer when he is not confined to his room as punishment. He rarely has friends over, preferring instead to go and hang out. He frequently misses his mother's curfew, but she is unable to provide consistent supervision due to her work schedule. While he treats his mother with respect most of the time, he has become increasingly verbally hostile to her and is quick to become angry, slamming doors, throwing things, and generally being unsociable and sulking.

CASE SITUATION D: JESSICA AND RICHARD

You are a social worker at the local Veteran's Administration (VA) behavioral health care clinic. You have been working with a 32-year-old African American female veteran named Jessica, who is pregnant with her second child. Her first child was removed to permanent foster care shortly after birth due to her established record of inability to provide care for the baby.

The biological father of the first child and the current pregnancy is a male veteran named Richard. Richard is a 35-year-old Caucasian male who is not living with Jessica but resides in the same town. He is a smoker, in recovery for alcohol abuse, and is successfully employed as a custodian. Richard is known as a hard worker, is medication compliant, and attends his outpatient appointments with his VA psychiatrist on a regular basis. He is overwhelmed by the current situation with Jessica, acknowledges paternity, and is currently residing in a Halfway House established for veterans. Richard manages his funds and has been able to independently and successfully meet his daily needs. Richard's immediate family consists of an elderly mother who lives 50 miles away and several siblings who assist their brother when they can, usually financially.

Jessica regularly attends her scheduled outpatient appointments with a VA psychiatrist and with you as her social worker at the clinic. She also sporadically attends art therapy classes and has been evaluated as having talent in this area. She has exhibited paranoid thinking, impulsiveness, and delusional thinking at times. She has a short fuse and is quick to anger, and she has been noncompliant with prescribed VA psychiatric and medical (diabetic) treatment/medications. Jessica is also irregular in her obstetric follow-up at a local public health department (the VA does not provide these services). She is a smoker and, at times, drinks to relieve stress.

Jessica has a legal fiduciary (a local bank) that has been established due to her inability to manage her finances and the fact that she has fled from two VA adult foster care placements and ended up in a local shelter, where she has been denied services upon occasion due to being intoxicated. She currently receives a VA disability payment and Supplemental Security Income (SSI), both of which are managed by the bank.

Jessica's immediate family lives over 500 miles away and has not wanted contact or a relationship with her since her return from service, when her first child was put into foster care.

The fiduciary has called you as Jessica's social worker, seeking assistance/guidance as they are worried about her overall medical and behavioral health, the pending birth of her baby, and her safety on the streets. They are also somewhat intimidated by her. They want to assist her by providing resources for her care but are not in a position to do anything but manage her funds.

Definition of the Social Work Profession
and Principles of the Profession

Let's explore how social work defines itself as a profession. We will first look at the definition of social work developed by the International Federation of Social Workers (IFSW), an organization that represents national social work organizations in over 80 countries. The IFSW (2008) defined social work in the following statement:

> The social work profession promotes social change, problem solving in human relationships and the empowerment and liberation of people to enhance well-being. Utilising theories of human behaviour and social systems, social work intervenes at the points where people interact with their environments. Principles of human rights and social justice are fundamental to social work.

This definition draws our attention to the importance of the role that social work has toward social change and empowerment of people to improve life conditions. This is an awesome responsibility and one that social workers throughout the world share. The definition also emphasizes the importance of our role in engaging in problem solving as we work with individuals, families, groups, communities, and organizations. Many of the problems that individuals and families bring to social workers are complex and often require solutions that not only involve the individual or family but also the neighborhood, community, and social systems that may have contributed to the problems in the first place and/or may be considered as part of the solution to the problems. Working as partners with people who are seeking change is rewarding and challenging. In the case examples, we see that individuals come to social workers with a range of needs and concerns, and our role is to assist these individuals in achieving the hoped-for outcomes in their lives. As we can note in the four case examples, Sean, Brenna, and Trevor; Frank, Helen, and Susan; Daivon and Monae; and Jessica and Richard will require the social worker to understand a range of human behavior theories and practice interventions in order to enhance their well-being.

At the heart of this IFSW definition is the importance of operating as social workers with a social justice and human rights lens. This definition helps to frame how social workers working in different countries share a common vision to make a difference in helping individuals, families, groups, and communities challenge inequities and injustices in order to enhance the well-being of all.

In the case examples, we need to be aware of how systems of discrimination, oppression, and poverty might influence the work we do in any helping situation. For example, in working with Sean, Brenna, and Trevor, we might need to consider how living in poverty conditions influences the opportunities for this family if they try to access treatment services for alcohol abuse and family violence. We need to consider how age discrimination impacts the life choices that Frank and Helen may make and how it relates to their desire to continue to live independently. We need to determine whose voice is most powerful in this situation—Frank, Helen, or Susan? We need to explore how experiencing discrimination due to racial and ethnic minority status affects the ways that Daivon and Monae interact with the school, court, and social service systems. We need to reflect on what ways living with a serious mental illness and the stigma associated with having a mental illness do indeed limit the choices available to Jessica and Richard in caring for a child. These are just of few of the many social justice issues that surface in working with individuals and families as illustrated by these cases.

In the United States, the Council on Social Work Education (CSWE, 2008) defined the purpose of the social work profession as follows:

> The purpose of the social work profession is to promote human and community well-being. Guided by a person and environment construct, a global perspective, respect for human diversity, and knowledge based on scientific inquiry, social work's purpose is actualized through its quest for social and economic justice, the prevention of conditions that limit human rights, the elimination of poverty, and the enhancement of the quality of life for all persons.

This purpose builds on the IFSW definition of social work by anchoring our work within the context of the United States with an emphasis on a global awareness and respect for each person while working toward social and economic justice. This purpose is shared by all social workers regardless of where one works in a community or organization or what specialized roles the social worker performs. This purpose brings to the forefront how important it is for social workers to understand not only the individual but also the different environments that influence the reality of the world experienced by the individual or groups of individuals. For social workers who specialize in working with individuals and families, this purpose helps to define our special niche in the helping professions. This niche requires social workers to not only know and understand individual and family theories and interventions that focus on individual and family change but also to understand social policies and community issues that impact the day-to-day lives of the individuals and families that they serve. Social workers have the added commitment to work to prevent conditions that oppress or discriminate against individuals or groups, to advocate for individuals and families, and to seek social and economic justice within the communities in which they work.

The Mission of Social Work

Now that we have reviewed the purpose of social work as a profession, we now need to define our unique mission. The National Association of Social Workers (NASW) Code of Ethics (1996) captures our social work mission in the following statement:

> The primary mission of the social work profession is to enhance human well-being and help meet the basic human needs of all people, with particular attention to the needs and empowerment of people who are vulnerable, oppressed, and living in poverty. A historic and defining feature of social work is the profession's focus on individual well-being in a social context and the well-being of society. Fundamental to social work is attention to the environmental forces that create, contribute to, and address problems in living.

The social work mission covers a range of activities that focus on intervening with at-risk populations in order to improve well-being for all individuals and to change policies and practices that oppress or discriminate against vulnerable individuals or groups of individuals. This mission builds on our purpose as a profession and helps to clarify how we seek to engage in change efforts. How can you or other social workers even begin to respond to this broad mission? What principles can help guide us in carrying out this mission? Finn and Jacobson (2003) identify five key themes consistent with the mission of the profession that structure a just practice framework. These themes include

1. meaning (How do people give meaning to the experiences and conditions that shape their lives?),

2. context (How do we apprehend and appreciate the contextual nature of human experience and interaction?),

3. power (What forms and relations of power shape social relations and experience? Who has power to have their interpretations of reality valued as true?),

4. history (How might a historical perspective provide us with a deeper understanding of context, help us grasp the ways that struggles over meaning and power play out, and enable us to appreciate the human consequences of these struggles?), and

5. possibility (How do we claim a sense of the possible as an impetus for justice-oriented social work practice?). (pp. 58–59)

When using a *just practice approach* in Case Situation B (Frank and Helen), it would be important for us to explore how Frank, Helen, and Susan give meaning to their current situation and to give voice to each person's perspective. We need to address Frank and Helen's desire to stay in the community where they have friends and support and Susan and her siblings' desire to have their parents move closer to them in order for them to better provide care for their parents. Often times, the voices of the elderly are minimized in society, and power differentials emerge that can result in the rights of Frank and Helen being ignored. In fact, Frank and Helen are not seeking social work services, but their daughter has reached out for help. While any intervention plan that emerges needs to ensure the safety of Frank and Helen, as a social worker, you must be aware of how age discrimination might influence the assessment and plan development.

Social Justice Lens

Let's consider further what we mean by a *social justice lens* in our social work practice. We will turn again to the IFSW and review the Ethics in Social Work Practice statement approved in 2004 to highlight the social justice commitment of the profession. In this statement, promoting social justice in society for the individuals with whom we engage in helping is viewed as a responsibility of all social workers. The IFSW (2004) statement adds that this means

1. challenging negative discrimination,

2. recognizing diversity,

3. distributing resources equitably,

4. challenging unjust policies and practices, and

5. working in solidarity.

The responsibility to promote social justice involves recognizing and acting to prevent discrimination on the basis of individual diversity characteristics such as ability, age, culture, gender or sex, marital status, socioeconomic status, political opinions, racial or other physical characteristics, sexual orientation, and spiritual beliefs. Further, we also need to ensure that resources are distributed fairly and unjust policies or practices are brought to the attention of employers, policy makers, and others in society in order to change these policies and practices.

In Case Situation C (Daivon and Monae), using a social justice lens, you need to consider, for example, how discriminatory practices in the juvenile justice system negatively impact Daivon and his mother, Monae. If Daivon was a Caucasian youth, would he have been placed in a Juvenile Detention Center? If Monae was not a single mother who missed appointments with juvenile court officials, school officials, and social workers due to her low-paying job schedule, would Daivon have other options and resources available to him to help address his behavioral issues? These are just a few examples of the types of questions we need to consider when working with diverse groups of individuals and families.

Using this core social justice lens, all levels of social work practice—from work with individuals, families, and small groups to community organizing to organizational and administrative practice to policy making and advocacy practice to research and evaluation—work collaboratively and in an interdependent framework to promote a just society for all.

REFLECTIVE LEARNING ACTIVITY

Review Finn and Jacobson's five key themes and the IFSW 2004 statement. How are these themes/responsibilities addressed in your field placement setting or social service agency where you have volunteered or worked? Are there open discussions with staff and consumers about just practice and ways to promote diverse opinions and perspectives within the organization?

Which of the cases presented at the beginning of the chapter seem to pose the most questions related to just practice and why?

Core Theoretical Perspectives

Let's now move to examining a few of the core theoretical perspectives that guide us in engaging and intervening with individuals, families, and small groups. We will look briefly at the following core theoretical perspectives: ecological systems, life model of social work practice, empowerment, sociocultural, and EI practice.

Ecological Systems Perspective and the Life Model of Social Work Practice Perspective

The first perspectives that we will examine are the ecological systems perspective and the life model of social work practice perspective. The ecological systems perspective emphasizes the importance of reciprocal relationships between person-environmental transactions. Underlying this perspective is the principle that everything affects everything else and a change in one part of a system will change other parts of the system. For example, in a family system in which a child is born with developmental challenges, an elderly parent can no longer manage living independently, or one parent loses a job, the other family members are also affected. Each family member will adjust and change to meet the new challenges within the family system. Sometimes these adjustments result in positive coping responses, and other times, these adjustments add additional strain and disruption in the family system, resulting in negative coping responses.

Using an ecological systems perspective, we focus on understanding the various systems that are nested around the individual and family systems, such as the school, neighborhood, social services, employment services, health services, religious or spiritual supports, and cultural supports, in order to intervene in ways that enhance the functioning of the individual and family systems. Figure 2.1 illustrates how the various systems are linked.

For many of us who work with individuals and families, the primary system of focus or concern is the *individual and/or family/small group system.* We look within the individual and/or family/small group system to understand how the problem or challenge has emerged, the ways that the problem or challenge is managed, and the goal(s) of the change effort and to identify all possible emerging solutions. We explore how other relevant systems, such as *neighborhoods, schools, work environments, or larger community systems,* contribute to or help to alleviate the problem or challenge that the individual and/or family system is experiencing.

The ecological system's perspective helps us to understand that there are different pathways that an individual and/or family may follow that result in the emergence of problems or challenges (equifinality) and also how individuals and/or families can have similar situations and experiences and some of these individuals and/or families will cope in positive and resilient ways while others will experience different problems or challenges (multifinality).

Using an ecological systems perspective, we look at exchanges within systems and across different systems and at how resources within systems can help to improve the problem or challenge experienced by the individual and/or family system. We are

Figure 2.1   Core Systems Involved in Change Efforts

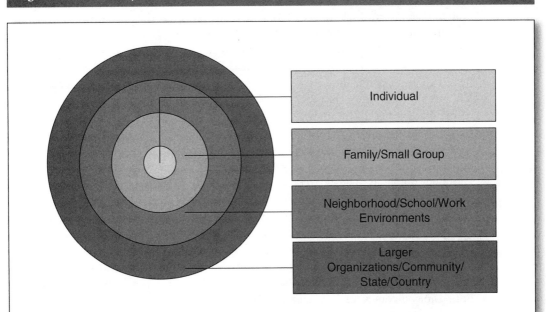

working to increase the fit between the individual or family system needs and the resources available within the individual, family, neighborhood, community, and other relevant social systems. We often have to work simultaneously with other systems (e.g., schools, courts, welfare system, child welfare system, behavioral health system, work environment) in order to improve outcomes for individual and/or family systems. In all four case situations, it is clear that the social worker will not only be working with the focal system (the identified clients) but also with the various systems that compose the environments that surround them.

Hepworth, Rooney, Rooney, Strom-Gottfried, and Larsen (2010, p. 16) propose that assessment from an ecological systems perspective requires knowledge of diverse systems involved in interactions between people and their environments, including:

1. Subsystems of the individual (biophysical, cognitive, emotional, behavioral, and motivational)

2. Interpersonal systems (parent-child, marital, family, kin, friends, neighbors, cultural reference groups, spiritual belief systems, and other members of social networks)

3. Organizations, institutions, and communities

4. The physical environment (housing, neighborhood environments, buildings, other artificial creations, water, and weather and climate)

In Case Situation D (Jessica and Richard), Jessica has several nested systems that need to be considered in the development of any intervention plan. The primary focal system (the system that we are engaging in changing) in this situation is Jessica, but Richard may also be considered part of the focal system. Let's consider some of the key systems that are involved in Jessica and Richard's case situation. We know that the VA system is involved because both Jessica and Richard have emotional and behavioral health challenges and they are receiving services from a variety of community-based VA sites. We also know that Richard lives in a Halfway House where he has been able to maintain his recovery, benefit from stable housing, and hold onto his job. While both Jessica and Richard have prior involvement with the child welfare system, both also have extended family members who might be resources for them. Of primary concern for us is that Jessica has several current challenges that are raising concerns about her potential to be a parent. Using an ecological systems perspective, in order to work with Jessica, we need to understand how each person in Jessica's network influences the current situation and how these individuals and systems might work together to support and empower Jessica in reaching her anticipated outcomes. We are doing a contextual assessment using the ecological systems approach in order to better understand how different systems interact and function in ways that contribute to the current problems or challenges and ways that these systems function to support more hoped-for outcomes for Jessica and Richard.

REFLECTIVE LEARNING ACTIVITY

Choose one of the cases presented in the beginning of this chapter. Make a list of the systems that you and the client(s) think will interface as a plan of action is developed.

The life model of social work practice perspective (Germain & Gitterman, 1996; Gitterman, 2011; Gitterman & Germain, 2008) builds on ecological systems constructs to address ways that help people strive to improve the fit between peoples' (individual, family, group, or community) perceived needs, capacities, and aspirations and the environmental supports and resources. Gitterman and Heller (2011, p. 205) articulate the importance of person and environment fit in the life model of social work practice perspective in the following statement:

> Level of person and environment fit refers to a person's perception of the "fit" between his/her physical, intellectual, emotional and motivational strengths and limitations and environmental resources (family, social networks, organizations, and physical space) to deal with a specific life stressor(s) or challenge(s). Over the life course, people constantly strive to improve the level of fit with their environments. When a person perceives the availability of sufficient personal and environmental resources to deal with a life issue, stressor or event, s/he experiences a positive fit with the environment. The

positive level of fit supports and resources release the person's potential for personal growth and sense of mastery. However, when a negative level of fit evolves between a person's perceptions of personal and environmental resources to deal with a life stressor, s/he experience stress. How overwhelming and disabling individuals experience their daily life stress will largely depend upon the perceived level of fit between their personal and environmental resources.

The life model of social work practice perspective incorporates a dynamic view of the person-environment exchanges. This model highlights that over the life course, individuals must cope with three interrelated life issues: difficult life transitions and traumatic life events, environmental pressures, and dysfunctional interpersonal processes. Through processes of mutual assessment using the life model of social work practice perspective, social work practitioners and clients together determine the practice focus, choosing to

1. improve a person's (collectivity's) ability to manage stressors through more effective personal and situational appraisals and behavioral skills,

2. influence the social and physical environments to be more responsive to a person's (collectivity's) needs, and

3. improve the quality of person-environment exchanges. (Gitterman, 2011, p. 285)

REFLECTIVE LEARNING ACTIVITY

Choose one of the cases presented in the beginning of this chapter. Make a list of the interrelated life issues, difficult life transitions, traumatic life events, environmental pressures, and dysfunctional interpersonal processes that you think might be identified by the client(s).

Now make a list of the positive coping strategies and resources that might be identified.

By thinking systematically, we work in partnership with individuals engaging in social work services to creatively reflect on potential targets for change and strategies across systems that can be employed to address the challenges identified. In Figure 2.2, you will find person-in-environment components that illustrate the centrality of transactions in developing intervention plans.

In Case Situation A (Sean and Brenna), Brenna has several environments where transactions are occurring that create additional stressors for her. For example, Brenna is experiencing verbal and physical abuse in her relationship with Sean. The transactions between Brenna and Sean are strained and negative. She is having challenges in the transactions between her role as a parent and her role with the school system as it relates to Trevor. The transactions between Brenna and the father of the young woman who works for her (Marisol) are increasingly strained due to the actions of Sean. These

Figure 2.2 Person-In-Environment Components

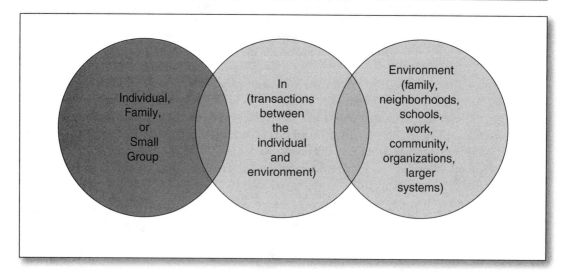

are just a few of the transactional areas where we might focus our work to improve the quality of the person-in-environment exchanges.

REFLECTIVE LEARNING ACTIVITY

One of the practice behaviors linked to the CSWE-EPAS (Competency 2.1.7 Apply knowledge of human behavior and the social environment) is to understand human behavior across the life course, the range of social systems in which people live, and the ways social systems promote or deter people in maintaining or achieving health and well-being. Using the four case situations in this chapter, how did the systems (e.g., individual; family; small group; neighborhood; larger community; organizations; and social, economic, and political systems) promote and/or deter the individuals and families in these cases from achieving health and well-being?

Empowerment Perspective

The empowerment perspective examines the ways that individuals and/or families can gain power or develop power to address current barriers and challenges. Lee and Hudson (2011, p. 160) define the empowerment approach as one that makes connections between social and economic injustices and individual pain and suffering. Adams (2008) further shares that empowerment is about taking control, achieving self-direction, and seeking inclusiveness rooted in connectedness with the experiences of other people. The social worker using this perspective promotes reflection, thinking, and problem solving by focusing on person-in-environment transactions, including the client's role in these transactions and their experiences of oppression (Lee & Hudson, 2011, p. 167).

In Case Situation A (Sean and Brenna), using an empowerment perspective, we need to understand Brenna's perception about what she would like to do to take control of her life and, at the same time, we need to be aware of the challenges she might face in making decisions that, at this time, appear to be overwhelming to her (e.g., filing charges against Sean for the verbal and physical abuse). We might provide information about options that Brenna has to address her challenges, engage in problem solving with her, and assist her in developing the skills she needs to take the actions she determines are best for her life.

In Case Situation C (Daivon and Monae), we might work with Monae to assist her in getting her needs met as she tries to raise her son as a single parent, meet the demands of her job, and address the different systems that are currently involved in her life (e.g., the court system, the school system). Again, from an empowerment perspective, we would provide information, assist in problem solving, and work with Monae to effectively deal with each of the systems to achieve her goal of improving the quality of life for herself and her son.

REFLECTIVE LEARNING ACTIVITY

Choose one of the cases presented at the beginning of this chapter and discuss why it is important for the social worker to understand not only the individual/family who may be seeking help but also the different environments that are influencing and impacting the individual/family's life in the case. Why is a person's environment a critical factor in assessing what led the individual/family to seek help? Why is it crucial in the case you chose in developing the plan of action? Share an example/case from your field placement or volunteer/work experiences where you have used an empowerment approach.

Sociocultural Perspective

Another important perspective that has recently emerged to help us better capture what is happening in the field of behavioral health as it relates to health disparities is the sociocultural framework developed by Alegría, Pescosolido, Williams, and Canino (2011). We are including this perspective since it really articulates the relationships among cultures, race/ethnicity, and health disparities in the health services sector. The core elements of this perspective can also be applied when we try to better understand disparities in other service sectors where social workers work, such as in school systems, the justice system, the welfare system, the child welfare system, and the aging system. Health disparities in this model are defined as "racial and ethnic differences in access, health care, quality or health care outcomes that are not due to clinical needs or the appropriateness of treatment" (Alegría et al., 2011, p. 364). Note in Figure 2.3 that this model assumes a meta-systems analysis to assist us in better understanding health service outcomes. This means that we examine not only the individual domains but also how those domains interact and function as a whole.

The *system domains* involve federal, state, and economic policy, operation of provider organizations, and provider/clinician/social worker factors. This domain requires us to examine policies and regulations to determine how these policies may support inclusion or exclusion of individuals who lack resources to afford services or who are members of oppressed groups within society. How organizations are designed to deliver core services is another area where we need to explore how issues such as provider burden, workforce diversity, and organizational climate and culture may discriminate against particular minority groups in society or other oppressed groups who are seeking our help. The providers and clinicians (including social workers) are trained to provide services within the organizations in which they are

Figure 2.3   Sociocultural Perspective Domains

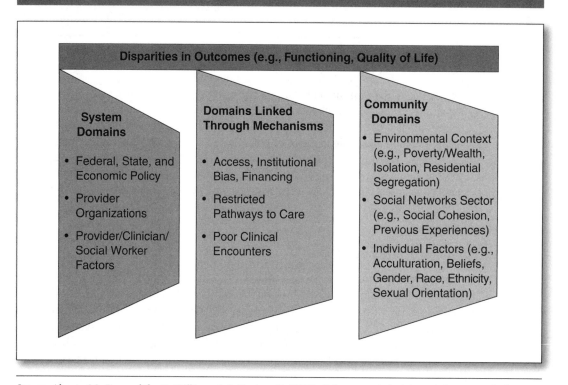

Source: Alegria, M., Pescosolido, B., Williams, S. & Canino, G. (2011). Culture, race/ethnicity and disparities: fleshing out the socio-cultural framework for health services disparities. In B. Pescosolido, J. Martin, J. McLeod & A. Rogers (Eds) *Handbook of the sociology of health, illness and healing: a blueprint for the 21st Century,* (363-382).

employed (host organizations), and this may limit how they perceive client groups and a range of client diversity factors.

The *community domains* include the environmental context, social network sectors, and individual factors. The *environmental context* refers to such factors as the level of poverty/wealth in a community, the degree of residential segregation, the level of social isolation, and the level of access to health care services. The operation of community system and *social network sectors* is important to us in all phases of our work. We need to scrutinize how the community perceives service use, the amount of social cohesion and support present in the networks, how the community recognizes problems, how the community perceives the effectiveness of the service systems, and how the community experiences the care system.

When we analyze the *individual factors context,* we need to take into consideration the degree of acculturation and language understanding, the beliefs individuals have, the competing needs individuals have, and the individual's prior experience in accessing the care system, and we need to understand the risks presented by an individual's gender, race, and ethnicity. It is important for us to understand how the system and the community domains are linked and that mechanisms such as market failure, restricted pathways to and of care, and poor clinical encounters impact our work. The market failure mechanisms we need to be aware of include lack of availability of services and accessibility of services, institutional bias, and limited financial challenges. The *restricted pathways to and of care* mechanisms refers to the differential pathways our clients may face when attempting to access services, poor client and provider interaction, and communication and mismatches in service offerings to meet the needs of our minority or oppressed groups. The *poor clinical encounters* mechanism focuses on lack of community trust in the providers (including social workers), misperceptions about what to expect from services, limited workforce availability, and limited training in work with specific minority or oppressed groups. Understanding the two domains and the mechanisms that link the domains helps us to better understand how disparities emerge.

Disparities in outcomes for our clients could result in differences in functioning, an uneven burden of illness being experienced by individuals and groups, and a varying level of social integration and participation, which impact the overall quality of life experience for those seeking help. This has the potential to result in a cumulative disadvantage being experienced by individuals from minority and oppressed groups when they interface with community and treatment systems. Using this perspective, we can see how a person's individual cultural factors, clinician factors, and system and community factors can result in a lifetime of disadvantage, resulting in poor outcomes particularly for individuals who are viewed as a part of an oppressed group and/or culturally diverse community. Applying this perspective to other key systems where we work (such as the child welfare system, the school system, the judicial system, the aging system, and the welfare system) will ultimately assist us in understanding how disparities surface in a range of client groups across a range of diverse factors. It is critical for us to think beyond the individual and family encounters in our work and to recognize that individuals have different pathways to services and often, these pathways may create additional burdens and challenges for them. This perspective helps us use a social justice lens to better understand the complexities involved in providing effective services in an environment where power and privilege can result in differential access to needed services for all clients.

Let's look at Case D (Jessica and Richard) to highlight how the sociocultural framework might explain the disparities in outcomes that we see for Jessica and Richard as it relates to their care in the VA system. Both Jessica and Richard are veterans and have been involved in the VA health care system. Jessica is an African American woman and Richard is a Caucasian male. Jessica appears to have more negative service outcomes than Richard, based on the information provided in the case situation. When we look at the system domains, both Jessica and Richard are eligible for services under the same federal policies. Using the sociocultural perspective, it is important for us to understand that Jessica, as an African American woman, and Richard, as a Caucasian male, might experience differences based on their race or gender identities in service access due to the design of the provider services or the organizational climate. We also would want to explore how provider/clinician/social work factors might impact the services either of these individuals receives. We should explore the providers'/clinicians'/social workers' training in working with diverse client systems and also what the attitudes or perceptions might be that could impact how potential individuals might perceive the provider's openness to helping them. Related to the community domains, it is important for us to explore whether Jessica receives different levels of community support than Richard based on her gender and racial identities. We need to determine how Jessica's prior experiences with the VA system and her beliefs about how the system works influence her ability to access and follow through with treatment recommendations/services. When we look at how the system and community domains are linked, do we find that there is institutional bias as it relates to serving African American women? Or that the pathways to care differ for Jessica based on her minority status? Or does a lack of trust exist between the VA providers and Jessica? While we would need more information, the negative functioning outcomes and the poorer quality of life that Jessica is experiencing may be related to the cumulative disparities in the system and community domains. The sociocultural perspective provides us with a way to examine how systems and the mechanisms put in place to help individuals and families in need may, in fact, not promote wellness and improved outcomes for these people.

REFLECTIVE LEARNING ACTIVITY

Using the sociocultural perspective, discuss how different pathways to services have created additional burdens or challenges for the clients in the case examples. How has this affected your clients at your field placement or those served by your volunteer/work agency? What do you see as the largest challenges involved in addressing the disparities that your clients or those in the cases may experience?

Evidence-Informed (EI) Practice Perspective

The final perspective that we will discuss in this chapter is the EI practice approach in our work with individuals, families, and small groups. In order to effectively use this approach, we are required to search the literature for the interventions that have the greatest chance of producing desired outcomes for our clients/consumers. In addition, the interventions selected need to respect and incorporate our client system's values and belief structures as well as fit with our skill sets when we deliver the interventions. We can operationalize this framework by using the five steps identified in the Client-Oriented Practical Evidence Search (COPES) developed by Gibbs (2003) and Straus, Richardson, Glasziou, and Haynes (2005). (See Figure 2.4.)

Figure 2.4   The COPES Process Diagram

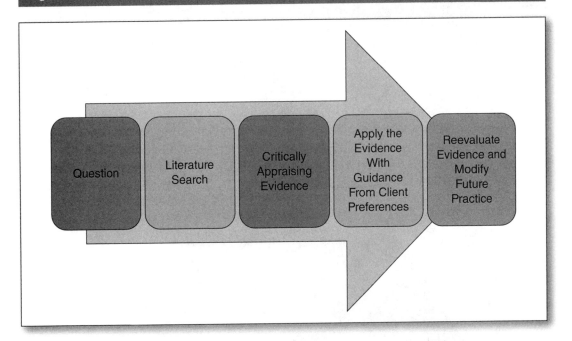

In the COPES process, you begin with a question based on the information provided during your initial assessment with the client (e.g., What is the best intervention to help a young African American girl [age 12] living with a bipolar disorder? Or what intervention works best to help families who are providing caregiving services to an adult family member living with Parkinson's disease? Or what interventions work best for helping adolescents at risk of dropping out of school to stay in school?). The second step involves you conducting a literature search to identify the evidence-supported resources that answer the question from your initial assessment. The third step involves critically appraising the evidence-supported resources to assess their value for your client situation. The fourth step requires you to apply the evidence-supported resource with guidance from your client, taking into consideration their preferences, the clinical state or level of distress, and your practice expertise. The fifth and final step involves reevaluating how you applied the evidence-supported resources to assist you in modifying your future practice. The EI practice framework challenges us to guide our work by using what we learn from research and integrating it with our practice wisdom.

A helpful diagram that captures the current thinking about how an EI practice framework can be implemented in day-to-day practice can be found in Figure 2.5 (Barth et al., 2011). As you can see from this diagram, the COPES process occurs continuously and encourages us to examine policy and values directives, practice principles, common factors, common practice elements, manualized evidence-supported treatments

Figure 2.5　A Framework for Conceptualizing the Role of Various Components of Evidence-Supported Social Work Practice

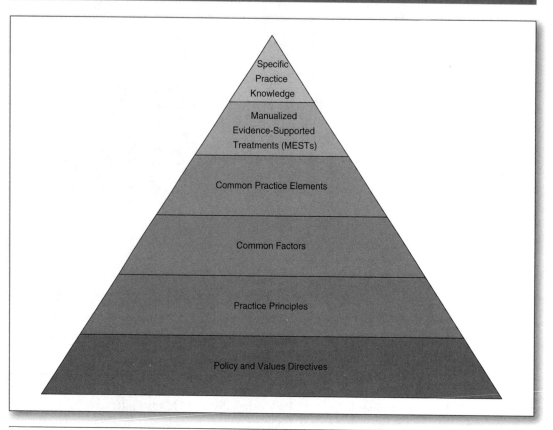

Source: Barth, T. P., Lee, B., Lindsey, M., Collins, K., Strieder, F., Chorpita, B., Becker, K. & Sparks, J. (2011) Evidence-based practice at a crossroads: the timely emergence of common elements and common factors. *Research on Social Work Practice.* Thousand Oaks: SAGE Publications.

(MESTs), and specific practice knowledge. The *policy and value directives* give our social work profession legitimacy through legal and agency mandates as well as provide us with the framework for the ethical conduct to guide our practice. *Practice principles* are specific models of care that operate within particular service sectors or agency-based practices, such as family-centered practice, person-centered practice, or recovery-oriented practice. *Common factors* include our personal qualities as a social worker, the understanding of the importance of the therapeutic alliance, and our client's hopes and expectations. *Common practice elements* refer to our individual treatment practices such as psychoeducation, positive reinforcement, and cognitive restructuring that emerged from EI practices (Chorpita, Daleiden, & Weisz, 2005). The MESTs are the manuals that were developed in randomized controlled trials (RCTs), which spell out the process steps, and the skills and techniques used in the trials that support the positive change observed for our client systems. The *specific practice knowledge* focuses on the importance of addressing culture, circumstances unique to our client system, and other diversity factors to enhance our practice effectiveness.

We have adopted an evidenced-supported social work practice framework in our organization of this book. In the skills chapters, you will note that we examine the cross-cutting skills that make up the common factors and common practice elements components contained in this model. As we shared in the introductory chapter, you need to have knowledge and skills that are shared by all social workers (generalist practice), and when you specialize, you will need to gain more in-depth knowledge and skills in a particular or more specialized area. Specialized knowledge and skills are often developed by becoming certified or trained in specific evidence-supported treatments (e.g., trauma-focused cognitive behavioral treatment, dialectical behavioral therapy, integrated dual disorders treatment) that include manuals and protocols that, if used with fidelity (as they were used in the RCTs), will produce positive outcomes for individuals and families (and small groups).

REFLECTIVE LEARNING ACTIVITY

Ask for a list of evidence-supported or EI practices that are used in your field placement or where you volunteer/work. Inquire whether you would be able to shadow those practitioners who are implementing evidenced-informed practices so you can learn more about them and see how they are applied.

Integrating Conceptual Perspectives

These conceptual perspectives (ecological systems, life model of social work practice, empowerment, sociocultural, and EI practice) capture for us different ways to make sense of the problems and concerns that individuals, families, and small groups bring to the helping process. These core perspectives contribute to our understanding of the challenges associated with engaging in effective change efforts.

In day-to-day practice, we seek to integrate the core themes from these different frameworks by using

1. a meta-systems framework (one that looks at the person-in-environment to better understand the contexts for change),

2. a bio-psycho-social-spiritual perspective in working with individuals and families (we will address this perspective in more detail in Chapter 6),

3. a strength orientation to change (the strengths-based orientation to practice moves us to search for competencies and capacities within individuals, families, and their nested environments and to look for ways to build hope and positive expectations for change while building resilience and resources to assist individuals and families in reaching their goals),

4. a perspective that values diversity and cultural norms (we engage in the helping process while remaining mindful of our commitment as a professional to promoting social justice),

5. an emphasis on informed practice that incorporates emerging evidence, and

6. an awareness of how the various service sectors that influence service delivery within the health and behavioral health sector, the justice sector, the child welfare sector, the schools, the welfare sector, the aging sector, and other relevant service sectors may influence outcomes.

REFLECTIVE LEARNING ACTIVITY

Take a moment to review the core perspectives and principles discussed in this chapter. Develop your own concept map of the core principles and perspectives that you will use to guide your social work practice. You might find it helpful to use a free web-based concept mapping tool to help you organize your thoughts for this map. Choose one case that was presented at the beginning of the chapter and make a list of the core principles and theoretical perspectives you might consider using if you were working with the case.

CHAPTER REVIEW QUESTIONS

1. How have the IFSW definition of social work, the CSWE purpose of social work practice, and the NASW Code of Ethics mission helped you to develop your professional identity as a social worker?

2. What does a just practice perspective include?

3. In what ways can you promote a social justice perspective in your day-to-day work?

4. Identify the core constructs associated with the ecological systems theory perspective, the life model of social work practice perspective, and the empowerment perspective.

5. Describe the sociocultural perspective as it relates to understanding relationships among cultures, race/ethnicity, and system disparities.

6. Why is it important to do a meta-analysis of the systems involved in providing care for your clients?

7. What does a COPES approach to social work practice involve?

8. Why is it important to integrate core theoretical perspectives when engaging in change efforts with our clients?

REFERENCES

Adams, R. (2008). *Empowerment, participation and social work.* Hampshire, England: Palgrave MacMillan.

Alegría, M., Pescosolido, B., Williams, S., & Canino, G. (2011). Culture, race/ethnicity and disparities: Fleshing out the socio-cultural framework for health services disparities. In B. Pescosolido, J. Martin, J. McLeod, & A. Rogers (Eds.), *Handbook of the sociology of health, illness, and healing: A blueprint for the 21st century* (pp. 363–382). New York, NY: Springer.

Barth, R. P., Lee, B., Lindsey, M., Collins, K., Strieder, F., Chorpita, B., . . . Sparks, J. (2011). Evidence-based practice at a crossroads: The timely emergence of common elements and common factors. *Research on Social Work Practice, 22*(1), 108–119. doi: 10.1177/1049731511408440

Chorpita, B., Daleiden, E., & Weisz, J. (2005). Identifying and selecting common elements of evidence based interventions: A distillation and matching model. *Mental Health Services Research, 7,* 5–20.

Council on Social Work Education (CSWE). (2008). *Educational policy and accreditation standards* (Revised in March 2010). Retrieved July 25, 2014 from http://www.cswe.org/File .aspx?id=13780

Finn, J., & Jacobson, M. (2003). Just practice: Steps toward a new social work paradigm. *Journal of Social Work Education, 39*(1), 57–78.

Germain, C., & Gitterman, A. (1996). *The life model of social work practice* (2nd ed.). New York, NY: Columbia University Press.

Gibbs, L. (2003). *Evidence-based practice for the helping professions: A practical guide with integrated multimedia.* Pacific Grove, CA: Brooks/Cole-Thomson Learning.

Gitterman, A. (2011). Advances in the life model of social work practice. In F. J. Turner (Ed.), *Social work treatment: Interlocking theoretical approaches* (5th ed., pp. 279–292). New York, NY: Oxford University Press.

Gitterman, A., & Germain, C. (2008). *The life model of social work practice: Advancement in theory and practice* (3rd ed.). New York, NY: Columbia University Press.

Gitterman, A., & Heller, N. (2011). Integrating social work perspectives and models with concepts, methods and skills with other professions' specialized approaches. *Clinical Social Work Journal, 39,* 204–211. doi: 10.1007/s10615-011-0340-7

Hepworth, D., Rooney, R., Rooney, G., Strom-Gottfried, K., & Larsen, J. (2010). *Direct social work practice: Theory and skills* (8th ed.). Belmont, CA: Brooks/Cole.

International Federation of Social Workers (IFSW). (2004). *Statement of ethical principles.* Retrieved July 25, 2014 from http://ifsw.org/policies/statement-of-ethical-principles/

International Federation of Social Workers (IFSW). (2008). *Definition of social work.* Retrieved July 25, 2014 from http://ifsw.org/policies/definition-of-social-work/

Lee, J., & Hudson, R. (2011). Empowerment approach to social work practice. In F. J. Turner (Ed.), *Social work treatment: Interlocking theoretical approaches* (5th ed., pp. 157–178). New York, NY: Oxford University Press.

National Association of Social Workers (NASW). (1996). *Code of Ethics of the National Association of Social Workers* (Revised in 2008). Washington, DC: Author. Retrieved July 25, 2014 from http://www.naswdc.org/pubs/code/code.asp

Straus, E., Richardson, S., Glasziou, P., & Haynes, R. (2005). *Evidence-based medicine: How to practice and teach EBM.* New York, NY: Elsevier.

From Evidence-Based Practice to Evidence-Informed Practice

As social workers, we regularly encounter complex problems for which there may not be a single *correct* solution. It is important that we approach the practice environment with a set of tools and strategies for sorting through and making sense of complex problems. Such tools and strategies should help inform a range of possible solutions that can be considered in light of their possible outcomes.

CHAPTER LEARNING OBJECTIVES

By the end of this chapter, you should

- know the contemporary definition of evidence-based practice (EBP) and evidence-informed (EI) practice,
- understand the major components of EBP and how they are interrelated,
- describe the challenges associated with using the EBP framework and the emerging EI practice perspective,
- recognize the role of critical and reflective thinking in practice,
- apply a collaborative decision-making approach in your work with clients/consumers and families, and

(Continued)

(Continued)

- understand the move to EI practice to expand the evidence we use to inform our work. This evidence may come from emerging promising practices for work with diverse populations and wider forms of data collected systematically through case studies, quality improvement efforts, and consumer-focused feedback.

The Council on Social Work Education Educational Policy and Accreditation Standards (CSWE-EPAS) Competencies that are highlighted in more depth in this chapter include the following:
2.1.3 Apply critical thinking to inform and communicate professional judgments.
2.1.4 Engage diversity and difference in practice.
2.1.6 Engage in research-informed and practice-informed research.

This chapter provides foundation knowledge and a general framework to inform collaborative decision making in social work practice. The focus of this chapter is on understanding EBP and the move to EI practice. We will examine the important components of EBP and the ways that we have broadened the EBP framework to encompass a range of evidence that supports us in systematically assessing how we are making a difference in assisting clients/consumers and families in reaching their hoped-for outcomes. This newer EI practice perspective is central to our work in social work today.

CASE SITUATION A: MICHAEL

Michael is a 34-year-old African American man who has struggled for many years with an anxiety disorder called *social phobia*. This disorder is characterized by a strong fear of being judged by others, and it is common for such fears to lead to problems in other life domains (e.g., social relationships, employment, school). Michael's anxiety has worsened over the past couple years, and at night, he has been drinking more alcohol to help take the edge off. Michael was recently arrested for driving under the influence of alcohol and was self-referred—under pressure by his family—to a community mental health agency. In the initial interview with Michael, he stated that his drinking problem would go away if he could manage his anxiety, suggesting that his anxiety should be the target of treatment. At the same time, it is plausible that alcohol can exacerbate anxiety problems, suggesting that his alcohol consumption might be a focus of treatment. In a following case consultation, the possibility of anxiety and alcohol reciprocally influencing each other was also considered—that is, Michael's anxiety is leading him to drink more alcohol to take the edge off. Although this gives some temporary relief to his anxiety problems, the higher levels of alcohol could be giving rise to further increases in anxiety. A decision needs to be made regarding the best course of treatment.

CASE SITUATION B: NAIMAH

Naimah is a 15-year-old Chaldean girl who has lived in foster care for one year. She was removed from her family of origin due to neglect charges soon after the family had immigrated. She has adjusted to her foster family, is doing well in school, and has a few close friends. She and her family of origin are in a reunification program that has been successful thus far.

Naimah has been labeled obese by her family physician and, as a result, is on medication for hypertension. She and her foster mother have been referred by the physician to a dietician for counseling, and the foster mother is trying hard to provide Naimah with a diet that will address her weight problem and help stabilize her blood pressure but she, too, struggles with her weight and is being treated for diabetes. Naimah does not think her problems are serious, so she eats what she wants when out of the supervision of her foster mother and on reunification visits. Her biological family doesn't appear to understand the seriousness of the hypertension diagnosis or weight problems experienced by Naimah.

At Naimah's last doctor's appointment, the physician expressed concern that she was headed into a major medical event as her blood pressure had escalated and she had gained additional weight.

Defining Evidence-Based Practice (EBP)

Let's first examine the development of EBP in social work. EBP is defined as the integration of the best available evidence with practice experience and the client's characteristics, treatment preferences, and cultural values (APA Presidential Task Force on Evidence-Based Practice, 2006; Sackett, Strauss, Richardson, Rosenberg, & Haynes, 1996). This definition is aligned with the Social Work Policy Institute (2010), which comprises the major federal organizations that are considered allies with the field of social work, including (but not limited to) the Institute of Medicine (2001), the National Institutes of Health (NIH), the Centers for Disease Control (CDC), and the Agency for Healthcare Research and Quality (AHRQ). This definition is commonly represented by a Venn diagram (see Figure 3.1) to show that our practice decisions should be firmly rooted in the integration of multiple sources of information. In fact, no single source of information by itself is considered sufficient or superior to another source.

Let's briefly look at the three components of this diagram. We will start with the *best research evidence* component. The ultimate goal for the social worker is to have an understanding of what works and for whom (see Roth & Fonagy, 1996). With respect to Case Situation A (Michael), we are interested in knowing what the range of treatment options are that might benefit him. What EBPs have demonstrated positive outcomes for individuals such as Michael who are experiencing anxiety or

Figure 3.1   Visual Depiction of Contemporary Definition of EBP

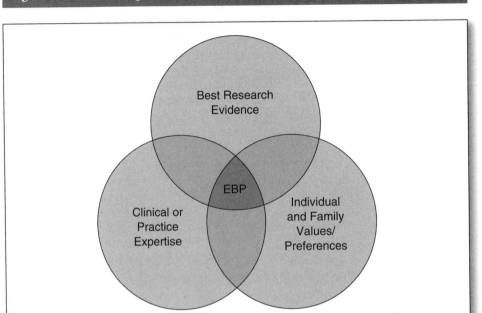

social phobia challenges? We also want to inquire about interventions for alcohol abuse. These are just a few of the questions that we need to consider as we engage Michael in a change effort. The EBP research is essential for building a knowledge base for understanding what works and for whom. Throughout your career as a social worker, you will need to stay current as new research becomes available.

Research also helps address a very important but often under-recognized issue—that is, the potential negative and unintended consequences of our interventions, or *iatrogenic effects* (Breton, 1994). We are aware that side effects from pharmacotherapy can be regarded as an iatrogenic treatment effect. Such effects are not limited to medical interventions, and research has helped us identify such problems that can occur with well-intentioned social workers providing psychosocial interventions. While we seek to "do no harm" in our work with individuals and families, it is important to understand that some interventions might have the potential for negative outcomes for clients/consumers. More specifically, we typically do not meet with clients/consumers after service or treatment has terminated, so we may not be aware of the long-term effects of the services we have provided. Unfortunately, reports of client/consumer satisfaction and short-term treatment outcomes are not always correlated with long-term effects.

One such example is critical incident stress debriefing. This involves providing counseling, typically a single session in a group format, immediately following a traumatic event (e.g., terrorist event, natural disaster, major accident). The session leader, often a social worker, guides participants in processing their experience and negative emotions, with the idea that working through and sharing intense emotions can help stave off the negative consequences, particularly symptoms of anxiety (e.g., post-traumatic stress disorder [PTSD]) and depression. While many participants in these services may self-report that the sessions were enjoyable or helpful, the research on this intervention actually shows that the persons who participated in these debriefing sessions actually had more symptoms of anxiety and depression compared to persons who received no treatment (Rose, Bisson, Churchill, & Wessely, 2002).

A variety of different organizations have put forth different taxonomies to characterize levels of evidence to help us in understanding what is known about particular interventions. In Table 3.1, we present a simplified version of levels of evidence that are common to social work practice.

The next component in the diagram in Figure 3.1 is the *clinical* or *practice expertise* component.

We see that decisions within the framework of EBP are not based solely on research evidence. Another source of information is our practice or clinical experience,

Table 3.1 Levels of Evidence

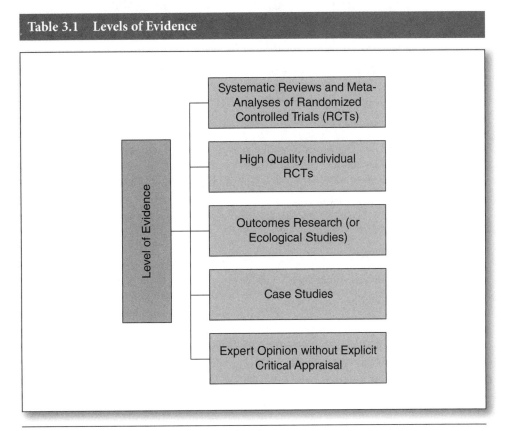

Source: Adapted from the Centre for Evidence-Based Medicine, 2001.

Note: The strength of evidence is presented from strongest at the top to weakest at the bottom.

which is essential to the effective integration of various sources of information. For example, our experience gives us important contextual information that is often essential to making good decisions. Practice experience is more than simply logging hours in the field. It is significantly more complex, and not all practice experience is equal. Much like research evidence, our practice experience is also subject to a variety of biases. For example, one common bias is called a *confirmation bias*, where we look for evidence that confirms what we believe to be true while ignoring refuting evidence. Significant research has been done on decision making to show that biases occur to a much higher degree than we might think they do. But biases do not characterize our practice experience, provided we approach our practice experience with the same rigor and critical appraisal that we use to examine the research evidence. Table 3.2 provides a list of the various ways our experience can be integrated within the broader framework of EBP.

Table 3.2   Practice Domains and Examples of Practice Experience in EBP

Assessment, Diagnosis, and Service/Intervention Planning

- Taking into account unique client characteristics and circumstances
- Selection of service goals and service strategies
- Integrating social work values and ethics in a service or service plan

Decision Making

- Remaining flexible in the delivery of interventions
- Identifying which outcomes to monitor
- Knowing when to make changes in a service or service plan

Interpersonal Expertise

- Building a therapeutic alliance
- Selecting best method of communication with other providers to coordinate services (e.g., electronic, face-to-face)

Self-Reflection and Skill Acquisition

- Recognizing biases that influence decision making
- Identifying limitations in knowledge and skills

Evaluating and Using Research Evidence

- Being able to critically evaluate the research
- Determining when research is and is not relevant

Understanding Sources of Diversity

- Determining the relevance of client characteristics and values in services
- Recognizing sources of diversity in service contexts

Seeking and Utilizing Available Resources

- Identifying relevant local resources and supports within the client's support system and community

Establishing a rationale for decisions

- Articulating the various reasons why specific services were selected

Source: Adapted from the APA Presidential Task Force on Evidence-Based Practice, 2006, pp. 276–279.

Let's explore these items from Table 3.2 in a bit more detail.

Assessment, Diagnosis, and Service/Intervention Planning

Practice experience lays the foundation for assessment, diagnosis, and service planning. For example, we may have tools with established psychometric properties that give us confidence in their reliability and validity. However, these psychometric properties do not consider the appropriate time to use these tools and how they are introduced to individuals in distress. Similarly, we can make diagnoses that are consistent with the latest version of the *Diagnostic and Statistical Manual of Mental Disorders* (*DSM-5*) of the American Psychiatric Association (2013), but the research is certainly not able to speak to the manner in which we talk about diagnoses with individuals and the potential impacts on their lives. Simply having knowledge of the best available evidence will never produce a quality service plan. We have to draw on our experience with the research and consider that in context with the locally available services. For example, when we examine Case Situation B (Naimah), our previous experience in working with youth who are involved in the child welfare system, our understanding of the physical health system, and our knowledge of successful engagement practices with immigrant families will influence how we examine the research evidence on different types of obesity treatments.

Decision Making

If decisions were to be informed simply by the available evidence, we could easily replace social workers with computer programs. However, as you will quickly discover in your field, volunteer, and work experience, even the best available research doesn't fit neatly into practice situations. With experience, we uncover where we lack an appropriate fit and discover how to make adaptations. Of course, such decisions often lack a clear right or wrong answer, but the active reflection and careful appraisal of decisions can improve our decision making over time. We are also regularly confronted with knowing what outcomes to monitor when providing services, as certain outcomes will be more important or relevant to clients than other outcomes. Furthermore, our research is not yet advanced enough to tell us when we need to make adjustments in the course of services. Social workers will regularly confront these decisions for which there are not right and wrong answers.

Interpersonal Expertise

A comprehensive knowledge of the research evidence will certainly be of great utility to social workers and their clients/consumers. But knowledge of the research does not necessarily improve our interpersonal competencies, especially when working with diverse populations. Thus, it is essential to acquire a diversity of experiences while looking for various feedback cues that can help shape our expertise. Not only do we need to know what to say to our clients/consumers but also through which channels. This is increasingly important, given that our interactions may no longer be simply face-to-face but may be mediated by electronic communication. Moreover, our interactions with others will also involve a variety of communication channels. In order to have a context for communicating with clients/consumers or assisting them in effectively communicating with others, we need to have a full range of experience of the different forms of communication.

Self-Reflection and Skill Acquisition

Identifying what we don't know is an essential part of learning. In fact, it is probably the most essential and most difficult aspect of the EBP framework. For example, lacking knowledge of a particular intervention strategy provides an opportunity for meaningful learning. However, how does one come to realize this knowledge gap? And how does one realize that practice could be improved through the acquisition of a particular skill? The role of supervision obviously plays an important role in filling these gaps in knowledge, but supervision by itself is not the complete solution. Social workers need to be actively engaged in lifelong learning (Cournoyer & Stanley, 2002), which is an active and ongoing process of continually reflecting upon successes and situations that may have revealed skill and knowledge deficits. It is only through the process of reflection that one can prepare a meaningful plan of learning that will ultimately enhance their overall knowledge and skill set. Therefore, the final chapter of this book concludes with guidance on lifelong learning.

Evaluating and Using Research Evidence

Much of this chapter has addressed the importance of evaluating and using research evidence. Thus, it is curious how this topic emerges again in the area of practice experience. You will soon discover that your practice experience will largely dictate how well you can evaluate and use the available research evidence. Evaluation and application are skills to be acquired, and it takes significant experience to perform them effectively and efficiently. Social workers experienced in the EBP framework can draw on their experience to quickly evaluate the relevance of research and know how it fits (and perhaps doesn't fit) with decisions to be made. You will soon discover that the skills involved in applying the EBP framework become refined with experience.

Understanding Sources of Diversity

Diversity is inherent in every aspect of social work practice. It can be found in every client/consumer population, among our colleagues, and across service contexts. No amount of social work practice experience will expose us to all possible forms of diversity. Thus, social workers have the ongoing challenge of recognizing and responding to different forms of diversity and thinking about how diversity fits within the decisions they make. In Case Situation A, we need to consider Michael's experience as an African American male, for example, as we look at the research evidence and plan together for change efforts. In Case Situation B, we need to address our understanding of Naimah's culture, her experience of being part of an immigrant family, her experience in being a foster care youth, and her developmental stage within the context of the health challenges she faces. In considering the research evidence, social workers need to think about how study results generalize to the diverse populations whom they serve. This process involves much more than simply matching up characteristics of persons in the study with the client/consumer populations. Social workers must be aware of the full range of client/consumer characteristics that can never be controlled for in research. This is not to suggest that the research is not important, but the process of EBP involves the thoughtful integration of practice experience and client values with research evidence. Thus, remaining cognizant of how individual differences affect all aspects of the treatment process places social workers in a position to more effectively apply research evidence.

Seeking and Utilizing Available Resources

Even the research that seems to be the best fit for a given practice decision can never have a perfect fit, and we often encounter situations in which we need to consider other resources to meet the client/consumer's needs. Our experience can contribute to our understanding of the local availability of services, allowing us to seek and utilize these resources as needed. And, within this context, social workers also need to consider the other integrative themes involved with social work practice. For example, how does our conception of social justice affect the access to certain limited resources?

Establishing a Rationale for Decisions

The EBP framework forces social workers to move beyond intuitive thinking— that is, making decisions that *feel right*—to careful, systematic, and reflective thinking. In doing so, and by drawing upon the major sources of information (i.e., best available research integrated with practice experience and client characteristics), social workers are firmly positioned to articulate rationales for their decisions. Again, this is a skill that is acquired through experience, and our rationales for decisions should become more fully explicated and articulated over time.

The third component in Figure 3.1 is the *individual and family values/preferences* component. This source of information refers to client/consumer characteristics, values, and preferences. Any service that ignores this source of information will likely be ineffective. Although this is the third component to be described, it is no less important than the other major components of EBP. At the most basic level, it is essential that social workers understand that individuals will not respond favorably to services that they don't want or don't value. So the social worker guided by the EBP framework will ensure the central role of the client/consumer throughout the service process. Thus careful assessment attends not only to the problems and strengths of the individuals, but the process should also recognize what the individuals want and don't want in the receipt of social work services. An entire section of this book is devoted to assessment to facilitate this process. When we talk about individual and family values/preferences, we are considering the different aspects of the individual that may be directly or indirectly relevant to the service process. What do the clients/consumers value and how do they make sense of their world and the challenges that they are facing? How do these values lead to building a change relationship that will move clients/consumers to their hoped-for goals? We also need to examine how an individual's preferences during the engagement, assessment, and service processes influence the helpfulness of the social work interventions. From our case examples, we would need to explore with Michael and Naimah how their life experiences and current challenges influence the ways in which they may engage in seeking help and in what form the help needs to be delivered in order for Michael and Naimah to be open to making difficult changes.

REFLECTIVE LEARNING ACTIVITY

Consider the last couple of days at your field placement/volunteer or work situation. Write down various decisions you have made in your work with clients/consumers. Then, describe the extent to which the decisions were informed by the three different (but interrelated) information sources of the EBP framework. Were all three information sources represented in your decisions? In what ways could you improve the integration of all three information sources?

The Challenges in Using the EBP Framework in Social Work

As you might note, this three-component conceptualization of EBP limits the importance of the context in our work with clients/consumers and families. It is important for us to consider in any change effort the broad contextual factors that influence our work. Haynes, Devereaux, and Guyatt's (2002) conceptualization of the elements of evidence-based social work policy and practice changes the core components in the initial diagram to incorporate professional expertise at the center and adds the various contexts, such as community sociopolitical climate, organizational resources/constraints and economic context, training and supervision and professional context, and organizational mandate and political context (see Figure 3.2). This diagram captures more of the ecological systems focus that we use in social work practice.

How we consider contextual factors in clinical decision making is still not clear in this conceptualization of EBP. In addition, having professional expertise in the center emphasizes to a greater degree the role of practitioners and values their expertise in deciding how the various components interact in practice. Satterfield et al. (2009) present an even more complex model called the *transdisciplinary model of EBP* that puts decision making at the center, since this is the action that turns evidence into contextualized EBP. The components of this transdisciplinary model still include best available research evidence; client's/population's characteristics, state, needs, values, and preferences; resources, including practitioner's expertise; and the environment and organizational context, but at the center is decision making, which intersects with

Figure 3.2   Ecological Context for EI Decision Making

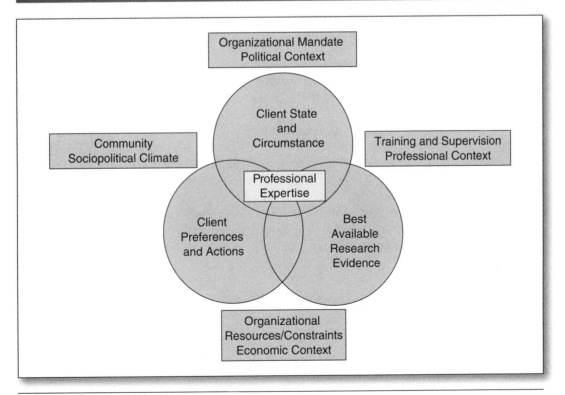

Source: Adapted from Haynes, R., Devereaux, P. & Guyatt, G. (2002) Clinical expertise in the era of evidence-based medicine and patient choice. *ACP Journal Club* 136, A11–A14.

each component. This newer conceptualization helps us to move to more collaborative and shared decision making with clients/consumers and families as we consider the range of evidence from these various components in developing effective interventions and service plans. For example, in Case B (Naimah), we may find several EBPs that address obesity issues and we have a solid understanding of the various contexts and resources available to address implementing some of these practices, but to make sense of these various inputs, we need to engage in collaborative decision making with Naimah. Her voice is critical in order to deliver the interventions in ways that promote helping her reach outcomes that she deems positive and central to her change efforts.

Steps in Applying the EBP Framework

The delivery of EBP is often presented as a set of steps, although in practice, EBP is highly iterative, with decisions and strategies being adjusted with new information that is acquired through the intervention process. Here, we present a simple five-step approach that is a useful starting point for understanding how the components fit together. The five steps involve converting an issue or problem into an answerable question, locating the available evidence, appraising the evidence, developing a plan, and evaluating the outcome.

Step 1: Convert an issue or problem into an answerable question.

Whether you are a new or seasoned social worker, the available research literature will appear overwhelming and fragmented. Thus, it is best to engage or approach the research literature with a specific question to guide your search for information. Generally speaking, we try to frame questions that include our population (e.g., older adults), the problem or issue (e.g., depression or anxiety), and the context (e.g., community setting vs. institutional setting). We can use any combination of these broad categories to help us formulate questions that ultimately help answer the fundamental issue of what works for whom. Such questions generally take the following forms:

- What are effective interventions for older adults with depression?
- Is cognitive behavioral therapy effective for adolescents with anxiety disorders?
- What are the various types of problems that problem-solving therapy has been shown to be effective in treating?

Ultimately, the quality of the question you ask will elicit the same quality information. Over time and with experience, you will begin to see how some questions elicit better answers. As previously noted, the EBP process is iterative, so it is unlikely that the first question you ask will lead you to the most useful information. Prepare yourself to reformulate your question multiple times. A good way to start is by formulating broad questions and then narrowing your focus after you see the relevance and amount of research available in response to each answer.

REFLECTIVE LEARNING ACTIVITY

Our ability to efficiently and effectively generate answerable questions comes from ongoing practice and experience. Take a moment to write out at least five answerable questions that are related to your current field placement or the Case Situations presented in this chapter.

Step 2: Locate the available evidence.

Now that we have formulated a question or set of questions, we have to start the process of finding the available evidence to help answer it. Again, the answerable question(s) helps guide the search process, as opposed to wandering aimlessly through a giant sea of information. From your question(s), you should be able to derive key words and use specific search terms for your initial search. Thus, your experience with searching the literature is critical, and at first, you probably won't enjoy much success. You need to learn the most common key words associated with your question in order to be both effective and efficient. One common mistake that social work students make is assuming that the language and terminology used in their field placements are consistent with the language of the research literature.

In addition to identifying the initial key words and search terms to be used, you will also have to be knowledgeable about the different databases that are immediately available to you. If you are a current social work student, you probably have a library system with access to various proprietary databases (e.g., Social Work Abstracts and PsychInfo). However, if you are searching for information at your field placement or another place that is not connected to a university library, you will need to rely on different databases (e.g., Google Scholar) and open access journals. The last section of this chapter provides an overview of different databases, search engines, and other types of resources for retrieving necessary information to apply the EBP framework.

Social workers who are proficient at retrieving relevant literature to inform the decision-making process typically use advanced search options and Boolean operators. Making an investment to learn about these advanced search skills can have long-term payoffs. They will make your searches more effective and efficient, allowing more time to be spent in meaningful interactions with the client and other important social work activities. The companion website for this book provides a series of video demonstrations for using some of the advanced search features of freely available databases.

It should be noted that the majority of journals require subscriptions in order to obtain full text access. While most social work students have access to journals through their university or college library system, it is generally cost prohibitive for social work agencies to pay for such subscriptions. However, this is becoming less problematic over time with the proliferation of open access journals and federal policies that require research funded by governmental dollars to be made freely available. The companion website for this book provides a list of databases, open access journals, and other supporting materials that can assist you with conducting literature searches and obtaining free full text articles.

REFLECTIVE LEARNING ACTIVITY

Refer back to the last reflective learning activity. Attempt to use the literature to answer one of your questions. Based on your initial search results, refine your question. If your search resulted in too much information that was irrelevant, narrow your question and search again. If your search produced too little information, consider broadening your question or using different key words.

Step 3: Appraise the evidence.

The concept of *best available evidence* is probably the most contentious and difficult aspect of the EBP. Thus, it is important to critically appraise the research we find in the context of our other EBP information sources. This helps us move beyond the overly simplistic idea of services or treatments as being either evidence based or non-evidence based. A more sophisticated understanding considers the strength and quality of the evidence and thinks critically about how the evidence applies to the specific practice situation. Thus, it is very well possible that the evidence for one practice situation will not be appropriate for another situation. The most common method of evaluating the strength of the evidence is evaluating the designs of the existing studies. The idea behind this approach is that the more rigorous the study, the better the evidence. In addition to considering the research design, Bond and colleagues (2009) present a list of attributes of research that should be considered in the EBP framework (refer to Table 3.3).

Step 4: Develop a plan.

The fourth step involves developing a plan of action. This step is much easier said than done, as it requires advanced skills in both critical and reflective thinking, which are covered later in this chapter. Developing a plan involves the integration of all information sources that define EBP. This involves critical and reflective thinking, considering the relevance of one information source relative to the others as well as involving the client/consumer in collaborative decision-making processes. The process of integration should elicit various choices to be made, and then each choice is systematically considered with respect to relative advantages and weaknesses. You may recognize that you have very few choices or perhaps no choice that seems appropriate. You may identify a particular service approach that might need to be modified or adapted. Or you may find yourself in a situation in which there seems to be no good answer.

Table 3.3   Important Attributes to Consider in the Appraisal of Intervention Research

Criteria	Attributes
Well-defined	Adequate operational definitions Clarifies and incorporates client/staff roles Specification of interventions used
Reflects client/consumer goals	Makes sense to client/consumer Aligns with client/consumer's reasons for seeking services
Consistency with societal goals	Applies interventions that benefit society
Demonstrates effectiveness	Research studies indicate consistent positive findings Findings are replicable in real-world settings
Minimum side effects	Side effects are not greater than/do not offset benefits
Positive long-term outcomes	Interventions lead to long-term positive changes Dependence on mental health services is reduced
Reasonable costs	Costs involved are appropriate and fit within budget limits
Ease of implementation	Clinicians can effectively practice without advanced training Minimal effects due to workforce training and turnover
Adaptable to diverse populations	Practices suit clients of varied backgrounds and values

Source: Bond, G. R., Drake, R. E., McHugo, G. J., Rapp, C. A. & Whitley, R. (2009). Strategies for improving fidelity in the national evidence-based practices project. *Research on Social Work Practice.* Thousand Oaks: SAGE Publications.

Step 5: Evaluate the outcome.

Part of the process of EBP is evaluating outcomes—that is, using a systematic process to determine whether the intervention or other strategy selected is effective. When thinking about this step, it is important to consider it part of an evolving process rather than the final or last step in EBP. More specifically, in the context of a service plan, it is used to help you make decisions as to whether the selected strategy is working or whether changes are necessary. Chapter 11 provides a more detailed description of evaluation of outcomes, including various designs that are useful for working with individuals or groups. The process of monitoring and evaluating outcomes in the course of services is much different than conducting research. However, it is still important to have a strong understanding of research, particularly knowing about the reliability and validity of the measures we select.

In addition to providing you with feedback on the service process, evaluating outcomes also provides the appropriate context for becoming a *reflective practitioner*. We need to find sources of information and experiences that challenge our biases and improve our understanding of the change process. Evaluating intervention outcomes and actively considering what worked and didn't work is an important part of this process.

Resources to Promote Evidence-Based Decisions

As you begin to work within the EBP framework, you will quickly recognize the challenge of locating resources to inform decision making. As a student, you are being trained within a resource-rich environment, with library resources that include subscriptions to journals and other resources that many social work agencies simply cannot afford. Thus, as social work students graduate and enter the field, they may be surprised at the level of difficulty in obtaining current information. However, with the proliferation of online resources, we have a much more positive attitude toward the availability of resources for fieldwork. This section provides an overview of various types of resources that will be of value to your future work. The majority of these resources are available online, so we encourage both social workers and their respective agencies to focus their limited resources to acquiring Internet access as opposed to purchasing print material.

- *Treatment Manuals:* Treatment manuals provide step-by-step descriptions of interventions. Significant heterogeneity exists regarding the amount of detail that is provided. For example, some treatment manuals provide actual scripts for providers that guide providers in what to say in the treatment setting. Such scripted manuals are more difficult to use, given the need to ensure that services are appropriately adapted to the service setting. Other manuals provide details on the overall structure of treatment and various treatment activities. When assessing the manuals, social workers should actively assess the extent to which the manuals are grounded in established theories and have corresponding empirical evidence. We strongly encourage social work students to build a collection of freely and publicly available treatment manuals, which are disseminated on the Internet. These can then become part of the resources to inform practice as well as to enhance an agency's overall set of practice-oriented resources. As a resource to the reader, we have identified and organized a collection of treatment manuals on a variety of topic areas (listed in the companion website).

- *Open Access Journals:* It is helpful to recognize two different types of journals—traditional subscription journals and open access journals. Traditional journals are subscription-based—much like magazines, although the cost of the subscriptions is often significantly more expensive. Thus, it is usually cost prohibitive for individual social workers and social work agencies to maintain subscriptions to these journals. However, open access journals help fill this void. Similar to traditional journals, open access journals contain high-quality original research, although the manner in which they operate allow them to be freely available to readers. We have compiled a list of open access journals that social workers can freely access with an Internet connection in the companion website.

- *Treatment Guidelines:* Treatment guidelines are summary statements that are intended to help persons get oriented quickly to major treatment approaches for specific conditions and problems. High-quality guidelines are based on a comprehensive review of the available knowledge and tend to include all different levels of evidence. Guidelines are a helpful way to become oriented to treatment approaches rather than doing a search. The National Guidelines Clearinghouse (www.guidelines.gov) maintains an archive of high-quality guidelines that are provided in a standardized format. The format provides both a detailed description of guidelines and executive summaries to facilitate their review. A video demonstration of how to search this site is available at the companion website.

- *Systematic Reviews and Meta-analyses:* The Cochrane Collaboration (www .cochrane.org) is an international nonprofit organization that assists in the preparation, maintenance, and dissemination of high-quality systematic reviews and meta-analyses. Thus, it is considered an essential source of information for locating high-quality evidence on the efficacy and effectiveness of interventions for various conditions. Although the Cochrane Database requires subscriptions to obtain full-text articles, this organization provides freely available *Plain Language Summaries,* which are a very efficient way to obtain the main findings of these studies. A video demonstration is provided on how to use this resource (see the companion website).

- *Original Research:* While Social Work Abstracts represents one of the major databases for indexing social work research, access to this database is by subscription only, which limits the opportunity for practicing social workers to conduct searches and access articles. As an alternative, particularly for social workers addressing health and mental health conditions (including addictions), we recommend the use of PubMed, which is maintained by the US National Library of Medicine and the NIH. Although this database contains primarily traditional subscription-based journal articles, it is useful for a variety of reasons. Foremost, unlike many other proprietary databases (e.g., Social Work Abstracts), anybody can access this database and conduct searches free of charge. Additionally, recent policy requires that research funded by the NIH, which is the major funding organization for health and health-related research, to be made freely available in PubMed one year following publication. Thus, social workers will have increased access to the best available evidence at no charge. Furthermore, this site also indexes many open access journals and other freely available articles, which are easily identified using the advanced search functions. The companion website provides video demonstrations of accessing these freely available articles in PubMed.

Moving from EBP to Evidence-Informed (EI) Practice

From this chapter presentation of EBP, we can see that evidence-based social work practice is evolving. The key concerns for us when working with clients/consumers and families is to know in the moment if the interventions we are using are moving them toward hoped-for outcomes.

We know from research on the effectiveness of psychotherapy that the type of treatment we choose is not necessarily the most important component (Carr, 2009) and that the outcomes of psychotherapy are similar across different approaches and with a diverse range of problem areas. The Council on Social Work Education's (CSWE) Education Policy and Accreditation Standards (EPAS) uses the term *EI practice* instead of *EBP* to capture a broader view of our work. EI practice requires that we use research-informed practice (e.g., EBPs) and practice-informed research (e.g., promising practices, consumer feedback) to guide our work. As we have noted, the level of evidence available to us for selecting interventions that will work for individuals and families often requires going beyond what is known. Implementing EBPs and disseminating research-informed interventions can be quite challenging. For example, in Case A (Michael), we will look collaboratively with Michael at the research on anxiety treatments or alcohol abuse treatments. We may find evidence-based interventions that work effectively for individuals who are experiencing anxiety only or alcohol abuse only but no practices that involve both problem areas or that have focused on individuals with the same racial or ethnic background as Michael. In Case B (Naimah), we need to take into account not only her struggles with obesity and hypertension but also we need to engage Naimah in change efforts that make sense to her based on understanding her current peer, family, and school challenges as well as her cultural beliefs and immigrant experiences. As you will note from these case situations, as social workers, we are involved in change efforts that often go beyond what is known from research. We need to adapt evidence-based interventions to meet the complex needs of the individuals and families we engage in change efforts. We engage in practice-based research to systematically collect data to inform us of the effectiveness of the interventions we use. We may be using quality improvement data, consumer feedback loops, or case studies to better understand what is working in a particular situation. The term *EI practice* seems to capture our evolving understanding of the science of social work practice.

CHAPTER REVIEW QUESTIONS

1. What are contemporary definitions of EBP and EI practice?

2. Provide a description of each component of EBP and the manner in which it shapes our decisions.

3. Describe the major steps of EBP decision making.

4. What are the different information sources to facilitate decision making within the EBP framework?

5. What are publicly accessible sources that you can use to keep your knowledge current on the emerging EBPs?

REFERENCES

American Psychiatric Association. (2013). *Diagnostic and statistical manual of mental disorders* (5th ed.). Arlington, VA: American Psychiatric Publishing.

APA Presidential Task Force on Evidence-Based Practice. (2006). Evidence-based practice in psychology. *American Psychologist, 61*(4), 271–285.

Bond, G. R., Drake, R. E., McHugo, G. J., Rapp, C. A., & Whitley, R. (2009). Strategies for improving fidelity in the national evidence-based practices project. *Research on Social Work Practice, 19*(5), 569–581.

Breton, M. (1994). On the meaning of empowerment and empowerment-oriented social work practice. *Social Work with Groups, 17*(3), 23–37.

Carr, A. (2009). *What works with children, adolescents, and adults? A review of research on the effectiveness of psychotherapy.* New York, NY: Routledge.

Cournoyer, B. R., & Stanley, M. J. (2002). *The social work portfolio: Planning, assessing and documenting lifelong learning in a dynamic profession.* ERIC Number: ED475334.

Haynes, R., Devereaux, P., & Guyatt, G. (2002). Clinical expertise in the era of evidence-based medicine and patient choice. *ACP Journal Club, 136,* A11–A14.

Institute of Medicine. (2001). *Crossing the quality chasm: A new health system for the 21st century.* Washington, DC: National Academy Press.

Rose, S., Bisson, J., Churchill, R., & Wessely, S. (2002). Psychological debriefing for preventing post traumatic stress disorder (PTSD). *Cochrane Database of Systematic Reviews, 2*(2), 1–34.

Roth, A., & Fonagy, P. (1996). *What works for whom? A critical review of psychotherapy research.* New York, NY: Guilford Press.

Sackett, D. L., Strauss, S. E., Richardson, W. S., Rosenberg, W., & Haynes, R. B. (1996). Evidence based medicine: What it is and what it isn't. *British Medical Journal, 312,* 71–72.

Satterfield, J. M., Spring, B., Brownson, R. C., Mullen, E. J., Newhouse, R. P., Walker, B. B., & Whitlock, E. P. (2009). Toward a transdisciplinary model of evidence-based practice. *The Milbank Quarterly, 87*(2), 368–390.

Social Work Policy Institute. (2010). *Evidence-based practice.* Retrieved June 4, 2012 from http://www.socialworkpolicy.org/research/evidence-based-practice-2.html

Professional Values, Ethics, and Professional Use of Self

This chapter will highlight social work's professional values and ethics. We will explore how to address ethical dilemmas that will surface in your day-to-day practice. This chapter will also examine the importance of developing a greater awareness of your values and beliefs and how these values and beliefs influence the professional use of self in social work practice.

(Continued)

The Council on Social Work Education Educational Policy and Accreditation Standards (CSWE-EPAS) Competencies that are highlighted in more depth in this chapter are:
2.1.1 Identify as a professional social worker and conduct oneself accordingly.
2.1.2 Apply social work ethical principles to guide professional practice.
2.1.3 Apply critical thinking to inform and communicate professional judgments.

CASE SITUATION A: PEARL

Pearl is an 82-year-old woman who was diagnosed with stomach cancer six weeks ago. Her family does not want her to be told that her condition is terminal. The family wants Pearl to be cared for in her home, where they are able to assist by providing some home health care support. Hospice was ordered by the attending physician but they were instructed not to tell Pearl that they are from hospice. The hospice staff is doing their best to respect the family's wishes, but they are also concerned about Pearl's deteriorating condition and the fact that she constantly asks about what is wrong and why she feels so ill all the time. Pearl has a living will and has made it clear that she doesn't want extraordinary efforts put in place should she not be able to make competent decisions. Due to Pearl's declining condition and her inability to eat, the family demanded that the physician order a feeding tube. The hospice social worker is conflicted about what to do as she is aware of the living will and the fact that Pearl has confided in her that she fears she is dying and no one is telling her the truth.

CASE SITUATION B: JUDY

Judy is a female social worker who is assigned to a short-term inpatient adult psychiatric unit and is responsible for providing group therapy for female patients who are newly diagnosed with a mental illness with the goal of stabilizing them prior to their discharge to an intensive outpatient program. During a group session, one of the patients told the group that she was having an intimate relationship with a male staff member on the unit. Judy spoke privately with the patient after group to investigate further. The patient, while diagnosed with bipolar disorder, was very convincing about this relationship and begged Judy not to talk to the male staff member or tell anyone else on the unit, reminding Judy that she had told the group when it began that the things they shared with everyone would remain totally confidential.

CASE SITUATION C: MOLLY

A 16-year-old female student named Molly was referred to the school social worker by a teacher who was concerned about her promiscuous behavior as seen in the hallways at school and because of the stories other students have shared with her about Molly's provocative behavior. Molly tells the social worker that she enjoys having sex with many young men, that she smokes pot a lot, and that she is allowed to stay out all night if and when she wants to. She lives with her divorced father, Joe, who currently has custody of her. He appears to not be aware of her behavior nor does he care about what she does. The girl's mother, Sarah, is in court fighting for custody, but this has dragged on and on. Molly forbids the social worker to tell or talk to either of her parents and threatens to harm herself if the social worker does. Molly has posted on her Facebook page that the social worker is having an affair with the principal, and she has refused to remove the posting when confronted by the principal.

CASE SITUATION D: TOM

An Iraq war veteran named Tom was receiving outpatient treatment for pain that was a result of a service-related injury. During a routine social work evaluation designed to evaluate psychosocial issues, the social worker observed that Tom was despondent, lethargic, and had a hard time functioning. The social worker suspected that Tom may have been overmedicated. When the social worker approached the treating physician about his concerns regarding the medication dosing, pain levels, and so on, the physician made it very clear that it was out of the social worker's scope of practice and that he himself was a veteran and he knew the level of opiates that his patient could tolerate. The physician indicated that it was his job to make sure his patient was consistently comfortable "because, after all, he will never amount to much and fit back into society."

CASE SITUATION E: SEBASTIAN AND ALICE

Sebastian is a 37-year-old Caucasian youth worker at an after-school program for youth, where he has worked successfully for several years in a large urban area. He is going to community college and studying for his nursing aid certification. Alice is a 29-year-old African American who is Sebastian's supervisor and, in addition, is responsible

(Continued)

(Continued)

for coordinating all the family activities and events that are held on a regular basis in the after-school program. Alice is a licensed social worker who has been promoted quickly to a supervisory position due to retirements in the organization. She has increasingly become concerned about Sebastian's nonprofessional relationships with some of the children and is considering issuing him a written reprimand. Sebastian openly disagrees with Alice on occasion, and he has been known not to follow the program's policies related to social media use. He has used texting with the youth to increase their attendance at the events that he has successfully coordinated, but he also has been making home visits and communicating with parents on Facebook, both of which are against the program's policies. He has told the kids not to tell Alice and acknowledges, when confronted, that he has broken the rules at times. Sebastian argues that he has been able to successfully arbitrate family conflicts, that the adults love him for his energy and passion for the kids, and that he has effectively kept them off the streets.

REFLECTIVE LEARNING ACTIVITY

These five cases raise several potential ethical dilemmas for the social worker. Read through the cases again and list at least three concerns you have about each case situation. How to resolve these concerns or dilemmas requires you to be aware of the professional values and ethics found in the NASW Code of Ethics that guides our day-to-day work. We will address the dilemmas in the cases and provide you with ways to think about resolving these dilemmas in everyday practice later on in this chapter.

Professional Social Work Values, Purpose, and Practice Principles

Becoming aware of our personal and professional values is core to understanding how we can best engage others in a change process. Inherently, values influence the development of ethical principles that become rules that shape our thinking and ethical conduct in the field of social work. Ethical conduct can be evaluated by analyzing decisions/options that have been made when based on ethical principles. The NASW Code of Ethics (1996) provides us with the core values that are central to the field of social work and that guide our everyday professional conduct. The NASW Code of Ethics also provides guiding principles to assist us in resolving dilemmas that may surface in our daily work.

It is important that you take a few minutes to review and begin to learn how to use this Code of Ethics in your daily practice. In addition to the NASW Code of Ethics, there are other codes and guiding principles developed by subgroups of social workers, such as clinical social workers, the National Association of Black Social

Workers, school social workers, and also by international social work organizations such as the International Federation of Social Workers (IFSW). Finally, depending on where you work, you may also be held accountable to additional standards that could include state licensing laws and state codes (public health, mental health, penal, school, etc.) as well as a certification and accreditation standards that may guide social work practice.

The NASW Code of Ethics identifies six stated purposes:

1. Identifies core values on which social work's mission is based

2. Summarizes broad ethical principles that reflect the profession's core values and establishes a set of specific ethical standards that should be used to guide social work practice

3. Is designed to help social workers identify relevant considerations when professional obligations conflict or ethical uncertainties arise

4. Provides ethical standards to which the general public can hold the social work profession accountable

5. Socializes practitioners new to the field to social work's mission, core values, ethical principles, and ethical standards

6. Articulates standards that the social work profession itself can use to assess whether social workers have engaged in unethical conduct

   NASW has developed formal procedures used to adjudicate ethics complaints filed against its members.

In the Code of Ethics, you will also find core values of social work that include the following: service, social justice, dignity and worth of the person, importance of human relationships, integrity, and competence. To better understand how these values are to guide our practice, the Code provides practice principles that help to operationalize these values in our day-to-day work with individuals/families and small groups. The practice principles in the Code that flow from our core social work values include the following:

- Social workers' primary goal is to help people in need and to address social problems. (service)
- Social workers challenge social injustice. (social justice)
- Social workers respect the inherent dignity and worth of the person. (dignity and worth of the person)
- Social workers recognize the central importance of human relationships. (importance of human relationships)
- Social workers behave in a trustworthy manner. (integrity)
- Social workers practice within their areas of competence and develop and enhance their professional expertise. (competence)

A more detailed presentation of each of these values and practice principles is located in Table 4.1.

In addition, there are several core concepts that are used to guide ethical practice. Houston-Vega, Nuehring, and Daguio (1997) identify the following:

- Self-determination
- Informed consent
- Competence
- Confidentiality and privacy
- Attention to conflict of interest
- Maintenance of professional boundaries
- Professionalism

These concepts should be evaluated in each and every client interaction and need to be applied appropriately given the context within which the client is seeking help. A helpful statement out of the NASW Code of Ethics includes the following:

> Social workers treat each person in a caring and respectful fashion, mindful of individual differences and cultural and ethnic diversity. Social workers promote clients' socially responsible self-determination. Social workers seek to enhance clients' capacity and opportunity to change and to address their own needs. Social workers are cognizant of their dual responsibility to clients and to the broader society. They seek to resolve conflicts between clients' interests and the broader society's interests in a socially responsible manner consistent with the values, ethical principles, and ethical standards of the profession.

So we can see that, as the principles and core concepts suggest, social workers have an obligation to ensure that we are helping and not instead actually harming individuals who seek our services due to unethical conduct. It is therefore important to recognize the special challenges we face in implementing these principles and concepts regardless of where we work but particularly when we are working in organizations where individuals and/or families may be mandated to receive services (e.g., in cases of child abuse and neglect, juvenile justice, or behavioral health). It is critical that we remember to highlight and use our social justice lens when focusing on individual/family well-being within a social context while at the same time focusing on the well-being of society. This is accomplished by constantly evaluating environmental forces that create, contribute to, and address problems in living that clients face on a daily basis. We need to recognize that sometimes when we seek to protect people by our actions, we may actually have the opposite effect. It is important, therefore, for you to reflect on your role in the organization, understand the practice principles, and make a conscious effort to take actions that ensure that individuals, families, and society are helped but at the same time protected. We must recognize that these practice principles play a central role in our professional relationships and that we need to respect individuals/families and embrace the diversity present in our work. The other important reminder to take away from these practice principles is that we, as a profession, must seek to work toward social justice so that when we encounter an injustice, we recognize that we have an obligation to take action. Inherent in taking action is the fact that we must also recognize that we are responsible for ensuring that we have the skill set required to carry out our helping role.

As you might start to recognize, our core values, practice principles, and concepts that guide ethical practice may often raise ethical dilemmas for us in the real-world setting. Several social workers who are prominent in the field of social work ethics have developed ways for us to think about how we can practice ethically. Strom-Gottfried (2008, p. 3) identified five common ways that ethical dilemmas can arise:

1. When the application or boundary of an ethical standard is unclear

2. When standards conflict with institutional demands

3. When there are conflicting loyalties

4. When a professional finds it difficult to adhere to an ethical standard

5. When good solutions seem unattainable

REFLECTIVE LEARNING ACTIVITY

Pick one of the cases presented at the beginning of the chapter and, using the Strom-Gottfried list above, reflect on each type of dilemma within the context of the case.

As a social worker, you often will be in a position where you must decide between two good or two or more compelling "right" choices or courses of action.

Reamer (2013), reflecting on the work of Beauchamp and Childress (2001), identified nine focal or critical virtues and moral principles that are important in social work practice. These include compassion, discernment, trustworthiness, integrity, conscientiousness, autonomy, non-maleficence, beneficence, and justice. Take a moment to review the definitions of these critical virtues in Table 4.2.

Let's consider the values and practice principles we have identified from the NASW Code of Ethics and these nine core virtues and moral principles as they relate to one of our case situations. In Case Situation A (Pearl), you may have listed concerns about how to implement the NASW Code of Ethics' values of service, dignity, and worth of the person and importance of human relationships and integrity as it relates to Pearl's desires and the desires of her family. In addition, when you consider the core virtues, Pearl's situation raises questions about how we implement our compassion, how we discern what steps to take, how trustworthy we are seen by Pearl and her family, how to maintain our professional integrity, and what the right course of action is in this situation. We need to consider how we address autonomy, our obligation not to bring additional harm to others, how we carry out our charity, and whether we are being fair and

Table 4.1   Ethical Principles from the NASW Code of Ethics (1996)

Value: *Service* **Ethical Principle:** *Social workers' primary goal is to help people in need and to address social problems.* Social workers elevate service to others above self-interest. Social workers draw on their knowledge, values, and skills to help people in need and to address social problems. Social workers are encouraged to volunteer some portion of their professional skills with no expectation of significant financial return (pro bono service).

Value: *Social Justice* **Ethical Principle:** *Social workers challenge social injustice.* Social workers pursue social change, particularly with and on behalf of vulnerable and oppressed individuals and groups of people. Social workers' social change efforts are focused primarily on issues of poverty, unemployment, discrimination, and other forms of social injustice. These activities seek to promote sensitivity to and knowledge about oppression and cultural and ethnic diversity. Social workers strive to ensure access to needed information, services, and resources; equality of opportunity; and meaningful participation in decision making for all people.

Value: *Dignity and Worth of the Person* **Ethical Principle:** *Social workers respect the inherent dignity and worth of the person.* Social workers treat each person in a caring and respectful fashion, mindful of individual differences and cultural and ethnic diversity. Social workers promote clients' socially responsible self-determination. Social workers seek to enhance clients' capacity and opportunity to change and to address their own needs. Social workers are cognizant of their dual responsibility to clients and to the broader society. They seek to resolve conflicts between clients' interests and the broader society's interests in a socially responsible manner consistent with the values, ethical principles, and ethical standards of the profession.

Value: *Importance of Human Relationships* **Ethical Principle:** *Social workers recognize the central importance of human relationships.* Social workers understand that relationships between and among people are an important vehicle for change. Social workers engage people as partners in the helping process. Social workers seek to strengthen relationships among people in a purposeful effort to promote, restore, maintain, and enhance the well-being of individuals, families, social groups, organizations, and communities.

Value: *Integrity* **Ethical Principle:** *Social workers behave in a trustworthy manner.* Social workers are continually aware of the profession's mission, values, ethical principles, and ethical standards and practice in a manner consistent with them. Social workers act honestly and responsibly and promote ethical practices on the part of the organizations with which they are affiliated.

Value: *Competence* **Ethical Principle:** *Social workers practice within their areas of competence and develop and enhance their professional expertise.* Social workers continually strive to increase their professional knowledge and skills and to apply them in practice. Social workers should aspire to contribute to the knowledge base of the profession.

Source: Copyrighted material reprinted with permission from the National Association of Social Workers, Inc.

Table 4.2	Definitions of the Nine Focal or Critical Virtues and Moral Principles

Focal/Critical Virtue	
Compassion	An attitude of active regard or caring for another's well-being
Discernment	Ability to make judgments with insight and understanding
Trustworthiness	Confidence that one will act with the right motives and the belief that the person will use moral norms
Integrity	Acting with fidelity to moral norms
Conscientiousness	Motivated to do what is right because it is right and using due diligence to determine what is right
Moral Principles	
Autonomy	Involves self-rule free from controlling interference by others
Non-maleficence	Obligation to not inflict harm on others
Beneficence	Acts of mercy, kindness, and charity
Justice	Fair, equitable, and appropriate treatment

Source: Reamer, F. (2013). *Social work values and ethics (4th edition)* NY, NY Columbia University Press.

equitable in our treatment interventions/courses of action. The other case situation examples raise similar types of value-related issues. That is why the Code of Ethics needs to be used, as it will give us guidance when we begin to address the emerging value-related conflicts. Using an ethical lens will assist you in developing the capacity to think of ethics as a process that derives from a context. Inherent in this process is also the fact that you must remember that your personal values may compete and/or conflict with individual/family, client, or consumer values and/or the values of the social work profession. This is why it is important for you to learn the profession's values, principles, and core concepts and explore your underlying personal values and identify where these conflict with the profession's. Two ways to accomplish this can be done by debating hypothetical cases and presenting/discussing issues/situations as illustrated by the cases utilizing an ethical lens. You can also address these conflicts with your supervisor as well as participate in case consultations with the goal of resolving these conflicts in ways to ensure that individuals/families and clients/consumers do not experience harm.

NASW Code of Ethics Standards

The next section of the NASW Code of Ethics addresses the standards that are used to ensure that we are engaging in ethical practice. These ethical standards involve five key areas: (1) responsibilities to clients, (2) responsibilities to colleagues, (3) responsibilities in practice settings, (4) responsibilities as professionals, (5) responsibilities to the social work profession, and (6) responsibilities to the broader society. When addressing responsibilities to clients, the standards outline the primary responsibility that we have, to promote the well-being of clients by ensuring that

- the rights of clients ensure that self-determination is fostered,
- clients are informed, and consent to the services is provided,
- social workers operate in their areas of competence,
- social workers develop the skills to engage in practices that reflect cultural competence and value social diversity,
- social workers address any conflict of interest and respect the privacy and confidentiality of the helping process,
- a process is in place for clients to access records,
- social workers do not engage in sexual relationships with clients and minimize or avoid physical contact (especially if it has the potential to promote psychological harm),
- social workers do not sexually harass clients or use derogatory language,
- social workers establish fair pricing/fees for services delivered,
- social workers take safeguards to protect clients who lack decision-making capacity,
- any interruption in services is addressed in order to minimize harm, and
- when terminating services, appropriate steps are in place to maximize the benefit of the helping process.

Many of the dilemmas raised in our case examples will be easier to address and resolve when we use these standards to sort out the dilemmas that arise, particularly when these focus on our responsibilities to clients.

REFLECTIVE LEARNING ACTIVITY

Return to the list you created in the first reflective learning activity, where you identified three ethical concerns you had about each case situation. Using this list, identify which Code of Ethics standards related to responsibilities to clients outlined above would apply to your concerns. List the challenges that still remain for you.

The next set of standards in the Code addresses issues related to our ethical responsibilities to colleagues. The Code articulates that social workers need to

- practice respect;
- respect confidential information that may be shared;
- value participating in interdisciplinary collaboration;
- avoid taking sides when disputes occur between colleagues and the employer;

- engage in consultation when in the best interests of clients;
- refer clients to colleagues with specialized knowledge or skills to best assist the client;
- avoid sexual relationships with colleagues when there is a potential for conflict;
- not sexually harass interns, supervisees, or colleagues;
- take action when one has direct knowledge that the colleague's impairment due to personal problems, psychosocial distress, substance abuse, or mental health difficulties is impacting on services to clients and a organization; and
- take action if a colleague is putting the client or organization at risk due to incompetence and when a colleague engages in unethical practice.

Taking action may involve different steps based on organizational policies and procedures and state laws. In Case Situations B (Judy) and D (Tom), we can see how the standards related to responsibilities to colleagues might help us address concerns about inappropriate sexual relationships with clients/consumers, our work on interdisciplinary teams, and our perceived incompetence of a colleague.

A third set of standards when addressing our ethical responsibilities in social work practice settings include

- supervision and consultation,
- education and training,
- performance evaluation,
- client records,
- billing,
- client transfer,
- administration,
- continuing education and staff development,
- commitment to employers, and
- labor management disputes.

The standards related to our ethical responsibilities as professionals focus on

- competence;
- discrimination;
- private conduct;
- dishonesty, fraud, and deception;
- impairment;
- misrepresentation;
- solicitations; and
- acknowledging credit.

The next set of ethical standards focus on our ethical responsibility to the social work profession and include

- integrity of the profession, and
- evaluation and research.

The last set of standards focus on our ethical responsibilities to the broader society and include

- social welfare,
- public participation,
- public emergencies, and
- social and political action.

Again, these standards can help us to sort out the dilemmas and help us resolve some of the conflicts or dilemmas you may have identified on your list using the case situation examples.

REFLECTIVE LEARNING ACTIVITY

Look at your remaining challenges and dilemmas. Do the other standards related to responsibilities to colleagues, responsibilities to practice settings, responsibilities as a professional, responsibilities to the social work profession, and responsibilities to the broader society help you to resolve some of the challenges or dilemmas that you noted earlier in the chapter?

Ethical Decision Making

When professional and personal values and practice principles conflict and when the standards do not provide us clear guidance, an ethical dilemma may emerge in our work that requires us to use a higher level of critical thinking to resolve. There are a range of frameworks that can be used to guide us in engaging in ethical decision making. One framework is called the ABCDE Multiple Perspectives Framework (Strom-Gottfried, 2008, p. 17). In this framework, the *A* stands for *assess options*, the *B* focuses on *being mindful of the process*, the *C* involves *consultation*, the *D* addresses *documenting the decision process*, and the *E* involves *evaluating the outcomes*. All the steps except *E* can be done simultaneously or in a different order, based on the context of the situation. In assessing options, you need to consider a wide range of ethical theories and principles, appropriate laws and policies, professional values, pertinent information, and appropriate standards. In being mindful of the process, you are being asked to explore multiple options, to think about how different decisions might be enacted, and to consider what might be possible outcomes. Consultation is extremely important and involves seeking input from your immediate supervisors or other experts about ways to approach and resolve the ethical dilemma. The documentation step is critical in order to capture how the ethical dilemma was resolved, particularly if there are legal implications or ramifications. Oftentimes, the documentation will be recorded in the client's/consumer's permanent case record or case consultation notes. The evaluation step involves exploring how the application of the ethical decision has impacted the client/consumer but also includes you as the worker, reflecting on the process you used to resolve the dilemma.

Reamer (2013) provides another framework for ethical decision making that clarifies some of these steps in more detail. In Reamer's framework (p. 78) there are seven steps:

1. Identify the ethical issues, including the social work values and duties that conflict.

2. Identify the individuals, groups, and organizations likely to be affected by the ethical decision.

3. Tentatively identify all viable courses of action and the participants involved in each, along with the potential benefits and risks for each.

4. Thoroughly examine the reasons in favor of and against each course of action, considering relevant

    A. code of ethics and legal principles;

    B. ethical theories, principles, and guidelines;

    C. social work practice theory and principles; and

    D. personal values (including religious, cultural, and ethnic values and political ideology).

5. Consult with colleagues and appropriate experts (such as agency staff, supervisors, agency administrators, attorneys, and ethics scholars).

6. Make the decision and document the decision-making process.

7. Monitor, evaluate, and document the decision.

Let's look at Case Situation A (Pearl). While many of the ethical dilemmas or challenges that you noted when you first read the case situation may have been resolved once you explored values, practice principles, and standards, some may still remain. One ethical dilemma from Case Situation A that would benefit from using the ABCDE Multiple Perspectives Framework or the more detailed seven-step framework is the question that surfaces related to conflicting demands from Pearl, who is receiving the services, and her family, who are paying for the services and are responsible for Pearl's care. How can you continue to engage in work with Pearl if you do not provide her with information related to her illness/condition and you continue to engage in the deception related to your organizational role and purpose? What would happen if you informed Pearl of her condition against her family's wishes and the family discontinues your agency's services? In Case Situation B (Judy), you have a client/consumer who wants you to keep to the rules of the group that indicate that what is shared in group sessions is to be held confidential, and you also have an obligation to report the potential ethical violation of a staff member related to engaging in intimate relationships with a client/consumer. In Case Situation C (Molly), there are several dilemmas that surface related to the minor status of the youth, the role of the parents, and social networking tools that may have been used to spread disinformation. In Case Situation D (Tom), your role to do no harm, the power differentials that appear to exist between your role as the social worker and the role played by the physician, and the best interests of the client/consumer all illustrate potential ethical dilemmas. In Case Situation E (Sebastian), there are several dilemmas related to responsibilities to practice settings, colleagues and professionals, and the use of social media. Using the steps identified in the two frameworks, you can see how important it is for you to engage in several critical thinking tasks in order to explore and resolve these dilemmas. Remember, if the answer is obvious and our personal and professional values, practice principles, or standards are clear, then you would not need to engage in this more intensive process.

REFLECTIVE LEARNING ACTIVITY

Choose two of the cases presented at the beginning of this chapter and apply Strom-Gottfried's ABCDE Multiple Perspectives Framework or Reamer's Seven-Step Framework to help you sort out and develop a plan of action that might resolve the ethical dilemmas you outlined in earlier reflective learning activities. Consult with a classmate to see if your conclusions are similar to their conclusions.

A Closer Look at Self-Determination, Informed Consent and Confidentiality, Privileged Communication, and Technology/Social Media Use

In this section, we will examine a few of the standards of self-determination, informed consent, privileged communication, and the expansion of technology/social media use related to ethical social work practice in more detail. In an earlier section of this chapter, we discussed how some of these core concepts are important as contextual influences that need to be taken into consideration when exploring ethical issues.

Self-Determination

In most situations, the right that clients/consumers have to self-determination is one of the most highly valued concepts in the social work profession. Even when working with mandated clients/consumers, we need to ensure that we seek to maximize choice and control for the client/consumer. In Case Situation A (Pearl), the issue of self-determination surfaces as we think about Pearl's right to know and be informed about her illness/condition and the family's concern that if we were to tell Pearl, it might result in negative outcomes for her that involve her inability to handle the news about her illness and impending death. Some social workers might agree with the family members and argue that telling Pearl will do more harm than good and that this justifies not informing her of her condition. Other social workers would argue that withholding information from Pearl is engaging in deception, which is unethical. Whenever social workers choose to withhold information or limit the right to self-determination of a client/consumer, they could be accused of acting in a paternalistic manner, and their motivations and actions could be construed as suspect. Think back to the NASW Standards related to responsibilities toward clients. Review in more detail this section of the NASW Code of Ethics as it relates to this issue (Section 1.02 and Section 1.03). Balancing the client/consumer's right to know and their right to be informed in order to assist them in making sound decisions about the situation they may be in and balancing this with the desire to protect the client/consumer from potential harm needs to be explored and addressed using the tools presented in this chapter in order to successfully address the ethical concerns.

Informed Consent and Confidentiality

Informed consent involves engaging with clients/consumers in discussions related to the purposes of intervention, benefits and risks involved in participating in the change process, limits of services and third-party payment requirements, presentation of reasonable alternatives, costs of services, and client/consumer's right to refuse or withdraw consent. The informed consent process usually involves documenting this understanding in a written form signed by the client/consumer and is usually time limited. Understanding how confidentiality will be protected in this helping process is also core to the discussion of informed consent. Clients/consumers have the expectation that, as professionals, we will keep their situation private and will protect their rights to confidentiality. Gambrill (2006, p. 49) defines *confidentiality* as regulating against disclosure of information about a client without the client's permission. The discussion regarding the purpose and the limits of confidentiality needs to occur as soon as possible during the initial engagement process. In fact, the NASW Code of Ethics specifies in detail the different ways we as professionals need to protect confidentiality as it relates to clients/consumers, our record keeping, and our reporting out of information about a case situation to third-party payers or during legal proceedings.

There are exceptions to confidentiality, such as state-mandated child abuse and neglect reporting laws, elder abuse reporting laws (usually referred to as *mandatory reporting laws*), and the Tarasoff court decision (*Tarasoff v. Board of Regents of the University of California, 1976*) regarding the duty to protect the client/consumer and others who might be harmed. This exemption to confidentiality is often referred to as the *duty to warn* when others are at imminent risk of harm. In the Tarasoff case, the therapist alerted his supervisor and the police that his client was threatening to kill a woman. The police detained the individual for a brief time but had insufficient grounds to hold him. The man did kill the woman. While the therapist did take action by alerting his supervisor and the police, the therapist failed to warn the woman of the danger from this man. He failed in his *duty to warn.*

Other laws are in place to ensure that we protect confidential information, and it increases our responsibilities to protect private information. Some of the key laws include the Confidentiality of Alcohol and Drug Abuse Patient Records (42 C.F.R. 2–1 ff.), the Health Insurance Portability and Accountability Act (HIPAA-Public Law 104–91), the Uniform Child Custody Jurisdiction Act (UCCJA) of 1968, the Uniform Child Custody Jurisdiction and Enforcement Act (UCCJEA) of 1996, the Parental Kidnapping Prevention Act (PKPA) of 1981, and the Family Educational Rights and Privacy Act (FERPA) of 1974. In Case Situation C (Molly), we can see how having a discussion related to informed consent would help you clarify with the parents and Molly your limits related to confidentiality when working with minors and would help you figure out how to address how you work with a noncustodial parent in the intervention process. In Case Situation B (Judy), when setting up the rules for the group, you should have used an informed consent process with Judy that would have identified exceptions to the confidentiality rule. In Case Situation D (Tom), the informed consent process steps would have helped address alternative approaches to treatment.

Privileged Communication

Privileged communication refers to the legal rights of clients/consumers to refrain from having their communications with the social worker revealed in court without their permission (Gambrill, 2006). The Tarasoff court decision referenced above provided the grounds for occasions when privileged communication can be waived. Some of these exemptions include if a client/consumer waives the right to privileged communication, if the client/consumer shares privileged material in court proceedings or litigation, if the social worker is called to testify in a criminal case, if the client threatens to commit suicide or harm others, if a minor is involved in criminal activity, or if child abuse or neglect is suspected. It is important for you to review the Tarasoff court decision and become familiar with the laws in your state related to exemptions to privileged communications.

REFLECTIVE LEARNING ACTIVITY

It is important for you to have an understanding of federal laws, state laws, and your own agency's rules and regulations regarding privileged communications.

Interview one or two social workers who are working in the area that you want to practice, and ask them how they understand and apply privileged communication laws. What sources do they use to help clarify when exemptions are permitted and under what conditions?

Technology/Social Media Use

With the expansion of the use of a range of technologies in storing client information (e.g., electronic medical records, third-party billing systems) and the use of different technologies to deliver interventions (e.g., online counseling, e-support groups), it is extremely important that we pay special attention to the ways that the different technologies have been designed to protect client privacy. Many of the popular ways that we communicate using technology do not ensure the levels of privacy that are mandated in order to protect a client's information. Be sure to investigate at your field internship site how technology is used and what protections are in place to ensure client privacy.

Though the official standards of the social work profession may struggle to keep pace with the ever-evolving presence of social media in our lives, social workers must be proactive by being mindful of their ethical and professional responsibilities related to the use of social media. A major challenge for the social work profession is that official practice standards continue to lag far behind the rapid growth of online social media, despite efforts by the NASW and Association of Social Work Boards (ASWB) as they attempt to address new technologies in social work practice. For example, in 2005, when Facebook was just a year old, the NASW and ASWB released their *Standards for Technology and Social Work Practice*, which was an attempt to establish overarching guidelines for ethical practice in the digital age; however, these failed to address specific precautions to take when using online social media. The specific goals of these standards are

- to maintain and improve the quality of technology-related services provided by social workers;
- to serve as a guide to social workers incorporating technology into their services;
- to help social workers monitor and evaluate the ways in which technology is used in their services; and
- to inform clients, government regulatory bodies, insurance carriers, and others about the professional standards for the use of technology in the provision of social work services.

The complete set of the NASW Technology Standards can be found online.

The NASW Code of Ethics is also behind the times. Since its last revision in 2008, many more popular social media sites (e.g., Foursquare, Google+, Instagram, Pinterest) have surfaced. When faced with any ethical dilemma, social workers are advised to consult the NASW Code of Ethics; however, this currently may be more confusing because the Code does not explicitly articulate ethical standards for the use of social media. It therefore becomes challenging to navigate the increasingly complex ethical dilemmas inherent in social media use.

We must be proactive by being mindful of our ethical and professional responsibilities related to social media use and realize that it is prudent to exercise caution in online activities. We suggest that in many social work practice settings, social work coherence may be best achieved through the development of comprehensive social media guidelines/policies. These policies and/or guidelines should be created as a means of clarifying expectations for employees, students in field placement, and client relationships. All social workers will benefit from guidance in several areas that focus on building intentional online identities as social work professionals, appropriate professional and personal use of social media in accordance with the NASW Code of Ethics, and risk management strategies for online behavior, thus ensuring that ethically sound social work practice expectations are clarified.

Particularly for those training to be behavioral health service providers during the Internet age, it has become imperative that potential online ethical issues be acknowledged and addressed in educational settings and by clinical supervisors (Lehavot, Barnett, & Powers, 2010, pp. 165–166). New practitioners, especially those who are more likely to regularly use social media, may not solicit guidance from more experienced clinicians because they perceive them to be lacking in knowledge and exposure to Internet-related ethical dilemmas (Guseh, Brendel, & Brendel, 2009, p. 584; Taylor, McMinn, Bufford, & Chang, 2010, p. 157). Being able to rely upon a social media policy would help new practitioners chart a professional course through murky ethical waters. According to Trimberger, "Professional social work boundaries and ethical behaviors are influenced by a worker's personal and professional environment" (2012, p. 74). This points to the need for continued exploration regarding how social media usage in our agencies impacts not only the development of your professional identity but also how social media usage guidelines/policies might affect the profession overall related to the established benchmarks for ethical practice.

New ethical challenges are surfacing on a daily basis as the boundaries between personal and professional lives are constantly being tested as a result of social media use, such as Facebook, LinkedIn, Twitter, Blogger, Tumblr, Flickr, and the use of texting. By using Google, clients can often locate personal information about us and may even seek to have us join ("friend") them on their social network sites. It is important for us to become familiar with how we can best implement ethical practice related to the use of technology.

The popularity of social networking and microblogging sites such as Facebook and Twitter has increased the amount of personal information people share online, while search engines such as Google enable people to find practically anything they might be looking for in seconds. Unfortunately, it has become easier than ever before for us to blur the boundaries between personal and professional relationships online. As an example, the uninvited discovery of personal information on both sides of a treatment relationship could have a devastating impact on the goals that have been established and could negatively impact the treatment outcomes. As simple as it would be to say, "Never Google clients without their consent," the ethical course is not always clear.

REFLECTIVE LEARNING ACTIVITY

A social worker decides that, in the interest of the safety of a client who has missed their last few appointments and who has been impossible to contact, they will search for the client on Facebook to determine if she is indeed safe.

Is this violation of the client's privacy or an attempt to ensure the client's well-being?

Is it permissible/ethically right to violate the client's privacy in the name of safety?

What happens if the social worker becomes privy to a lot of previously undisclosed information about the client that is not related to the issue of client safety?

What other course of action/resources might be available to the social worker instead of searching for the client online?

Blurring the boundaries by being friends with a client on Facebook also poses issues such as dual relationships, conflicts of interest, and potential confidentiality/privacy violations. An organization's social media guidelines/policy should make clear that under no circumstance should a student or employee be friending a client from a personal Facebook page, following a client on Twitter, or engaging in any other type of online relationship with a client, as this constitutes a dual relationship (Section 1.06(c) of the NASW Code of Ethics). Social workers do not need to fear social media, but they do need to understand it and make a place for it in their ethical awareness, which will help them to adapt to the ever-changing social media landscape.

In Case Situation C (Molly), you are confronted with the way that Molly has used social media (Facebook) to share false information in ways that could potentially damage your and the principal's reputation. Even once the information is removed from Molly's Facebook page, the number of people who would have read this false accusation is often unknown, and there is the growing alarm that once posted, nothing can really ever be removed. Since social workers believe that "once a client, always a client," the issue of access to personal information through social media does raise ethical issues when boundaries are too fluid. Agencies should have policies related to the use of technology and social media as these relate to client information sharing and professional boundary setting by employees/students. In general, it is important to address dual relationships, confidentiality, boundary issues, and privacy concerns when using technology and social media with your supervisor as it relates to your professional role and the type of helping relationships that are supported by your organizational roles. Case Situation E (Sebastian) also raises several concerns related to the use of social media.

> **REFLECTIVE LEARNING ACTIVITY**
>
> Using Case Situation E (Sebastian), list 2–3 positive attributes that might prove useful when using technology/social media related to the mission of the work of the program. Then list 2–3 ethical issues of concern related to the use of technology and social media. Given what you have learned in this chapter, discuss the course of action that you would recommend given the ethical concerns you have identified.

Addressing Malpractice and Unethical Behavior

As social workers, we have a responsibility to our clients/consumers to alert state licensing boards and/or appropriate governing authorities when we witness or become aware of unethical behavior or malpractice by colleagues. Social workers who are found guilty of unethical behavior or malpractice may have their professional licenses suspended/removed and may face criminal charges, depending on the type of offense. In recent situations, complaints against social workers have included things that have been copied from various social media sites to substantiate the complaints. Some examples include the social worker posting statements about how they feel about their clients, about buying and selling things that involved clients, and so on. In one situation, a young woman was advertising her services on Facebook. She had her master of social work (MSW) degree, and her services were within the scope of the licensing law. A client entered an official complaint with the state licensing board by copying things that were on her Facebook page. Right under her picture, she had written "I am a social worker." It turned out that she had let her license lapse, so she was formally charged with practicing without a license. Her response was that she was not working as a social worker because she was working online and that she was calling herself a "social work designee." She was sanctioned and a fine was imposed.

In another situation, a man started a website offering online therapy. He used Facebook and LinkedIn to advertise his services. He was charged by the state licensing board with practicing without a license because he was licensed only by the state he was living in but was offering and providing services to residents who lived in another state. He was sanctioned with probation, limitations were placed on his license, and he was fined and required to enroll in continuing education coursework.

Reamer (2013, p. 191) notes that a substantial portion of claims filed against social workers allege some form of misconduct or unethical behavior and fall into one or more of these categories: informed consent, the delivery of services, and boundary violations. In Case Situation B (Judy), the social worker is challenged to report a colleague to authorities within her own organization and also potentially to the state licensing board for unethical behavior related to the colleague possibly having an intimate/inappropriate relationship with a client/consumer. In determining whether a social worker has violated professional standards, the state licensing board references the NASW Code of

Ethics, current laws in the state, and what are considered best practices during the investigation and proceedings. Allegations of improper assessment or intervention, such as in Case Situation D (Tom), may cause the reporting to be taken to a different licensing board based on the profession of the individual engaged in problematic and/or unethical practice. Again, the importance of supervision and consultation cannot be overstated as these relate to understanding ethical practice.

Professional Use of Self

Social workers bring to the helping relationship their own experiences, values, and beliefs that influence how they engage others in a change process. Becoming aware of how our personal experiences, values, and beliefs can enhance our connections to those we seek to help or can hinder the helping process is a critical component of effective social work practice. In social work practice, the most important tool that we have is our professional use of self in helping to promote positive change for individuals/families and small groups. If we think about ourselves as a tool for promoting change, then we need to also be aware of how our personal and professional values influence the way we engage others in change, how our knowledge and skills can be used to facilitate movement forward, and how our actions convey preferred ways of engaging in change efforts. Reflecting on our own journeys into the helping profession of social work and exploring our motivations for helping others are important components of developing our professional use of self in our work with others. This is a lifelong process, and as we reflect through supervision and in discussion with colleagues how we are using our professional self in our work, we will be able to continually refine our tool (ourselves) and enhance our ability to create opportunities for positive change for diverse groups of individuals/families and small groups.

REFLECTIVE LEARNING ACTIVITY

Set aside 15–30 minutes and reflect on what has led you to want to practice the profession of social work. Take a few moments to engage in a "free write" exercise where you put your thoughts, feelings, and motivations in writing. This reflection can be the beginning of your journey in understanding the role that the professional use of self plays in your role as a developing social worker.

CHAPTER REVIEW QUESTIONS

1. Identify two purposes of the NASW Code of Ethics and use one of the cases presented in the beginning of the chapter to illustrate why these purposes are important.

2. Using the NASW Code of Ethics, discuss three of the core values and three practice principles that will guide your work with individuals/families and clients/consumers.

3. Using one of the cases presented in the beginning of the chapter, discuss three core concepts that would be important to focus on when deciding a course of action to take. Apply the ABCDE Multiple Perspectives Framework to one of the dilemmas you identified in Case Situation E (Sebastian).

4. After reviewing the critical values and moral principles found in Table 4.2, discuss why these are important to your development as a social worker.

5. Discuss your understanding of what is meant by *privileged communication* and list 2–3 exceptions to this type of communication that you have become aware of in your state.

6. Discuss how you would engage individuals/families and small groups in relation to informed consent procedures.

7. Discuss three reasons why it is important for agencies to establish social media guidelines/policies.

8. Discuss three reasons why it is important for you to establish a professional online identity.

9. Discuss why the professional use of self is an integral aspect of the helping process.

REFERENCES

Beauchamp, T. I., & Childress, J. F. (2001). *Principles of biomedical ethics* (5th ed.). New York, NY: Oxford University Press.

Gambrill, E. (2006). *Social work practice: A critical thinker's guide* (2nd ed.). New York, NY: Oxford University Press.

Guseh, J. S., Brendel, R. W., & Brendel, D. H. (2009). Medical professionalism in the age of online social networking. *Journal of Medical Ethics, 35*(9), 584–586.

Houston-Vega, M. K., Nuehring, E. M., & Daguio, E. R. (1997). *Prudent practice: A guide for managing malpractice risk.* Washington, DC: NASW Press.

Lehavot, K., Barnett, J., & Powers, D. (2010). Psychotherapy, professional relationships, and ethical considerations in the MySpace generation. *Professional Psychology: Research and Practice, 41*(2), 160–166.

National Association of Social Workers (NASW). (1996). *Code of Ethics of the National Association of Social Workers* (Revised in 2008). Washington, DC: Author. Retrieved July 25, 2014 from http://www.naswdc.org/pubs/code/code.asp

Reamer, F. (2013). *Social work values and ethics* (4th ed.). New York, NY: Columbia University Press.

Strom-Gottfried, K. (2008). *The ethics of practice with minors: High stakes, hard choices.* Chicago, IL: Lyceum Books.

Taylor, L., McMinn, M. R., Bufford, R. K., & Chang, K. B. T. (2010). Psychologists' attitudes and ethical concerns regarding the use of social networking web sites. *Professional Psychology: Research and Practice, 41*(2), 153–159.

Trimberger, G. E. (2012). An exploration of the development of professional boundaries. *Journal of Social Work Values & Ethics, 9*(2), 68–75.

5

Engagement and Relationship-Building Skills

As we begin to explore engagement and relationship-building skills in work with individuals, families, and groups, it is important to understand that our role is one of a partner and change facilitator. As social workers working in a range of service settings (e.g., behavioral health, health, child welfare, aging services, welfare, criminal/juvenile justice, developmental disabilities services), we provide a continuum of services that require core engagement and relationship-building skills that emphasize individual and/or family strengths, that activate resources to support change efforts, that respect individual diversity, and that build hope for a better future for the individuals and families who engage in change work.

CHAPTER LEARNING OBJECTIVES

By the end of this chapter, you should be able to

- understand the core relationship-building values that guide us in the engagement phase when working with individuals/families and small groups;
- build collaborative helping relationships that emphasize a strengths-based orientation, value diversity, and utilize an empowerment approach;
- identify skills to promote the likelihood that individuals, families, and small groups who could benefit from services seek the services they need and follow through with change efforts; and

(Continued)

(Continued)

- understand the Stages of Change Framework and identify the skills needed to implement this framework in social work practice to support readiness of individuals/families and small groups in engaging in the change processes.

The Council on Social Work Education Educational Policy and Accreditation Standards (CSWE-EPAS) Competencies that are highlighted in more depth in this chapter include the following:
2.1.3 Apply critical thinking to inform and communicate professional judgments.
2.1.4 Engage diversity and difference in practice.
2.1.6 Engage in research-informed practice and practice-informed research.
2.1.7 Apply knowledge of human behavior and the social environment.
2.1.9 Respond to contexts that shape practice.
2.1.10 (a–d) Engage, assess, intervene, and evaluate with individuals, families, groups, organizations, and communities.

In this chapter, we will use the following two case situations to illustrate key engagement and relationship-building skills.

CASE SITUATION A: PAUL AND LISA

Paul and Lisa are in their 30s and have been married for 13 years. They have three daughters (Maddy, who is 13; Sophia, who is 11; and Bea, who is 3). Paul is a naturalized American citizen. He moved with his parents to the United States from Chile when he was 10 years old. Lisa's parents were from Mexico, but Lisa was born in the United States. Paul and Lisa are fluent in Spanish and English.

Paul is currently out of work but is actively seeking employment. He is very quiet and appears depressed at times. Lisa works at a local convenience store, and her shift varies between the midnight and the early morning times. Lisa is viewed as the family organizer. They live in a rental house in a very rural area. Lisa's parents live in the area, as do Paul's parents. The family enjoys a good relationship with the maternal grandparents, but there has been no contact with the paternal grandparents for over 10 years.

Maddy has a very stubborn case of eczema, which requires her to wear gloves to school in order to protect her open wounds. She is a track and field star at her school and loves animals. She is in charge of caring for the six-month-old dog they adopted as a stray.

The family has had contact with the Department of Human Services' Child Protective Services (CPS) unit over the last 3–4 years for charges of medical neglect, which have not been substantiated.

Recently, Maddy contracted Norwegian scabies, most likely from her maternal grandparent's house. This is a very stubborn parasite that burrows under the skin and can live without a human host for 24–36 hours. The family has tried unsuccessfully to eradicate the scabies. The landlord found out about the outburst of the scabies and has threatened eviction.

Maddy is getting bullied at school, her grades are slipping, and she fusses about having to go to school in the morning when the bus arrives. The teachers at the school are unsympathetic to her situation, most likely due to their fear of the risk of contracting the scabies.

Paul and Lisa are under a great deal of strain due to constant calls from the school and the landlord. In fact, Lisa's job is in jeopardy. She has found it difficult to be on time for work due to the demands placed on her by the school and the landlord. She has been working hard to try and maintain some sense of normality for her family. The family has attempted to treat their home to get rid of the scabies, but these attempts have been unsuccessful. The school indicates that they may have no choice but to suspend Maddy from school until this can be resolved.

Another CPS referral was made (probably by the school) that substantiated medical neglect. As a last-chance effort prior to removing the children to foster care for reasons of medical neglect, the family was referred to the social worker at the Family's First program. This program provides intensive support, advocacy, and access to available resources/services.

The younger children are thriving and doing well in school and have not contracted the scabies, nor has either parent.

CASE SITUATION B: SAM AND ANNA

Sam is a 34-year-old Caucasian Marine Corps veteran who has served two tours in Afghanistan. He married Anna 18 months ago, and they are the proud parents of a new baby boy. Anna also identifies as Caucasian and is 25 years old. Anna has become a full-time mother, having quit her job shortly after the baby was born. They had been living on the base where Sam was assigned but when he "re-upped" for another tour in Afghanistan, Anna's family insisted that she return to her hometown to live so that she wouldn't be alone without family support.

The couple agreed, and Anna moved shortly before Sam was deployed. Prior to her marriage, Anna had been a very high achiever, was successfully employed as a manager in a bank, was very active at the gym, participated in a book club, volunteered at her church, and had a large group of friends. Soon after her marriage, Anna became more withdrawn, stopped going to the gym, and recently confided in a few friends that she feels like she can't breathe and that she feels like she is under Sam's thumb constantly.

Shortly after Sam was deployed, she tried to access their bank account to purchase a dehumidifier that the baby needed due to some respiratory issues and found that she had to have Sam's permission in order to access the funds. Anna has contacted your agency to seek counseling related to her feeling down and her increasing frustration with the marriage. Her mother had encouraged Anna to get help.

Core Values That Guide Engagement and Relationship-Building Efforts in Social Work Practice

Gambrill (2006, pp. 13–15) identifies 13 key value guideposts for social workers to address when engaging in social work change efforts. The guideposts (see Figure 5.1) address areas such as how we make decisions, how we help clients reach their outcomes, how we problem solve, and how we ensure that clients are not harmed. Keeping these guideposts in mind, we can see that for social workers, engagement and relationship-building activities must involve the dynamic participation of the individuals, families, and small groups in the change efforts in order to ensure that we are using the practice interventions available that will successfully support change actions.

In the evidence-based *Family Psychoeducation: Training Frontline Staff* (Substance Abuse and Mental Health Services Administration [SAMHSA], 2009), five core relationship-building values that emerged from research are identified (see Figure 5.2). These five core values include building hope, recognizing consumers and families as experts in their own experience of mental illness, emphasizing personal choice, establishing a collaborative partnership, and demonstrating respect. These values are consistent with the values of the social work profession discussed in Chapter 4. When we look at building hope, it is important for us to foster within clients and families a sense that the future can be better and that learning new skills will help them cope in meeting the challenges of today. We need to be aware that as professionals, we bring expertise about the change processes in our role that involves knowing about the resources that are available to support the individuals/families and clients in making change happen and possessing knowledge expertise. Our clients however, are experts, too, as they are bringing expertise in the lived experience of dealing with the challenges or problems they face each and every day. We must value client and family choice. Helping clients and families identify options involves not only addressing current challenges but also, in many situations, advocating for needed changes in other systems (e.g., schools, work settings, communities, laws/policies) that can impact and prevent future difficulties for these clients and others in similar circumstances. The value of collaborative partnership must be at the center of each helping encounter. *Collaborative partnership* means wanting to foster opportunities for clients and families to ensure that they have an active voice in the assessment, intervention, and evaluation of social work change efforts. Demonstrating respect means that we always value the diversity present in our encounters with clients and that we are aware of the power that differentials have to impact change efforts positively or negatively. Clients' unique experiences need to be understood within their social, cultural, political, and economic contexts. Communicating empathy and genuineness in our interactions with clients is a skill that is critical in the initial phase of engagement. We need to learn to address discrepancies that arise due to power differentials as well as those that are from cultural or other diversity factors. It is important that we apply a holistic approach that incorporates an understanding of the body/mind/spirit dimensions and that we are aware of the larger context/system issues during the engagement phase. These are critical to the success of being able to engage clients effectively in the helping relationship.

Figure 5.1 Value Guideposts for Social Work Practice

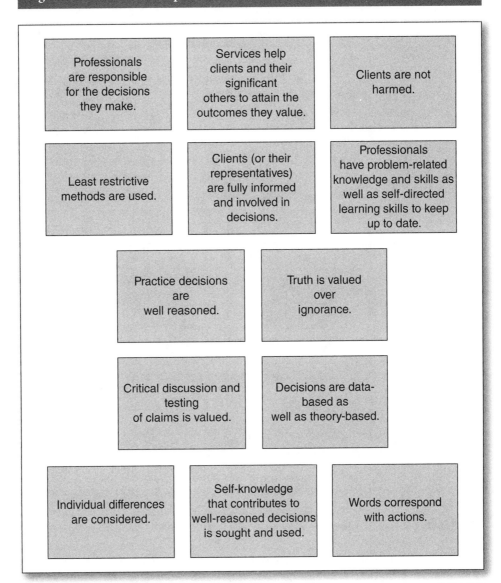

Professionals are responsible for the decisions they make.

Services help clients and their significant others to attain the outcomes they value.

Clients are not harmed.

Least restrictive methods are used.

Clients (or their representatives) are fully informed and involved in decisions.

Professionals have problem-related knowledge and skills as well as self-directed learning skills to keep up to date.

Practice decisions are well reasoned.

Truth is valued over ignorance.

Critical discussion and testing of claims is valued.

Decisions are data-based as well as theory-based.

Individual differences are considered.

Self-knowledge that contributes to well-reasoned decisions is sought and used.

Words correspond with actions.

Source: Social Work Practice: A Critical Thinker's Guide, 2nd Edition by Gambrill (2006). 13-15. By permission of Oxford University Press, USA.

Figure 5.2   Five Core Relationship-Building Values

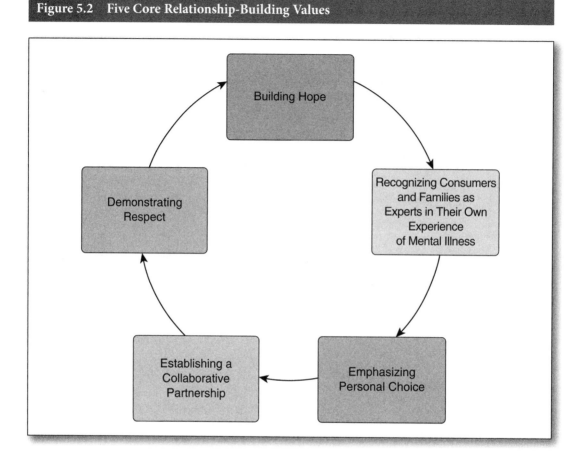

REFLECTIVE LEARNING ACTIVITY

Using both of the case situations presented in the beginning of this chapter, use the value guideposts and relationship-building values identified in this section to discuss how you might engage and build collaborative relationships with these clients.

Pathways to Services

It is important for us to constantly and consistently examine ways to build collabora-tive helping relationships that emphasize individual and family strengths, support empowerment, and value diversity.

The pathways to social work services are often difficult for many individuals/ families and clients. Paul and Lisa in Case Situation A are beginning services in order to keep their children from being removed and put into foster care, while Anna in Case Situation B is seeking services to help her with depression and marital/family adjustment issues. As social workers, we need to be aware that we may be perceived by individuals/families as positive sources of support and help; at the same time, we may be seen as agents of power who are capable of implementing negative consequences, such as the removal of children from the home. It is important for us to recognize that all pathways to services experienced by individuals/families will be impacted during the engagement and relationship-building phase of work.

Social workers need to learn how to use a strengths-based orientation in the engagement process, which means that we need to take actions that normalize the struggles our clients are experiencing. Greene and Lee (2011) captured the key points in the engagement process with clients, particularly when working with diverse populations and especially when these clients are referred by others for social work services. They have highlighted the following tasks that you should use to ensure that a strengths-based approach is utilized:

1. Convey one's openness, respect, and curiosity about the clients' culturally embedded perceptions.
2. Convene interventions as a collaborative process.
3. Ask about and clarify the information presented.
4. Use cultural resources and strengths.
5. Use clients'/families preferred help-seeking methods.
6. Use face-saving techniques.
7. Use language that implies the fewest assumptions.
8. Focus on what clients/families have done well.
9. Focus on positive motivations for change.
10. Establish meaningful goals.
11. Establish clear indicators of progress.

REFLECTIVE LEARNING ACTIVITY

In Case Situation A (Paul and Lisa), make a list of three questions that you would ask that would help to clarify the information presented.

Madsen (2011) suggests that one tool that can assist us in beginning to establish a collaborative relationship in family-centered services is a collaborative helping map. The collaborative helping map (see Figure 5.3) encourages us to focus our

Figure 5.3   Collaborative Helping Map

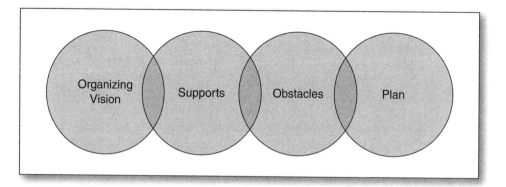

initial engagement activities by collaborating together with clients/families in these four key areas:

1. Organizing Vision (Where would you like to be heading in your life?)

2. Supports (What might help you get there?)

3. Obstacles (What might get in the way?)

4. Plan (What needs to happen next?)

Exploring these areas together with the client and/or family will allow them to tell you their story using this brief but powerful outline. The outline serves to assure your client that together, you can organize the important information that will assist you both in collaborating on a plan of action. During this process, it is important for you to remember to also focus on the core relationship values we talked about earlier, as this will provide you with another way to find out from your clients what they are worried about, what is going well for them, and what they hope will happen next. Building a collaborative relationship is key to any and all subsequent actions that occur in the helping process and will help us understand why the guideposts are critical elements in social work practice.

REFLECTIVE LEARNING ACTIVITY

Using the Collaborative Helping Map tool with Case Situation A (Paul and Lisa), list one specific question you would ask for each of the four areas that would demonstrate your ability to collaborate with these clients.

Once you complete this, discuss one potential strength and one potential limitation that you have identified while using this mapping process.

Approaches That Positively Impact the Engagement Phase

Solution-focused brief therapy (SFBT) approaches are often viewed as critical in the initial and ongoing engagement and relationship-building phases of work. The basic tenets of SFBT can be found in Table 5.1 (Franklin, Trepper, Gingerich, & McCollum, 2012). It is important for us to learn how to use these tenets as a guide, which would allow us to focus on the client's potential for change rather than on diagnosing and treating their presenting problems.

The main interventions that have demonstrated positive outcomes for clients when using the SFBT approach include the following:

- Establishing a positive, collegial, solution-focused stance
- Looking for previous solutions
- Looking for exceptions
- Using present- and future-focused questions
- Acknowledging change through compliments
- Building on what is working

There are several key types of questions that have been developed for use with the SFBT approach. Some of these might include the following:

Table 5.1   Basic Tenets of SFBT

- The approach is based on solution building rather than problem solving.
- The therapeutic focus should be on the client's desired future rather than on past problems or current conflicts.
- Clients are encouraged to increase the frequency of current useful behaviors.
- No problem happens all the time. There are exceptions—that is, times when the problem could have happened but didn't—that can be used by the therapist and client to co-construct solutions.
- Therapists help clients find alternatives to current undesired patterns of behavior. Cognition and interaction that are within the client's repertoire or can be co-constructed by therapist and client qualify as such.
- Differing from skill building and behavior therapy interventions, SFBT model assumes that solution behaviors already exist for clients.
- It is essential that small increments of change lead to large increments of change.
- Client's solutions are not necessarily directly related to any identified problem by either the client or the therapist.
- The conversational skills required of the therapist to invite the client to build solutions are different from those needed to diagnose and treat client problems.

Source: Solution-Focused Brief Therapy: A Handbook of Evidence-Based Practice by Franklin, Trepper, Gingerich & McCollum (2012). 21. By permission of Oxford University Press, USA.

Scaling Questions

These questions help clients to focus on changes and allow us to ask follow-up questions once the initial scaling question is answered (e.g., "On a scale of 1 to 10, where a 10 means that things are going very well and you feel that you are solidly on the path to reaching your goals and a 1 means that the things that brought you here are worse than ever, how would you rate how things are going during the past week?"). This type of question helps them to think about how things are currently, but it also provides them with an ability to see what would need to happen for them to be able to move up to the next number on the scale in the future.

Difference Questions

Difference questions allow us to help clients focus on comparing and contrasting what is happening in one situation with other similar situations (e.g., "So what is different about the way you handled the situation today? What happened that was different about the way you approached the situation?").

Accomplishment Questions

By using these questions, we can help clients recognize positive change and the ways their actions make a difference (e.g., "How did you do that? How did you make this happen?").

Goal Questions

We can use goal questions to help clients focus on identifying what needs to happen for them to establish an end point to our work (e.g., "How will you know that you have met your goals for why you sought help? What needs to have changed for you to say that you have met your goals?").

Description Questions

These questions provide us with a way to help clients describe their solutions in observable terms (e.g., "How did you know that you were better today? What was the first sign that you noticed? How would others know that you were better today?").

REFLECTIVE LEARNING ACTIVITY

In working with Anna in Case Situation B, you have determined that the SFBT approach would be appropriate. When using a SFBT approach, list five questions you would use to engage Anna in talking about her situation.

In Case Situation A (Paul and Lisa), discuss why the SFBT approach would work with this family. List three ways that you would apply this approach to engage them in change efforts.

Skill Building That Emphasizes Collaboration to Improve Follow-Through

One of the challenges we have in working with a diverse population of clients and families is finding ways to increase the likelihood that clients and families who need services will seek services with us and then follow through with change efforts. We have found through research that many clients and families who reach out for help often do not follow through with making the first appointment, and even if they make their first appointment, they may not continue with change efforts. Alegría and her colleagues (2008) found in working with Latino clients and families that using a *Right Question Approach,* which builds on activation and empowerment components in the initial stages and throughout the intervention process, actually resulted in more clients and families engaging effectively with services. Let's look a little closer at what we mean by activation and empowerment and the Right Question Approach in relationship building. Alegría et al. (2008), defined *activation* as developing experience with question formulation and building information-seeking skills that result in increased collaboration between the client and the social worker. For example, a client who is engaged when using activation might ask questions about medications, such as "How will this medication work for me?" Or, if children are in foster care, a parent might ask, "Once I complete the parenting program, how soon can I get my children back?" Alegría et al. defines *empowerment* as a capacity-building process where clients

- increase their belief that they play an active role (i.e., taking action to solve their problems),
- participate in decision making (i.e., seeing themselves as capable of making decisions and of feeling confident of the decisions they make), and
- manage their situation to achieve a greater measure of control (i.e., being able to accomplish what they set out to do and making their plan work).

REFLECTIVE LEARNING ACTIVITY

When reviewing Case Situation A (Paul and Lisa) and Case Situation B (Sam and Anna), list two ways that using the Right Question Approach may foster collaboration.

List the top three things you would focus on when developing questions to use in your initial phase of work with Paul and Lisa or Anna.

The primary goal when using the Right Question Approach is to remember to shift our focus in the initial engagement process with clients and families from asking questions and finding answers or solutions to an approach where we support clients and families in defining their own questions, help them look for ways that they have already tried to solve problems, examine the solutions they have tried, and work with them to advocate for their own priority needs as well as provide information that empowers them to seek answers they need about their own situations. What are some of the implications for social work practice when using this approach? It means that we need to engage in more active listening, we need to take a "one down" position in order to better hear the client and family perspectives, and we need to focus our initial engagement approach on being more client- and family-centered.

REFLECTIVE LEARNING ACTIVITY

Think back to the last time you met with a new client and or their family. How much of the initial session was spent focusing on your agenda for the session, and how much time did you spend helping clients and families find their own voice related to the challenges they were facing?

Take a moment to review your initial relationship-building approach. List three ways that you can formulate your questions so that they demonstrate activation and empowerment by eliciting more information that highlights the questions or concerns from your client's perspective.

The previous section of this chapter provided us with ways to think about the change process in the engagement and relationship-building phase of our work and provided us with some ways to format questions that support a strengths- or solution-based approach or the Right Question Approach when working with clients/families. In this section, we will focus on additional skills needed to effectively build a working relationship with clients/families who may be reluctant about engaging in change efforts or who might have been referred by others for services. The skills we will focus on developing include reflection/empathy skills and motivational enhancement skills.

Reflection and empathy skills involve communicating to clients and families that we accurately perceive their feelings and that we understand their feelings (Hepworth, Rooney, Rooney, Strom-Gottfried, & Larsen, 2010). This is a very challenging skill to learn and requires practice so that we learn how to actively acknowledge client or family feelings. By communicating our understanding, we are encouraging clients and families to engage in further exploration of their challenges/feelings. This skill requires that we engage in *active* or *attentive listening*, which involves focusing on the actual voice of clients and families (e.g., their tone, the speed of their words, their inflection) as well as nonverbal communications that might be evident. We might use *simple reflections* that simply repeat or rephrase a statement, substituting words with synonyms (e.g., "You are frustrated that nothing has worked"). We might also seek to engage in more complex reflections. *Complex reflections* may involve overstating feelings (e.g., "You're furious about your partner's reaction"), anticipating the next sentence (e.g., "This makes you angry and you want to get even"), or using double-sided reflections (e.g., "On the one hand, you like that your parents are gone most of the time, and on the other hand, you want your parents to be more involved in your life"). With complex reflections, we need to remember to be prepared to hear that our reflections may not be accurate from the client's or family's perspectives. Encouraging the clients and families to challenge our assumptions and clarify their feelings is an important step that will promote an ongoing relationship-building process.

Another way we can communicate our understanding of a situation and encourage further reflection and dialogue is by using metaphors. Metaphors can be simple (one or two sentences or a word) or more complex (using stories). Metaphors create a picture that often allows clients and families to explore how this picture/phrase/story captures their experiences or how it might be different from their experiences. As we begin to develop our skills in learning to be empathetic in our questions and responses, Figure 5.4 provides us with a concise way to think about and practice some common empathic responses (Hepworth et al., 2010, p. 101).

Figure 5.4   Sample Leads for Empathic Responses

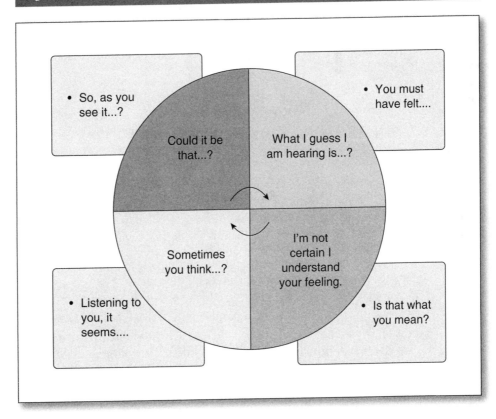

REFLECTIVE LEARNING ACTIVITY

In Case Situation B (Sam and Anna), using complex reflection skills, identify two reflections that might help Anna to challenge her assumptions and clarify her position/feelings.

Motivational enhancement therapy is emerging as an evidence-informed approach for building effective relationships with a wide range of clients, including adolescent youth. The motivational enhancement core skills that are used in this approach are derived from the motivational interviewing methods developed in the substance abuse field (Miller & Rollnick, 2013) and build on active listening and empathic responses. Motivational interviewing is a collaborative, person-centered form of guiding to elicit and strengthen motivation for change (Miller & Rollnick, 2013). This means that all decisions are made jointly in partnership with the clients and that we can inform and advise, but the decision to change and the choices about how to change remain with the clients. We should use motivational enhancement skills when it has been demonstrated that our clients or families have low motivation for change, have problems with implementing a change, or are reluctant to engage in change efforts. Addressing the ambivalence that clients experience is at the core of this approach. The general principles of motivational enhancement interviewing (see Figure 5.5) include

- expressing empathy,
- developing discrepancies,
- supporting self-efficacy, and
- rolling with resistance.

The first principle, *expressing empathy,* asks us to listen actively, engage in skillful reflective listening, communicate acceptance, and recognize that ambivalence is a normal part of any change effort. *Reflective listening,* as we noted earlier in the chapter, means showing an interest in what the client is saying and having an interest in understanding how the client views their current situation.

The second principle, *developing discrepancies,* requires that we help clients to examine where they are and where they want to be. This means that the client rather than the social worker makes the arguments for change.

The third principle, *supporting self-efficacy,* promotes the belief that change is a possibility and that we believe that clients have the ability to change.

The fourth principle, *rolling with resistance,* encourages us to avoid arguing for change, to not directly oppose resistance, to support new perspectives, and to recognize that resistance is a signal whereby we need to respond differently.

Figure 5.5   Principles of Motivational Enhancement Interviewing

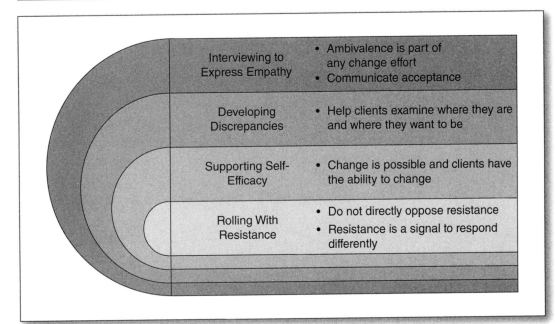

Interviewing to Express Empathy	• Ambivalence is part of any change effort • Communicate acceptance
Developing Discrepancies	• Help clients examine where they are and where they want to be
Supporting Self-Efficacy	• Change is possible and clients have the ability to change
Rolling With Resistance	• Do not directly oppose resistance • Resistance is a signal to respond differently

REFLECTION LEARNING ACTIVITY

Using Case Situation A (Paul and Lisa), discuss three reasons why using Motivational Enhancement Interviewing might work with Paul and Lisa.
   Would you recommend this approach for Case Situation B (with Anna)?

In order to effectively carry out the principles in motivational interviewing, we may find it helpful to use tools such as the OARS, which will assist us in enhancing our client's motivation for change. OARS stands for

- O= Using open-ended questions
- A= Affirming the clients
- R= Reflecting on the dialogue
- S= Summarizing what has been said

In this approach, the clients do most of the talking. We guide the process by using open-ended questions, asking our clients to look at both sides of the coin, showing appreciation and understanding, acknowledging strengths, listening more than telling, reflecting using statements (not questions), and summarizing and reinforcing what has been said. During this process, it is important for us to look for strength of commitment to change and readiness to change talk. For example, we may start by asking an open-ended question such as, "What concerns you most about. . . ?" or, "Tell me more about. . . ." Then, we might affirm the client by sharing that, "I am glad that you are talking today about your challenges," or "I know this must be difficult and I am glad that you are sharing your feelings." We might then reflect on the exchange by stating, "I hear your concern about X and I also see that when you do Y, you feel better in the short-term." We would then summarize by saying, "Let me see if I am on target with what you have told me so far. . . . Did I miss anything?"

REFLECTIVE LEARNING ACTIVITY

Let's practice using OARS. Select one of the case situations from the beginning of the chapter or a current case situation that you might be involved in at your field placement or volunteer/work setting. Then find two other students to role-play with. You will need to set aside 15 to 20 minutes to conduct this role-play.

Have one student role-play the client and talk about the situation in the case situation.

Have a second student respond using OARS by using open-ended questions, affirmation statements, reflection statements, and a summary of the key points.

The third student should be taking notes throughout the role-play about the types of responses they heard and the overall interview process.

Once you have completed the role-play, discuss how it felt to be the social worker and how easy or difficult OARS is to use.

Take time to switch roles so that everyone gets a turn to use OARS.

The Stages of Change Framework

One of the ways that we have learned to move toward engaging clients and families successfully by starting with where they are comes from the work that has been done in the substance abuse field focused on the Stages of Change Framework. Prochaska, Norcross, and DiClemente (1994) have developed a Stages of Change theory that can help us to better understand how ready and prepared clients and families actually are to engage in change efforts. There are six stages of change that have been identified when looking at the change process. Knowing at what stage of change the client and/or the family is in will help us establish a relationship that has a better chance of success. The six stages of change are found in Figure 5.6 and include the following:

- Precontemplation
- Contemplation

Figure 5.6   The Six Stages of Change

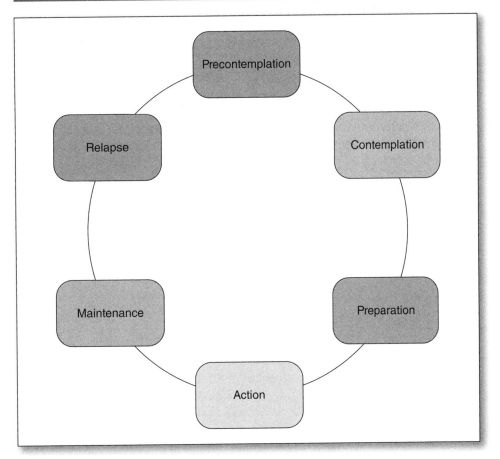

- Preparation
- Action
- Maintenance
- Relapse

The Stage of Change theory recognizes that change is an evolving process and that relapse is a natural part of any change effort. Let's think about a recent change that you might have attempted to make, such as exercising more, improving your diet, or using better time management skills. When we examine these changes in detail, we see that change was not a linear process and that we may have often relapsed or experienced a setback and fallen backward into our earlier pattern of behavior. It is important that we identify how strong our motivation was to change our behavior and also what steps were needed in order for us to move forward with our change plan. Let's look at these six stages in more depth.

The first stage, *precontemplation,* involves us understanding that people who are in this stage usually have no intent on changing and are often considered to be in denial. We might hear individuals in this stage say things such as, "There's nothing I really need to change," or, "What problem?" In the second stage, *contemplation,* the individual is aware that a problem exists but is ambivalent about changing. You will hear statements such as, "I'm thinking I might have a problem but I am not ready to decide to do anything yet," or, "It might be something I need to work on, but it is too hard." The third stage, *preparation,* involves getting ready to change and making a plan for change. You will hear individuals make statements such as, "I am making some small changes," or, "I have a problem and I am starting to think about how to change." The fourth stage, *action,* is when individuals are trying to change but are still having to work hard at consistently making a change. In this stage, individuals might say, "I am working hard on following my change plan," or, "I am making changes." In the fifth stage, *maintenance,* we will see individuals who are practicing the change and are relatively stable in carrying out their change work. Individuals in this stage might say, "I am doing well and I have changed." In the sixth stage, *relapse,* individuals may experience a setback and thus they return to previous behaviors for a brief time. The key is to prepare individuals for the reality that relapse is a part of the cycle of change. You may hear from individuals who have experienced a relapse, "How can I get back on track?" It is important for us to remember when working with any individual, family, or small group that the cycle of change is an ever-evolving process and that it is also a challenging one that requires considerable effort. It will be helpful to your practice as a social worker to use the Stages of Change theory to assist your clients in making the changes they identify as important to improving the quality of their lives. They have likely been living with situations or exhibiting behaviors they have identified as those they want to change for a while, so when they are ready to move forward, this model will assist you and them in the work ahead.

REFLECTIVE LEARNING ACTIVITY

In Case Situation B (Sam and Anna), discuss which stage of change you think Anna is in from the information provided and share three reasons for your conclusion.

There are ten principles that have emerged from the Stages of Change theory that will help us in understanding and applying this perspective with our clients (DeBonis, 2013). These principles include the following:

1. Change is a process rather than an event.

2. Change is characterized by stages.

3. Identifying the person's stage of readiness is essential to tailoring interventions that will be most effective.

4. Moving one stage at a time is the most reasonable goal.

5. Knowing the changer's stage helps to individualize the approach.

6. Insight is necessary but not sufficient for permanent change.

7. People who are not in the action stage may still be actively changing.

8. Understanding how to maintain change is also a key to successful change.

9. People can be at different stages for different problems.

10. The goal is for full freedom from the problem.

The Readiness to Change Ruler (see Figure 5.7) can be used to capture the level of readiness of the client. However, it goes a step further by asking them to rate how ready they are to change, how important the change is for them, and how confident they feel that they can make the change happen. The Readiness to Change Ruler rates how *ready* they are to change using a scale of 1 to 10 (1 = not prepared to change, 10 = they are already changing). When working with your client, you might ask, "Are you not prepared to change, already changing, or somewhere in the middle?" The Importance Ruler, another tool you can use, easily illustrates how important it is to make a change now, based on a scale from 1 to 10. The Confidence Ruler uses a similar concept and the same scale from 1 to 10, but it asks the client to rate how confident they feel that they can make a change happen.

Figure 5.7   The Readiness Ruler

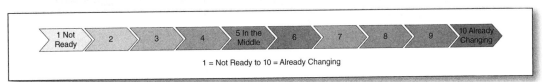

1 = Not Ready to 10 = Already Changing

REFLECTIVE LEARNING ACTIVITY

- Take a moment and think about a change you might like to make in your life. Briefly write down the change you want to make.
- List the reasons to change and the reasons not to change.
- Reflect on the stage of change you are in now related to the area you want to change.
- Rate yourself using the Readiness to Change, Importance, and Confidence Rulers as they relate to the change area.

  How difficult will it be for you to implement this change?

  What are statements you are telling yourself about the change possibility?

Alliance Building

Now let's move to looking more closely at the process of relationship building. We have spent some time already exploring core values that guide relationship building and several approaches and tools that will positively impact the engagement phase of work, including asking the right questions, using reflective listening skills, demonstrating empathy, and using motivational enhancement skills. These are all critical skills that must be demonstrated in the initial engagement and relationship-building phase. Another common feature that has emerged as central to any individual or family change effort is the concept of *alliance building*. In alliance building, it is imperative that we focus on the relationship between the social worker and the client and/or family. This alliance must be a collaboration between the social worker and the client or family, and it will predict the outcome of the change efforts. Therefore, if a positive alliance/relationship has been established, then it has been shown that the client and/or family will be more likely to experience better outcomes during the change process. We have learned that the client's perspective of the relationship is the most consistent predictor of a positive outcome. Therefore, it is critical that we learn how to develop positive alliances with our clients and that we use the theories and tools available to us in order to accomplish this goal.

CHAPTER REVIEW QUESTIONS

1. Using Figure 5.1, identify four areas that you will learn to focus on in your practice and list several reasons why these are important to you and your work.

2. List four reasons why it is important to engage in collaborative partnerships with clients and how these can influence the success of the helping process.

3. List several reasons why clients may be reluctant to follow through with change efforts. Identify tools you can use to address each of these reasons.

4. Discuss why the Stages of Change theory is important and how it will influence your work. Which three principles stand out to you at this point in your learning?

5. Discuss why you think the Readiness to Change Ruler is a useful tool.

6. Discuss why alliance building is an important skill and outline three ways that you will work to develop positive alliances.

REFERENCES

Alegría, M., Polo, A. J., Gao, S., Santana, L., Rothstein, D., Lyons, M., & Normand, S. L. (2008). Evaluation of a patient activation and empowerment intervention in mental health care. *Medical Care, 46*, 247–256. doi: 10.1097/MLR.0b013e318158af52

DeBonis, J. (2013). *Applying theories, perspectives, and practice models to integrated health* (Module 3). Retrieved August 6, 2014 from http://www.cswe.org/File.aspx?id=62752

Franklin, C., Trepper, T. S., Gingerich, W., & McCollum, E. (2012). *Solution-focused brief therapy: A handbook of evidence-based practice.* New York, NY: Oxford University Press.

Gambrill, E. (2006). *Social work practice: A critical thinker's guide* (2nd ed.). New York, NY: Oxford Press.

Greene, G. J., & Lee, M. Y. (2011). *Solution-Oriented social work: A practice approach to working with client strengths.* New York, NY: Oxford University Press.

Hepworth, D., Rooney, R., Rooney, G., Strom-Gottfried, K., & Larsen, J. (2010). *Direct social work practice: Theory and skills.* Independence, KY: Brooks/Cole.

Madsen, W. (2011). Collaborative helping maps: A tool to guide thinking and action in family-centered services. *Family Process, 50*(4), 529–543.

Miller, W. R., & Rollnick, S. (2013). *Motivational interviewing: Helping people to change* (3rd ed.). New York, NY: Guilford Press.

Prochaska, J. O., Norcross, J. C., & DiClemente, C. C. (1994). *Changing for good.* New York, NY: William Morrow.

Substance Abuse and Mental Health Services Administration (SAMHSA). (2009). *Family psychoeducation: Training frontline staff.* HHS Pub. No. SMA-09-4422. Rockville, MD: Center for Mental Health Services, Substance Abuse and Mental Health Services Administration, U.S. Department of Health and Human Services.

Assessment in Social Work With Individuals and Families

In this chapter, we will explore ways that social workers engage in the assessment process with individuals and families. In the previous chapter, we discussed the importance of engagement and relationship building. In this chapter, we will build on this work by exploring how assessment processes should be incorporated into the initial stages of work with individuals and families as well as throughout the time you meet with clients during the course of working with a case. In fact, Hepworth, Rooney, Rooney, Strom-Gottfried, and Larsen (2010, p. 181) state that an "assessment is a fluid and dynamic process that involves receiving, analyzing and synthesizing new information as it emerges during the entire course of a given case."

(Continued)

- the special screening elements used in suicide risk assessments and trauma informed assessments; and
- how the *Diagnostic and Statistical Manual of Mental Disorders* (*DSM-5*) diagnostic criteria and the International Statistical Classification of Diseases and Related Health Problems (ICD-10) coding system are used during the assessment process.

The Council on Social Work Education Educational Policy and Accreditation Standards (CSWE-EPAS) Competencies that are highlighted in more depth in this chapter include the following:

2.1.3 Apply critical thinking to inform and communicate professional judgments.

2.1.4 Engage diversity and difference in practice.

2.1.5 Advance human rights and social and economic justice.

2.1.6 Engage in research-informed practice and practice-informed research.

2.1.7 Apply knowledge of human behavior and the social environment.

2.1.9 Respond to contexts that shape practice.

2.1.0 (a–d) Engage, assess, intervene, and evaluate with individuals, families, groups, organizations, and communities.

CASE SITUATION A: BILL, APRIL, AND CECEE

Bill is a divorced 62-year-old African American male who came to the clinic today because he needed to have his hypertension medication reviewed. He is also depressed. Bill has been under stress from taking care of his mother, April, who is experiencing signs of dementia and is still recovering from a broken hip. She fell when she was walking up the steps at their home. Bill has not been taking his medications for hypertension or depression on a regular basis. His last visit to the clinic was two months ago. Bill works part time at an accounting firm and has to rely on his 20-year-old daughter, CeCee, to watch his mother when he is at work. Bill talks of feeling hopeless and blames himself for not taking better care of his mother. Bill's minister thinks that Bill doesn't need the depression medication. Bill is not sleeping well and has lost over 20 pounds since the last visit. The physician referred Bill to you as the social worker at the clinic to assess the situation.

CASE SITUATION B: SUE, TINA, AND KIM

You are working as a social worker at the neighborhood senior community center. Sue, an 80-year-old Asian American female immigrant, has several chronic health conditions, including diabetes, obesity, hypertension, and early signs of dementia. Sue has, in the past, participated in several of the activities at the center. She lives with a daughter, Tina, who is a reluctant caregiver to her mother. Tina and her partner, Kim, have been living together for over ten years. Having Sue in the home has put a strain on their relationship, especially since Sue disapproves of Kim. Tina has two adult children from a previous relationship but they do not have frequent contact. Tina reported that the health care team is concerned about Sue's diabetes. It has been out of control and causing problems that might result in the amputation of her foot. Tina says that she cannot do anything more to get her mother to follow the doctor's orders related to the diabetes. Tina is in tears in the office. She tells you that she is a failure as a daughter, partner, and mother and that her whole life is falling apart.

CASE SITUATION C: MARIA, SOPHIA, GUILLERMO, AND CARLOS

The Cortez family was referred to the family clinic by the school due to Maria's problems at school and with the law. Maria, a 17-year-old Latina youth, has been arrested two times for drug possession. Maria used to be a good student but recently has been missing classes and failing tests. She wants to drop out of school. Maria's mother, Sophia, works during the day as part of the housecleaning staff at a local hotel. Her father, Guillermo, is often absent from home due to construction projects that take him to other cities during the week. He belongs to the local union and works primarily as an electrician. Guillermo was born and raised in the United States, but his parents were illegal immigrants from Mexico who worked as migrant farm workers. Sophia came to the United States as an adult from Colombia, and she has limited English-speaking skills. Carlos is Maria's 12-year-old brother who has also been getting into trouble at school.

CASE SITUATION D: EMILY AND JENNA

Emily is the parent of four-year-old Jenna. Emily is a single mother who works at the local grocery store in the evening/night. Emily and her extended family are members of the Onondaga Indian Tribal Nation. Four years ago, Emily moved with Jenna's biological father, Clay, across the state (more than five hours away from her family). Clay left the home; and for the past three years, Clay has not had any involvement with Emily or Jenna. Emily and Jenna continue to live in the new community. When he was living with Emily, he was physically abusive to her. Emily has no idea where Clay lives, and he provides no child support. When Emily is at work, Jenna stays with a sitter. Usually when Emily returns home, Jenna is still up. Emily has a hard time getting Jenna to go to bed.

(Continued)

(Continued)

Emily feels like she has no control over Jenna. Jenna has temper tantrums when she doesn't get what she wants. Jenna also has trouble getting along with other children in the neighborhood. At the preschool, Jenna has similar behavioral problems. She does not follow the rules at the center. The sitters that Emily hires to watch Jenna at night usually only stay a few weeks due to Jenna's defiant behavior. Emily and Jenna were referred to the American Indian Outreach Center by Emily's aunt, who is concerned that Emily has no one to talk to about her situation. Last week, Emily's employer put her on notice that if she misses any more days at work this month, she will lose her job. Emily is having significant difficulties making ends meet financially and is afraid that she and Jenna will be homeless soon.

Defining Assessment

There are many definitions of assessment, but the two central purposes of assessment are

1. to reach an understanding about what causes the individuals or family members to partner with you in a change process and

2. to construct a collaborative plan to work on the challenges identified through this process.

The role of assessment often can be viewed as "laying the groundwork for selecting plans. It should indicate how likely it is that hoped for outcomes can be attained" (Gambrill, 2006, p. 309).

Initial assessments in social work practice may be brief or comprehensive, depending on the practice setting where you are working. For example, if you are part of an interdisciplinary team in an integrated behavioral health or primary care setting, you may find that the assessment protocol can be accomplished in 30 minutes or less. In that time, you would have identified and clarified the presenting problem(s), conducted a brief functional assessment of these problem(s), explored change plan options, and initiated a change plan with the client/patient and his/her family. In other settings (such as a family service center, for example), the first interview with the client(s) may take 60 minutes or more. This first interview would be followed by additional sessions, which would give you time to complete a more comprehensive assessment protocol.

Assessment is a continuous process for us as we work with individuals and families. Each time we meet with an individual or family, we will continue to collect new information (e.g., around the presenting issues, new issues that may have emerged), and we reassess how the individual or family is doing as they work to reach their goals for engaging in work with us. For example, in Case Situation A, if CeCee is no longer able to help Bill care for his mother, then we would need to reassess the situation and revise our goals to better meet the current needs of Bill. Another example would be, in Case

Situation B, the need to assess at each session the health conditions of Sue, since her various chronic health conditions impact on the type of care that Tina provides to Sue.

Being consistent with our collaborative partnership-building approach when engaging individuals and families in change is central to any change process. We will first examine how we may collect assessment information consistent with the bio-psycho-social-spiritual perspective. This approach incorporates a strengths-based resiliency approach that allows us to gather information about the presenting issues. Then we will review some key tools that support the screening and diagnosis aspects of assessment processes. We will focus on what you need to know about conducting a suicide assessment, and we will examine assessment procedures related specifically to trauma-informed care. We will also learn about the mandated reporting responsibilities of social workers who engage in work with families, specifically children and older adults. Finally, we will introduce the cultural assessment tool in the *DSM-5* and the new *DSM-5* classification system due to the fact that diagnosis is often a part of the assessment process, particularly in the behavioral health field, and is, at times, a requirement for continued access to services in many practice settings. The *DSM-5* is a classification and diagnostic tool that is based on a brain-disease model of mental disorder that is the universal authority for psychiatric diagnosis. We will also address the importance of the link between the *DSM-5* and the ICD-10 coding system as it relates to cross-cultural work with individuals and families. The World Health Organization developed this medical classification list and has over 14,000 codes and additional subcodes for diseases, signs and symptoms, abnormal findings, complaints, social circumstances, and external causes of injury or diseases.

As noted earlier, it is important that while we recognize that assessment is an ongoing process, we also need to be aware that our own perspectives on how people make changes and our clinical training/preferred approach (e.g., psychodynamic approaches, behavioral therapy, cognitive behavioral therapy, solution-focused therapy) often influence what type of data we decide to collect and how we subsequently make sense of or synthesize this information. When using some approaches, it is important to gather assessment data that help to answer the *why* questions first and to focus on underlying causes (e.g., Why do you think this problem is happening now?). Another approach may focus primarily on *what* and *how* questions and is considered more present focused (e.g., What is happening now? How does this current problem situation change how you act, feel, or think about your problem today?). Additional approaches emphasize gathering assessment data about what is the hoped-for future (e.g., How will things be different in the future if this problem is gone? What will your life look like when the problem is gone?). Whatever approach you use, you need to ensure that the assessment process helps you and the individual/families seeking help to identify ways to reach valued and hoped-for outcomes. Gambrill (2006, p. 310) suggests that the assessment should include

1. objectives that if attained would resolve problems,

2. what must be done to achieve these objectives,

3. how objectives can be pursued most effectively, and

4. the probability of attaining these objectives, given current resources and options.

Gambrill's approach captures the dynamic and spiral nature of assessment. The importance of the role of assessment in the helping process is critical to the success of identified hoped-for outcomes. Therefore, establishing clear objectives is central in the assessment process.

REFLECTIVE LEARNING ACTIVITY

For each case situation found at the beginning of this chapter, develop an outline of questions you might consider using when completing the initial assessment with each case. What guides your selection of the types of questions you want to ask and the data you want to collect?

In this next section, we will discuss common assessment approaches consistent with the bio-psycho-social-spiritual perspective, the problem-based approach, and a strengths-based/resiliency approach to the assessment process.

Bio-Psycho-Social-Spiritual Perspective, the Problem-Based Approach, and the Strengths-Based/Resiliency Approach to the Assessment Process

When using a bio-psycho-social-spiritual perspective and focusing on a strength-based/resiliency approach in assessment, we understand the significance of collecting data from multiple dimensions and sources and organizing this information in a way that summarizes the key points collected so that it can guide us in the development of a collaborative action plan where we partner with individuals and families. In most practice settings, social workers are responsible for summarizing information that has been gathered in the initial phase of work to create a bio-psycho-social-spiritual history summary (especially when working on interdisciplinary teams in health and behavioral health settings, child welfare settings, or family service settings).

Now, let's explore further the problem-focused approach and the strengths-based/resiliency approach to assessment. As Lee, Ng, Leung, Chan, & Leung (2009, p. 82) stated, "A useful assessment process should lead to clients and families that are more able to self-assess their situation and develop clear and specific goals that will bring beneficial changes to their life." We can see from this statement that it is necessary for us to use a balanced approach to assessment in our practice, which incorporates a greater understanding of the presenting problem(s)/challenges(s) as well as provides us with a means to measure and evaluate strengths.

Multidimensional Functioning (MDF) Assessment

Let's start by looking at one of the ways that we can begin the complex process of assessment using the multidimensional functioning (MDF) assessment, which is a problem-focused assessment tool. The MDF assessment tool focuses on the presenting problem(s)/challenge(s) that bring our clients to the helping process. Using the MDF assessment process involves the following five steps (O'Hare, 2009):

1. Determine the sources of data.

2. Decide on the methods for obtaining the data.

3. Conduct a thorough MDF assessment.

4. Consider the implications of the data for intervention planning.

5. Delineate a plan for monitoring client progress and evaluate the intervention.

The first step in the process is to determine from whom you will be collecting the information and what types of data you will need. The individual or family members who engage in the helping process are usually our primary sources of data for the assessment, which is specifically related to their particular problem situation(s) or challenges. In Case Situation B (Sue, Tina, and Kim), since Tina has come to you for help, the initial information you will collect will be from Tina's perspective. With Tina's permission, you may expand your data collection to include information from Sue and Kim. It may also be important to gain additional information from other professionals working with the individual or family, such as doctors, psychiatrists, teachers, social service workers, and so on, as this could assist in the assessment process. In Case Situation C (Maria, Sophia, Guillermo, and Carlos), obtaining additional information from the school and court systems seems like a logical step in developing a better picture of what is happening for Maria. In addition, we may seek data from neighbors, extended family members, coaches, work supervisors, or other individuals whom the individual or family identifies as important supports in helping to cope with the problem(s)/challenges. When we seek information beyond the individual or family members engaged in the assessment process, we need to remember to obtain written permission from the individual/family in order to talk with these other professionals or support persons so as not to violate confidentiality.

We may request, with the individual or family member's written permission, records from other professionals that would help to supplement the information we have collected to minimize the potential of duplicating information the individual or family members may have already provided to other professionals about their situation. For social workers employed in health and behavioral health settings, the electronic medical record, which integrates physical and behavioral health information, may be a major source of material and may help to minimize the time needed during an assessment, as it can provide relevant past history related to the client's physical or behavioral health issues.

The second step focuses on the methods you will use to obtain data, which may include face-to-face interviews, telephone interviews, direct observation, use of established screening protocols, and record reviews. In face-to-face interviews, we will often use a semi-structured interview format that encourages the client to tell their story related to the problem situation or the challenges they have been encountering and to share how they have handled these issues. In Case Situation A (Bill, April, and CeCee), helping Bill to tell his story through a semi-structured interview format may help him to capture what is happening in his life, not just in relation to his mother's situation.

The third step is when you will actually perform a MDF assessment. In this phase, you begin by gathering information about the presenting issue(s)/problem(s)/ challenge(s). Your goal is to understand the reason for the referral or the reason(s) the individual or family members are seeking help at this time. You will need to determine (using the Stages of Change process discussed in the previous chapter) how motivated the individual or family members are in engaging in a change process and what they see as potential solutions to their problem(s)/challenge(s). In discussing the problem(s)/challenge(s), you will collect information related to the duration of the problem(s)/challenge(s), what the triggers are (events or causes), the frequency of the problem(s)/challenge(s), and the intensity of the problem(s)/challenge(s). Finally, you will explore all of the factors that have impacted the problem(s)/challenge(s) by making it better or worse. You will evaluate the client's physical, emotional, behavioral, environmental, social, cognitive, and spiritual responses and experiences while living with the problem(s)/challenge(s) that have been identified. In the final phase of this problem analysis, you will look at the degree to which the client has experienced functional impairment (e.g., changes in work/school performance, changes in relationships or social activities, changes in sleep/energy/concentration, changes in substance use and medications). An illustration of a problem-based functional assessment in an integrated behavioral health or primary care setting can be found in Figure 6.1. While the individual or family members are usually your primary sources of data about the current situation, remember that you may have also collected additional information from a range of other sources. It is important in the assessment process to use, when possible, standardized measures/tools (e.g., functioning measures, social network maps) to ensure that you have as complete a picture as possible, which will allow you to create a comprehensive assessment summary.

Sometimes it is easier to think about the data you need to collect in the assessment process as similar to taking a series of pictures: when you put them together, they help you unfold the client's story. Each additional piece of data helps you to develop a more comprehensive understanding about their story related to their experiences with the problem(s)/challenge(s) that they have encountered. It is important for you to remember that the purpose of assessment is to gain a greater understanding and appreciation of what exactly is happening in the individual's life or family's life. The skill of active listening and being present and in the moment with the individual or family is central to the successful data-gathering process.

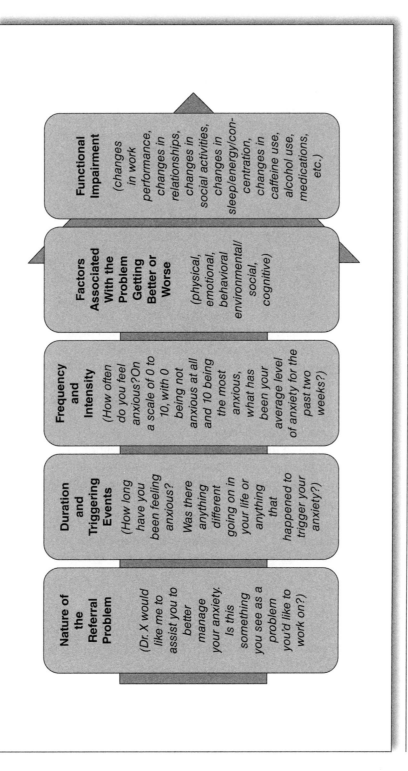

Nature of the Referral Problem

(Dr. X would like me to assist you to better manage your anxiety. Is this something you see as a problem you'd like to work on?)

Duration and Triggering Events

(How long have you been feeling anxious? Was there anything different going on in your life or anything that happened to trigger your anxiety?)

Frequency and Intensity

(How often do you feel anxious? On a scale of 0 to 10, with 0 being not anxious at all and 10 being the most anxious, what has been your average level of anxiety for the past two weeks?)

Factors Associated With the Problem Getting Better or Worse

(physical, emotional, behavioral environmental/ social, cognitive)

Functional Impairment

(changes in work performance, changes in relationships, changes in social activities, changes in sleep/energy/con-centration, changes in caffeine use, alcohol use, medications, etc.)

Source: Adapted from Hunter, Goodie, Oordt, & Dobmeyer, 2009.

REFLECTIVE LEARNING ACTIVITY

Review each case situation found at the beginning of this chapter.

List 2–3 triggering events you think might be occurring in the case situation.

List two factors that you could associate with the problem(s)/situation(s) getting better.

List two factors that you could associate with the problem(s)/situation(s) getting worse.

Upon completion of the MDF assessment, you are prepared, in collaboration with the individual and/or family members, to evaluate the implications of the data you have collected and determine the level of importance of the data so that intervention planning can begin, which is the fourth step. Your primary focus in intervention planning is to understand the individual's or family member's understanding of the problem(s)/challenge(s); their expectations for change; and the resources available within the person, the family, the professional community, and the informal support networks that would be able to assist them in reaching their hoped-for outcomes. It is critical that we use language that is understandable and relevant to the individual and/or family members we are helping as we develop the intervention plan. In this the final phase of the MDF assessment, through discussion with the individual and/or family members, you will be collaborating on an intervention plan and establishing a method for the plan to be monitored and evaluated over time. The individual's or family member's voice and goals need to be at the heart of the intervention planning process.

Lee et al. (2009, pp. 51–52) identified several advantages of conducting problem-focused assessments such as the MDF. These include the following:

1. It directly and explicitly acknowledges the primary concerns of the client.

2. The linear step-by-step assessment process is logical and rational, making it easier to understand and to explain to the individual, family, and other professionals.

3. When problems are clearly defined, it is easier to have specific, measureable indicators of treatment outcomes.

When we use a problem-focus assessment approach, we are making an assumption that there is a direct relationship between the presenting issue(s)/problem(s) and the solution(s) needed to reach the hoped-for outcomes.

Systemic and Strengths-Focused/Resiliency Approach

An approach to assessment that uses a more systemic and strengths-focused/resiliency focus is when the individual's or family's strengths are identified while examining the connectedness between the underlying systems to help you gain a more holistic understanding of their current challenges. The assumption is that we need to view the presenting problem(s)/challenge(s) as only one of the many factors that may be contributing to the current system imbalance that has precipitated the individual or family to seek help. This systemic strengths-focused/resiliency approach builds on the person-in-environment theory/philosophy important to social work practice, which highlights the importance of not only focusing on understanding the individual or their environment but also paying close attention to the balance or the transactions between the person and their environment. You should be interested in gathering data about the subjective, physical, emotional, psychological, and social well-being of the individual and/or family member(s), but at the same time, you should also gather information about the informal support networks and environmental resources available to the individual(s) and/or family member(s) seeking help. According to Simmons and Lehmann (2013, pp. 11–12), *subjective well-being* refers to cognitive judgments about the quality of and satisfaction with one's life; *physical well-being* is the person's subjective report of how healthy he or she feels; *emotional well-being* addresses life satisfaction, positive feelings, and the balance of positive to negative affect; *psychological well-being* includes personality, successful resolution of developmental milestones, and being mentally healthy; and *social well-being* refers to the relationships the individual has with others.

While there are multiple ways to collect information about systemic issues, strengths, and resiliencies, Rapp and Goscha (2012), in their work on the strengths model and recovery-oriented approaches in behavioral health with individuals and families, suggest that you use open-ended questions, questions that reflect on behavior as well as opinion, and probing questions to gain a better understanding of what is being reported and help people see the positive coping parts of themselves.

They propose that strengths-focused/resiliency assessment should contain three primary components: (1) current strengths of the individual or family, (2) desires and aspirations of the individual or family, and (3) the individual's or family's social and environmental resources. You would explore each of these primary components within the following seven system domains: (1) home/daily living, (2) assets (financial/insurance), (3) employment/education/specialized knowledge, (4) supportive relationships, (5) wellness/health, (6) leisure/recreational activities, and (7) spiritual/cultural beliefs. To gather the information you need for this type of assessment, your questions will explore recent successes, focusing on accomplishments and examining what positive changes may already be in place.

During the assessment process, you are actively engaging the individual or family members in a conversation about assets and resources in order to develop a plan of action that builds on existing resiliencies/strengths and that emphasizes the outcomes that the individual and/or family member desires. This plan of action can be modified or changed over time based on the progress toward hoped-for outcomes or changes in the current understanding of goals.

Whether you are using a problem-focused assessment process, a systemic strengths-focused/resiliency assessment process, or a balanced assessment process that incorporates multiple approaches, you need to remember to use these in partnership with the individual and/or family member, thus allowing you to evaluate their potential to engage in the desired outcomes during the change process, the potential benefits of these outcomes, and the likelihood of success for each outcome as time goes on. Table 6.1 highlights the key components of each of these types of assessments.

Table 6.1 Key Components of the Multidimensional Functional Assessment and the Strengths-Focused/Resilience Assessment Process	
Multidimensional Functional (MDF) Assessment	**Strengths/Resiliency Assessment**
Determine the sources of data.	Examine current strengths of the individual or family.
Decide on the methods for obtaining the data.	Explore the desires and aspirations of the individual or family.
Conduct a thorough MDF assessment.	Consider the individual's or family's social and environmental resources.
Consider the implications of the data for intervention planning.	Gather data from several domains: (1) home/daily living, (2) assets (financial/insurance), (3) employment/education/specialized knowledge, (4) supportive relationships, (5) wellness/health, (6) leisure/recreational activities, and (7) spiritual/cultural beliefs.
Delineate a plan for monitoring client progress and evaluate the intervention.	

The Bio-Psycho-Social-Spiritual History

You will often find when you are a member of an interdisciplinary team or due to agency requirements that you need to translate the findings from your assessment process into what is called a *bio-psycho-social-spiritual history summary*. Figure 6.2 highlights the key areas typically included in a bio-psycho-social-spiritual history summary, adapted from the work of Lee et al. (2009). This diagram illustrates a systemic perspective that highlights the importance of balancing information related to body/mind/spirit connections. The areas that connect the mind and the body include behavior, emotions, cognition, relationships (including family, friends, and other supports), health/lifestyle, self-concept, world views, spirituality, and life goals. We need to recognize that the individual and/or family is part of a sociocultural-economic-political system that also contributes to how we might begin to understand the current

Figure 6.2   The Body/Mind/Spirit Connections

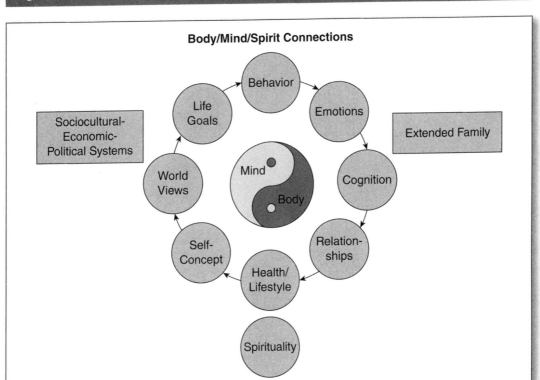

Body/Mind/Spirit Connections

Source: Adapted from Lee, M., Ng, S., Leung, P. & Chan, C. (2009). *Integrative Body-Mind-Spirit Social Work: An Evidence-based Approach.* NY: Oxford University.

problem/situation. This is especially important when you are working with individuals or families who are experiencing oppression, discrimination, limited access to resources/services, or other types of social injustices. As a social worker, you need to understand and appreciate how these contextual forces are present and impacting the current situation(s) and learn how to advocate for changes to improve these conditions. While this is extremely important for the individual or family you are working directly with, it is also important that these changes have the ability to be generalized to other individuals and families who are in similar situations.

In each area of the body/mind/spirit, you should summarize the relevant past history, the current situation(s), and the strengths/resources within a particular area that can be used to address the challenge(s) faced by the individual or family members. According to Lee et al. (2009), we need to pay attention to two notions: *balance* and *dynamic flow. Balance* refers to the system at a particular point in time and *dynamic flow* captures the interchanges among all components. Therefore, it is important when gathering data to pay close attention to how the information you receive from all areas is linked so as to ensure that the summary you create is comprehensive and reflects an accurate picture, because the bio-psycho-social-spiritual history summary is often used by other professionals who may work with the individual or family. Your summary can be used to assist your colleagues in gaining insight into the client's important stories and/or history that are influencing the current problem(s)/situation(s).

Key Screening Tools

In this section, we will explore and discuss important tools available that social workers use to assist them in screening and assessing functioning and wellness as well as methods used to diagnose particular problem(s) or challenge(s) related to behavioral health functioning.

Functioning and Wellness Screening Tools

In conducting assessments, you may find that using screening tools that have been established as reliable and valid when working with individuals and families can assist immensely in identifying key areas for subsequent work. In evidence-informed social work practice, the use of valid and reliable screening tools is frequently incorporated when you are completing the initial assessment interview. For example, when an individual reports being depressed, a screening tool such as the Patient Health Questionnaire (PHQ-9) may be used, as it will provide you with additional insight into what is currently happening for that individual regarding their experience with depression. In Case Situation A (Bill, April, and CeCee), this type of assessment measure could assist in understanding Bill's level of depression and for monitoring change over time. The questionnaire was developed by Drs. Kroenke, Spitzer, and Williams (2001) with the support of an educational grant from Pfizer, Inc. The PHQ-9 requires individuals to reflect on the past two weeks and to identify how bothered they have been by particular problems that are linked to our current understanding of depression, such as having trouble falling or staying asleep, feeling tired/having little energy, or having trouble concentrating on things such as reading the newspaper or watching TV. This nine-item screening tool then asks the individual to rate how difficult these problems are in relation to carrying out his or her daily tasks/functions. A copy of this questionnaire is located online.

There are also several other screening tools that focus on different aspects of psychiatric or behaviorally specific problems (e.g., anxiety, bipolar disorders, alcohol dependence); these also have good reliability and validity when used with individuals who may belong to a range of diverse cultural and racial groups. Remember, before using a screening tool, it is important for you to be sure you understand how the screening tool was developed and know what population/set of individuals this screening tool was shown to be effective in assessing for psychiatric or behavioral problems.

The genogram, the eco-map, and the social network map are three visual screening tools used to capture complex information. Each of these screening tools diagrams key information that can highlight particular relationships or key systems that are working or not working for the individual or family. These visual screening tools are usually done in a session with the involvement of the individual or family members providing the information to complete the visual representation of their family or their networks.

Genogram

The genogram is often used to gain a better understanding of a family's history over time. It asks individuals to identify people in their family tree (which includes several generations) and to also share particular aspects about these individuals such as their gender, marital/relationship status, birth date, age at the time of death, and any physical/psychiatric/substance-use-related problems they may have experienced. While this visual tool is used frequently by social workers to gain some insight into a family's history, it has not been studied in a rigorous manner, so its usefulness is questionable when assessing widespread family issues. Usually, the genogram is seen as a problem-focused tool that can be used to look for patterns of behavior within families as well as uncover histories of particular problems individuals have experienced. A solution-focused or strengths-based assessment may, at times, also use the genogram; but instead of evaluating problems over generations, you would ask the individual to track the strengths and successes of each family member. Figure 6.3 illustrates a traditional genogram map. This particular one highlights both physical illnesses and psychiatric/behavioral disease patterns in the family. In Case Situation C (Maria, Sophia, Guillermo, and Carlos), developing a genogram will assist you in getting a better understanding of family problems and strengths across generations, which may provide some insight into the current dynamics experienced by the family.

Eco-map

The second visual tool that helps you to examine the individual's or family's connections to the external environments is called an *eco-map*. An eco-map usually captures the current strengths of relationships among the individual and family members, the neighborhood, school/work settings, the community (e.g., law enforcement, social service agencies, local government), and religious/spiritual supports. When creating an eco-map, the individual or family would describe the relationships with these external systems using arrows and lines that indicate whether the relationship with that external system is a positive connection or strength (solid line); a conflicted or stressful connection (solid line with crosses through it or a wavy line); or a disconnected, tenuous, or weak connection (a broken line). Each line in the map also has arrows that direct the flow of the established relationships/connections (one-way or two-way). Again, this visual picture assists you and the individual/family in seeing what is happening in context and also helps you to see how these different systems might be contributing to current difficulties. When using this tool, you are also able to see how these systems might be used in intervention planning, with the goal of building on current relationship strengths with external systems. A sample eco-map is located in

Figure 6.3   Simple Family Genogram

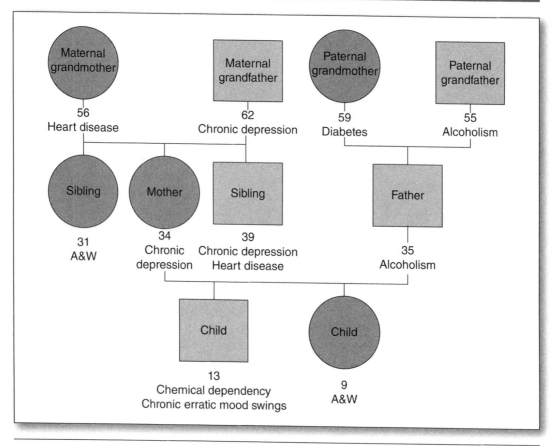

Source: Farlex, 2014.

Note: A&W = "alive and well"

Figure 6.4. In Case Situation D (Emily and Jenna), an eco-mapping tool can provide critical information that may help in developing an intervention plan that addresses the complexity of the situation that this family is experiencing across systems (e.g., work, preschool, extended family).

Social Network Map

A social network map focuses on examining specific types of social supports and resources in the individual's or family's environment. This tool is often called a *personal* or *family network map*. The social network map often uses three concentric circles to indicate the degree of connectedness or intimacy with the various individuals identified as part of the social network. The inner circle includes family members,

Figure 6.4   Sample Eco-Map

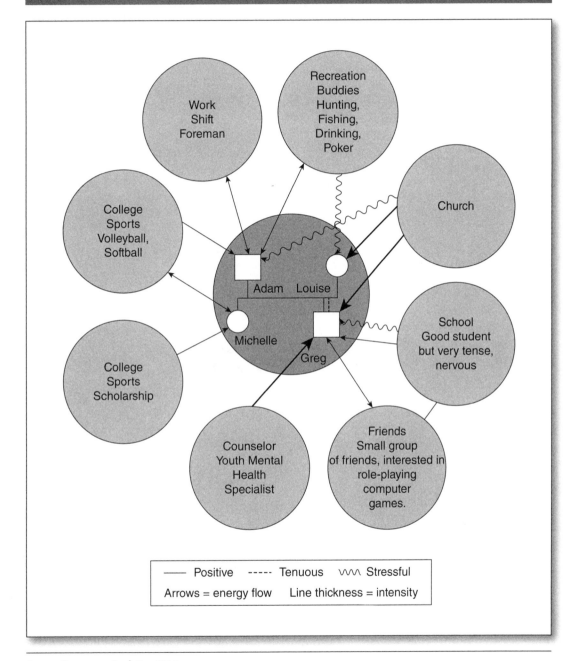

Source: Genogram Analytics, 2014.

spouses/partners, and important relationships (e.g., clergy, close friends). The second circle includes people whom the individual or family is connected to, but the relationships may not be as intimate. These types of relationships/friendships may include people whom individuals go to dinner with, attend sporting events or social events with, socialize with at work with, and the like. The third circle comprises people whom the individual sees infrequently or acquaintances with whom the individual interacts when carrying out daily tasks (e.g., store clerks, staff at service organizations). When we develop a social network map with an individual or family, we are evaluating the density of the relationships in each circle, the strength of the relationships, and whether these relationships have a positive or negative impact on the well-being of the individual or family. Figure 6.5 shows you a model for social network mapping. For example, in both Case Situation B (Sue, Tina, and Kim) and Case Situation C (Maria, Sophia, Guillermo, and Carlos), a social network map would provide a visual picture of the different relationships that have a positive or negative impact on the situation.

In conjunction with using a social network map, you might also follow up with additional questions that will enable you to assess whether the individual or family has social supports and how they are used. For example, you might want to explore who the individual or family would call if they needed help, who they might lean on to help them deal with emotional problems, who they would seek out to help them

Figure 6.5   Social Network Map

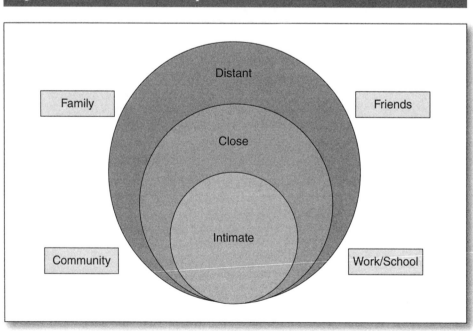

meet concrete needs (e.g., housing, food, transportation), and who they might turn to in the case of an emergency.

Suicide Risk Assessment Tool

In this section, we will take a special look at how the suicide risk assessment screening tool can be used, because in your role as a social worker, you will need to learn how to work to ensure the safety of individuals who seek your services. In addition, you need to learn how to take action if the individual you are assessing is a danger to themselves or others. This action may involve assisting the individual in getting into emergency care/inpatient hospitalization, involving other individuals close the person you are working with to implement a safety plan, notifying the police/law enforcement about the alleged threats of harm, and informing other individuals who may be at risk of harm from the person you are working with. In *Tarasoff v. Regents of the University of California* (17 Cal. 3d 425 [1976]), the courts found that when an individual threatens suicide, commits or threatens a criminal act, or threatens to harm others, privileged communication between the individual and the social worker is waived. This is significant when we remember the discussion in Chapter 4 on ethics related to the provisions on confidentiality. Because of this court ruling, in cases where harm is alleged (self-harm or harming others), the social worker is *not* bound by confidentiality to protect their client(s) and *must*, in fact, take action to address the issues related to the alleged harm. Due to some of the limits to confidentiality (this being one), you have an obligation to seek supervision/consultation in situations such as these in order to ensure that you take the appropriate action to protect the individual and others.

So let's now learn what is involved in conducting a suicide risk assessment. When using this tool, you need to ask open and closed questions that focus on the severity of the client's perceived suicidal ideation, which may well involve a specific plan that they may have in mind. You will need to uncover the frequency of their suicidal feelings and thoughts as well as the level of intensity of these suicidal feelings/thoughts (see Figure 6.6). You may ask questions: "Have you ever thought you would be better off dead?" "Have you ever had thoughts of taking your own life?" "Do you have a plan or have you ever thought of a plan to take your own life or take the lives of others?" "Have you ever attempted suicide before?" "In any given day or hour, how much time do you spend thinking about suicide?" "How have you been able to stop the urges to take your life or to harm others?" "What is keeping you from acting on your suicidal urges?" You *must not* be afraid to ask these questions directly! By engaging in a discussion and asking these questions, you will not increase the likelihood that the person will make a suicide attempt or successfully commit suicide. If the person indicates a positive response to any of the above questions, probe further and seek examples of what they have thought about or done to put their plan into action. The goal is for you to try and better understand and appreciate the level of hopelessness that the individual may currently be feeling/experiencing. Figure 6.7 gives you a scale to consider when questioning someone related to assessing their level of hopelessness. The Suicide Assessment Five-Step Evaluation and Triage (SAFE-T) tool, developed for use by mental health professionals, is also an excellent tool for you to use to conduct the initial risk assessment for suicide. The steps include the following:

1. Identify risk factors

2. Identify protective factors

3. Conduct suicide inquiry

4. Determine risk level/intervention

5. Document

After you have completed your initial risk assessment for suicide, you will need to move into the *taking action* phase. This may involve the development and negotiation of a safety plan with the client whom you have determined is at risk for suicide. This includes addressing warning signs you have determined are present and assessing and determining the internal strategies that the individual has exhibited that will support them in resisting their suicidal urges. Identifying the external strategies may involve the support and actions of others. Finally, your goal is to make the environment safe and document the steps you have taken. If you have determined that the suicide risk is present, you must make sure that during the safety planning stage, you work with the individual and others to remove all physical threats of harm, which might include

Figure 6.6   Assessing Suicide Risk

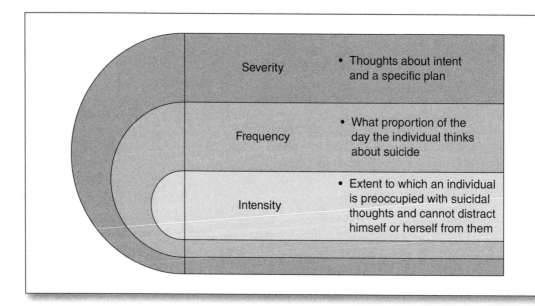

Figure 6.7   Assessing Hopelessness

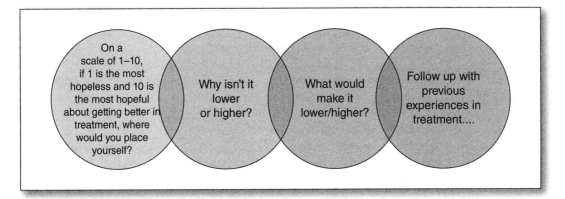

firearms (even firearms in locked cabinets), other weapons, medications that could be used in an overdose, and any other items that you deem as possibly posing a risk for the individual and potentially allowing them to carry out the suicide intent.

REFLECTIVE LEARNING ACTIVITY

Conduct a role-play with a class member or colleague where you have an opportunity to practice conducting a suicide assessment interview.

Discuss with your supervisor how the agency/clinic/organization handles situations when a client is actively suicidal and at risk of harming himself or herself or others.

The next section of this chapter will discuss the role that trauma can play throughout the assessment process and social work's inherent reporting responsibilities.

Trauma Assessments and Mandated Reporting Responsibilities

Another critical area during an assessment process is determining whether trauma-informed care is needed and whether you suspect that child or elder abuse is occurring. Current statistics suggest that more than two-thirds of individuals who have sought services in the behavioral health field have also experienced trauma of some nature (Substance Abuse and Mental Health Services Administration [SAMHSA], 2014). The National Center for Trauma Informed Care (2014) defines *trauma* in the following way:

> Traumatic experiences can be dehumanizing, shocking or terrifying, singular or multiple compounding events over time, and often include betrayal of a trusted person or

institution and a loss of safety. Trauma can result from experiences of violence. Trauma includes physical, sexual and institutional abuse, neglect, intergenerational trauma, and disasters that induce powerlessness, fear, recurrent hopelessness, and a constant state of alert. Trauma impacts one's spirituality and relationships with self, others, communities and environment, often resulting in recurring feelings of shame, guilt, rage, isolation, and disconnection. Healing is possible.

While conducting a bio-psycho-social-spiritual assessment, the experiences of trauma are often uncovered. Using screening tools specifically designed to assess trauma can assist you in determining how central the role of trauma will play during your intervention work. Prins, Ouimette, & Kimerling (2003) developed a brief screening tool that has been tested and found reliable within a range of diverse adult populations. This tool is called the Primary Care Post Traumatic Stress Disorder Screen (PC-PTSD). PC-PTSD is a four-item screening tool that was designed for use in primary care and other medical settings and is currently used to screen for post-traumatic stress disorder (PTSD) in the VA health system. Please refer to this tool in Figure 6.8. As we can note, this PC-PTSD screening tool first has the individual identify whether they have ever experienced an upsetting or frightening time. Then the tool explores four key areas that may indicate the individual is experiencing symptoms of PTSD. These areas include having nightmares, having a hard time not thinking about the situation, being constantly on guard or watchful, and feeling numb or detached from activities. Current research suggests that the results of the PC-PTSD should be considered positive if a patient answers "yes" to any three out of four items.

A similar screening tool has been developed for use with youth. The Trauma Events Screening Inventory (TESI) is a 15-item screening tool that assesses a child's experience with a variety of potential traumatic events, including current and previous accidents/injuries, hospitalizations, physical abuse, sexual abuse, domestic violence, community violence, and disaster-related situations (Ford & Rogers, 1997). A sample questionnaire includes the following questions:

- Have you ever been in a really bad accident, like a car accident, a fall, or a fire?
- How old were you when this happened?
- Were you hurt? [What was the hurt?]
- Did you go to the doctor or hospital?
- Was someone else hurt in the accident? [Who? What was the hurt? Did they go to the doctor or the hospital?]

REFLECTIVE LEARNING ACTIVITY

Review each case situation found at the beginning of this chapter. Discuss two screening tools that you might consider using with the individual/family in the case, share your rationale for why you chose them, and share what you hope to uncover/determine.

Figure 6.8 PC-PTSD

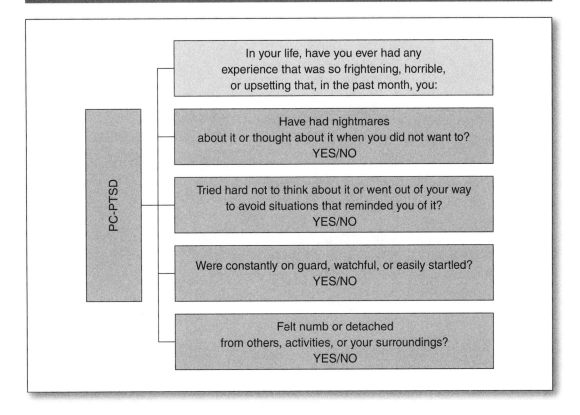

While these are just two trauma-screening instruments that have been determined to be reliable and valid, there are several other, more detailed screening tools and more intensive procedures for conducting trauma assessments that are beyond the scope of this book and have been developed especially for working with children who have experienced physical, emotional, or sexual abuse and older persons who are living in abusive conditions. The important task for you as the social worker in the assessment phase is to determine whether trauma has occurred by using a valid tool and, if so, decide whether further screening and/or treatment would be appropriate. You need to remember that you are considered a mandatory reporter for child abuse and neglect concerns. In this mandated role, you are required to report any suspicion of child maltreatment to the child protective authorities in your area. Please note that you are not responsible for or involved in the actual investigation of the alleged child maltreatment—you are only reporting your concerns based on your assessment, which could well be critical to the safety of your client. If the investigation itself results in the allegation not being substantiated, this should not dissuade you from reporting suspicions you may have now or in the future. Because all social workers are considered mandatory reporters, 24 hours a day/7 days a week, your assessment and subsequent documentation and actions are critical. You also want to ensure that during the assessment process, you convey to the individual that you have heard their concerns and that you will work to ensure their safety.

In addition, you are also considered a mandatory reporter should you suspect elder abuse, and you are required to report the abuse to the appropriate adult protective authorities. Not all states have designated elder abuse reporting laws, so be sure to explore the laws in your state. A complicating factor in working with older adults who are experiencing abuse is that many are afraid to report abuse due to their complex relationships with family that range from being dependent on family members to being afraid of retaliation by family/caregivers to feeling reluctance and possible guilt about charging family/caregivers with abuse. It is therefore important when working with older adults that you spend a lot of extra time with the individuals to help you discern what they want to change while at the same time weighing their decision-making capacity and ability.

Diagnostic and Statistical Manual of Mental Disorders (DSM-5), Cultural Assessment Tools in the DSM-5, and International Statistical Classification of Diseases and Related Health Problems (ICD-10)

In this last section of this chapter, we will highlight and discuss how to incorporate diagnoses using the *DSM-5* in the assessment process when required by your practice setting. While there are several concerns that social workers and other professionals have about using the *DSM-5* classification system due to a range of issues, it is currently the major tool used in the behavioral health field to determine the diagnosis of psychiatric and behavioral disorders/illnesses. The *DSM-5* diagnoses are aligned with the ICD-10 system, which includes subclassifications that can be used to classify/code diseases and other health disorders for a range of purposes. According to the authors of the *DSM-5* (which include hundreds of international experts in mental health), a mental disorder is "a syndrome characterized by clinically significant disturbance in an individual's cognition, emotion regulation, or behavior that reflects a dysfunction in the psychological, biological or developmental processes underlying mental functioning" (American Psychiatric Association, 2013, p. 20). In conducting the diagnostic interview, Nussbaum (2013) recommends that the following outline/structure be used for a 30-minute interview:

1. Asking why the person is seeking treatment/help.

2. Listening to the individual tell their story of illness.

3. Exploring history of the present illness, past psychiatric history, and safety concerns.

4. Reviewing the systems (mood, psychosis, anxiety, obsessions and compulsions, trauma, dissociation, somatic concerns, eating and feeding, sleeping, substance

and other addictions, personality and elimination) by addressing common symptoms and exploring in more detail the positive responses using the established *DSM-5* criteria.

5. Reviewing past medical history, allergies, family history, developmental history, and social history.

6. Conducting a mental status examination (MSE) that addresses the following components: appearance, behavior, speech, mood, affect, thought process, thought content, cognition, and intellectual resources and insight/judgment using the Mini-Mental State Examination (MMSE) to get a handle on types of difficulties the individual may be experiencing. The MMSE comprises name, date and time, place, immediate recall, attention (counting backward from 100 by 7s, spelling *world* backward), delayed recall, general information (president, governor, five large cities), abstractions, proverbs, naming, repetition, three-stage command, reading, copying, and writing. (Nussbaum, 2013, p. 27)

7. Checking to see that you have covered the major concerns of the individual.

In addition to this outline for conducting the diagnostic interview, the *DSM-5* stresses the importance of recognizing the influence and role that culture plays in an individual's experience of distress and has developed an additional structured tool, the Cultural Formulation Interview (CFI) with the goal of modifying the diagnostic interview in order to capture the cultural meanings of illness more effectively. When using the CFI interview format, you would open the session by asking the individual the following:

> I would like to understand the problems that bring you here so that I can help you more effectively. I want to know about your experience and ideas. I will ask some questions about what is going on and how you are dealing with it. There [are] no right or wrong answers. I just want to know your views and those of other important people in your life. (Nussbaum, 2013, p. 209)

You would then explore cultural definitions of the problem, cultural perceptions of cause and context, role of cultural identity, cultural factors affecting self-coping, and current and post help-seeking strategies.

This Cultural Formulation Interview structure is consistent with our earlier discussions focusing on the importance of relationship building and listening to the voice of the client. It is essential to learn from the client and family members how they view the current crisis (based on their cultural beliefs and identity) and what the acceptable ways of coping and seeking help for this crisis/illness are.

When a *DSM-5* diagnosis is made, you will discover that individuals will often have more than one diagnosis, so it is important to consider/review the order of the diagnosis. The first diagnosis is called the *principal diagnosis*. The secondary and tertiary (third) diagnoses should be listed in order of need for clinical attention. Subtypes for a diagnosis can be used to help communicate greater clarity and are mutually exclusive. Specifiers, on the other hand, are not mutually exclusive, and more than one can be used. Some diagnoses offer an opportunity to rate the severity of the symptoms as well.

CHAPTER REVIEW QUESTIONS

1. List four reasons why assessment is a critical component in the helping process and discuss why these reasons are important.

2. Discuss three reasons why it is important to seek information/data from multiple dimensions during the assessment process.

3. Discuss three reasons why creating a summary assessment using a bio-psycho-social-spiritual perspective is important.

4. Of the screening tools presented in this chapter, which one is the most interesting to you and why?

5. List the five steps involved in completing a suicide risk assessment.

6. Discuss at least three reasons why creating a safety plan is important.

7. List three reasons why using a trauma-informed assessment approach is important.

8. Which three steps in Nussbaum's diagnostic interview would you like to learn more about and why? Use the *DSM-5* to assist you. List several steps you would take to become more proficient when completing a diagnostic interview.

REFERENCES

American Psychiatric Association. (2013). *Diagnostic and statistical manual of mental disorders* (5th ed.). Washington, DC: Author.

Farlex. (2014). [genogram image]. Retrieved August 24, 2014 from http://medical-dictionary .thefreedictionary.com/genogram

Ford, J., & Rogers, K. (1997). *Traumatic Events Screening Inventory (TESI).* Retrieved August 8, 2014 from http://www.ptsd.va.gov/professional/pages/assessments/tesi.asp

Gambrill, E. D. (2006). *Social work practice: a critical thinker's guide* (2nd ed.). New York, NY: Oxford University Press.

Genogram Analytics. (2014). [sample ecomap]. Retrieved August 24, 2014 from http://www .genogramanalytics.com/

Hepworth, D. H., Rooney, R., Rooney, G., Strom-Gottfried, K., & Larsen, J. (2010). *Direct social work practice: Theory and skills* (8th ed.). Belmont, CA: Brooks/Cole, Cengage Learning.

Hunter, C., Goodie, J. L., Oordt, M. S., & Dobmeyer, A. C. (2009). *Integrated behavioral health in primary care: A step-by-step guidance for assessment and intervention.* Washington, DC: American Psychiatric Association.

Kroenke, K., Spitzer, R. L., & Williams, J. B. (2001). The PHQ-9: Validity of a brief depression severity measure. *Journal of General Internal Medicine, 16*(9), 606–613.

Lee, M. Y., Ng, S-M., Leung, P. P. Y., Chan, C. L. W., & Leung, P. (2009). *Integrative body-mind-spirit social work: An empirically based approach to assessment and treatment.* Oxford, UK: Oxford University Press.

National Center for Trauma Informed Care. (2014). [website]. Retrieved August 24, 2014 from http://www.nasddds.org/resource-library/behavioral-challenges/mental-health-treatment/trauma-informed-care/national-center-for-trauma-informed-care/

Nussbaum, A. M. (2013). *The pocket guide to the DSM-5 Diagnostic Exam*. Arlington, VA: American Psychiatric Association.

O'Hare, T. (2009). *Essential skills of social work practice: Assessment, intervention, and evaluation*. Chicago, IL: Lyceum Books, Inc.

Prins, A., Ouimette, P., & Kimerling, R. (2003). *Primary Care PTSD Screen (PC-PTSD)*. Retrieved August 8, 2014 from http://www.ptsd.va.gov/professional/assessment/screens/pc-ptsd.asp

Rapp, C. A., & Goscha, R. J. (2012). *The strengths model: A recovery-oriented approach to mental health services* (3rd ed.). New York, NY: Oxford University Press.

Simmons, C. A., & Lehmann, P. (2013). *Tools for strengths-based assessment and evaluation*. New York, NY: Springer.

Substance Abuse and Mental Health Services Administration (SAMHSA). (2014). *Trauma-Informed care & alternatives to seclusion and restraint*. Retrieved August 8, 2014 from http://www.samhsa.gov/nctic/

7

Change Planning

We spent considerable time during the previous chapter talking about the importance of various assessments and the processes that are used to build a comprehensive understanding of the client's problems, strengths, values, and needs. We engage in these processes to better understand the client's current state and the client's desired state.

The next step in treatment involves developing a strategy that will help support the client in achieving and sustaining this desired state. In social work, this planning process is commonly referred to as *treatment planning*, but we are using more general terminology, *change planning*, to reflect the fact that not all social workers provide treatment. As described in the previous chapter, we use assessments to build a comprehensive understanding of the client's problems, strengths, values, and needs. This information is then used as the basis for developing a plan for change. In this chapter, we focus on how to create a plan for change.

You are likely to encounter terminology in various social service settings that is different from the terminology we use here. It is important to reiterate that we are providing a general framework that can be easily adapted to fit any given setting. However, it is essential that any adaptation of the framework maintains the core principles of change planning.

CHAPTER LEARNING OBJECTIVES

By the end of this chapter, you should know

- the core principles of change planning,
- how change goals are used to direct the delivery of services,
- the process of selecting interventions,

(Continued)

(Continued)

- how to formulate objectives, and
- how to write a change plan.

The Council on Social Work Education Educational Policy and Accreditation Standards (CSWE-EPAS) Competencies that are highlighted in more depth in this chapter include the following:

2.1.2 Apply social work ethical principles to guide professional practice.

2.1.6 Engage in research-informed practice and practice-informed research.

2.1.7 Apply knowledge of human behavior and the social environment.

2.1.10 (a–d) Engage, assess, intervene, and evaluate with individuals, families, groups, organizations, and communities.

CASE SITUATION A: TRAVIS

Travis is a 13-year-old whose parents are divorced. He lives with his mother and visits his father, who lives in another state, every summer—a decision that was made in the custody decree. Travis has had serious emotional and behavior problems that have resulted in several psychiatric admissions during the school year. He was placed on medication that has helped to stabilize his behavior. When Travis made his annual summer trip to see his father, he told him that he doesn't like taking the medicine because it makes him feel weird. He begged his father to not make him take the medicine, and his father agreed. When the mother found out, she contacted the child's psychiatrist, who referred her to the clinic's social worker.

CASE SITUATION B: KIMI

Kimi is a 14-year-old who was referred for treatment due to disclosure of sexual abuse by her mother's boyfriend since she was 12 years old. She later disclosed that she had also been sexually abused by her paternal grandfather during this same time period. The social worker engaged the mother in sessions (where appropriate) and found that while she faithfully brought Kimi to appointments, she became very defensive and resistant when confronted with issues related to her relationship with Kimi and what had happened to her. On several occasions, Kimi told the social worker that following her appointments, her mother would be openly angry with her, punitive, and moody. Kimi reported living with her mother was like having to constantly walk on eggshells. Attempts to get the mother to engage in treatment for her were unsuccessful. Kimi has threatened to run away and frequently complains that her mother requires that she do the bulk of the household chores and that she has to constantly babysit her younger stepsister, who is the child of her abuser.

What Is Change Planning?

Change planning represents the development of a strategy intended to move a client from her or his current level of functioning to a desired or target level of functioning. *Level of functioning* commonly refers to an individual's performance in specific areas of a person's life. The specific level of functioning is established through careful assessment, typically guided by the use of scales or other standardized assessment tools. We use the concept of *level of functioning* broadly to include emotions, behaviors, or relationships that will be a target of change (i.e., change goals). For example, referring to the foregoing case situations, we would have a primary focus on Travis' behavior. His current level of functioning would be a description of his abilities for managing his present behavior. We would then consider his potential and set that as his target level of functioning. Kimi's level of functioning could be conceptualized in a few different ways. One possibility might be her ability to cope with her mother's expression of emotions and changes in mood, where her current level of functioning is characterized by frustration and plans to run away. The target level of functioning might be a pattern of responding that is more controlled and involves systematic problem solving. Keep in mind that these case situations are not fully detailed and can be conceptualized in different ways, but the idea is to consider the difference between the client's current level of functioning and their potential in setting a target level of functioning.

Change planning covers the activities that have been carefully selected and systematically organized in order to reduce the gap between the current and target level of functioning. Change planning emerges from the process of assessment and continues until the change goals are met. The actual change plan is a physical or electronic document that provides a detailed description of the change strategy. Change plans will look different across various social service sectors and agencies, but the overall function is essentially the same.

Change planning is a critical activity that social workers perform in nearly every area of social work practice. It is most common in the provision of direct services with clients, but we can easily apply the concept of change planning to virtually any other area of social work practice that requires a change to be based on systematic and coordinated efforts. While change planning may be considered an important duty of social workers, it can be a compulsory activity in certain areas of practice. For example, federal regulations (42 CFR §483.20) require that any United States health facility receiving money from Medicare or Medicaid create and submit a care plan (synonymous with a *change plan*) for those clients (Vongxaiburana, Thomas, Frahm, & Hyer, 2011). These change plans must abide by federal standards, which include accuracy, completeness, and reproducibility—all attributes that are covered in the ensuing chapter.

Core Principles of Change Planning

Before moving into the specifics of change planning and how to write a change plan, we need to look at a number of core principles that should be reflected in all change planning efforts and in written change plans. In referring to these as *core principles,* it is important to remember that they are not hard-and-fast rules that apply to all encounters with clients. Rather, they reflect best practices in treatment planning and need to be adapted to meet specific circumstances. In other words, we are interested in maintaining the spirit that underlies the principles as opposed to strict guidelines that must be applied as written. As you review this section of the chapter, consider how these different principles could be applied to the case situations presented at the beginning of the chapter.

Program-Driven Versus Tailored Change Plans

It is important to distinguish between program-driven change plans and individually tailored change plans. Program-driven plans tend to reflect a one-size-fits-all approach. This occurs in service settings where each client receives roughly the same kind of services. Program-driven plans are usually implemented to standardize a process in order to ensure efficiency and consistency in the delivery of services. It is much easier to train staff in a single set of services or treatment activities than to have a variety of service methods. It is also much easier to ensure the fidelity of services with program-driven change plans—that is, ensuring adherence to a protocol that helps minimize deviations from its key ingredients. Here are a few examples of a program-driven approach to change planning:

- A drug or alcohol treatment program offering a standardized 30-day curriculum for every client and requiring attendance to Alcoholics Anonymous
- A medical social worker referring every client affected by cancer to the same support group
- An employment specialist helping every client prepare a resume using the same format
- A mental health clinic providing eight sessions of counseling to persons with depression

An individually tailored change plan, on the other hand, is one that is customized to the unique needs and values of each client. Thus each client within the same agency would be pursuing different change goals, and the services for each client would be matched to her or his unique needs and values. While program-driven plans are well intentioned, the advantages do not outweigh the importance of tailored plans.

Program-driven plans often assume that the needs and values of each client can be met by the same plan—an assumption that is rarely, if ever true. They also lack the flexibility and comprehensiveness to address co-occurring problems.

Many of the problems that social workers address do not occur in isolation. For example, a myriad of other problems occur with alcohol use disorders (Kessler et al., 1996). Problems with relationships, employment, and the law are ubiquitous, and it is nearly impossible to make meaningful progress toward the goal of reduction or abstinence by ignoring co-occurring problems. Also, not all clients with alcohol-related problems have the same co-occurring problems, so it is not a good use of either program resources or the client's time to provide unnecessary or improperly matched services.

Another important reason for individually tailored plans is that they provide an important foundation for promoting engagement with the client. Clients are more likely to be engaged in services and achieve better outcomes when their change plans are aligned with their needs and values. It is more difficult to build engagement with a one-size-fits-all approach to services. Referring back to the case situations presented at the beginning of the chapter, it would be difficult to imagine how any social service agency could address the full range of challenges without a set of services that are tailored to the specific needs of these individuals.

While we emphasize the importance of tailored change plans, we cannot ignore some of their challenges. Foremost, tailored change plans require comprehensive assessments to fully understand the various needs and values of the client. Social workers face many complex challenges and decisions in the assessment process. Social workers need to determine how much assessment data needs to be collected in order to get an adequate representation of the needs and values of the client in change planning. They also need to know how to properly integrate various types of assessment data to meaningfully inform a change plan. Unfortunately, no straightforward answers exist for these challenges and decisions.

The final—and probably the most significant—barrier to constructing tailored change plans is the limited range of services that any given social service agency can provide. More specifically, clients typically present with co-occurring problems, and it is rarely the case that a single agency can address the full range of co-occurring problems. This requires referrals to be made to other service providers as well as a lot of coordination and integration of services. Although there are a number of challenges to developing individually tailored change plans, the principle of tailoring plans to individual clients should not be lost.

Change Plans Developed Collaboratively

The development (and implementation) of a change plan should be a collaborative process between the client and social worker. This is very different from the prescriptive approach, which is common in medical settings. A social worker using a prescriptive approach would prepare a change plan based on what she or he thinks is best for the client, but a *collaborative approach* means that the client's views are reflected throughout the entire change planning effort.

The collaborative relationship is important for two main reasons. First, working collaboratively is a necessary way to foster client engagement—a critical ingredient to the achievement of change goals. A client who takes on a passive role in social work services will be less likely to engage in the change process. This is particularly important if the major goals are oriented around changing specific behavior, such as the development and use of coping skills, smoking cessation, exercise, and so on. In a comprehensive review of the psychotherapy research, Tryon and Winograd (2001) found that a collaborative relationship—in which the client and the social worker agree on therapeutic goals and each party is equally involved in the course of treatment— improves the client's chances of success at meeting his or her change goal. This finding was also confirmed in a meta-analysis of therapeutic variables in youth and family therapy (see Karver, Handelsman, Fields, & Bickman, 2006), and such results can be observed in many other areas of social work practice (Clarke, Oades, Crowe, & Deane, 2006; Graham & Barter, 1999). A meta-analysis is a study procedure that involves combing or *pooling* the results of many comparable studies to get an estimate of the averaged effect across the studies. In other words, a meta-analysis is essentially creating a large study from a number of smaller studies.

The second reason the collaborative relationship is important is that it can be used to further increase the client's capacity for change. That is, the collaborative relationship provides a context for teaching the client about the change process. Collaboration provides the client with exposure to all aspects of the change process and allows the client to gain a greater understanding of systematic, planned change. This can become a very important and highly generalizable skill that the client can use outside of formal social work services. This skill will help promote independence and higher levels of functioning, thereby reducing the need for future services.

Change Plans Informed by Comprehensive Assessment

Change planning emerges from a careful and comprehensive assessment of the client in order to fully reflect the client's needs and values in the change process. This holds true for nearly all change planning efforts, except for crisis situations or other situations where there is an immediate risk to self or others. In these circumstances, assessment still occurs, but the progression from assessment to change planning (and implementation of a change plan) is much faster.

As previously stated, comprehensive assessment is necessary to understand the client's needs and values. Unfortunately, there are no rules that can guide the social worker in making the decision about whether enough assessment data have been collected before moving on to change planning. As a general guideline, you should have collected enough data to construct a set of hypotheses that reasonably explain why the problem is occurring. These are causal statements that explain how the parts of the problem are causally related. Be cautious of taking an intuitive approach where you "feel" that enough assessment data have been collected. You want to ensure that the assessment data have led to a set of treatment hypotheses that not only give a reasonable explanation for the problem but can also be used to define a full range of options for change. Additionally, as described in the earlier chapter on assessment, assessing for client strengths is associated with client empowerment (see Cowger, 1994).

Be sure to keep in mind that assessment doesn't stop when you begin change planning. In fact, assessment is important throughout the service process, although the purpose of assessment changes. At the beginning of service provision, an assessment helps the social worker build an understanding of the needs and values of the client in order to develop a change plan. When change planning begins, assessment continues so that the social worker can check the accuracy of her or his understanding of the problem as well as monitor the client for the emergence of new or related problems. As the change plan is implemented, assessment serves as a vehicle for monitoring any change that occurs. It is also used to measure the progression toward change goals. Assessment can be viewed as an iterative approach, where assessment is continually used to measure change and modify or establish new goals for treatment.

Flexible Change Plans

While the change plan is often considered a road map for directing services, it is important that change plans allow for flexibility. Many of the problems that clients experience within a bio-psycho-social-spiritual framework can be extremely dynamic, giving rise to new problems or changing unexpectedly. A change plan needs to have enough flexibility to be responsive to these dynamics.

Social workers face many difficult decisions in the delivery of social work services, and deciding when to revise a change plan is certainly one of them. No specific rules or guidelines exist to assist a social worker in deciding when to change the plan. For example, consider a school social worker who is helping administer a behavioral intervention in a classroom for a young child with serious behavior problems. Although a comprehensive change plan may have been developed, the social worker still needs to think carefully about when changes are expected to be observed. It is impossible to estimate the exact amount of change that will occur, so having clarity on the expected range of change is important. The social worker needs to consider how long to wait before making revisions and how much of the change plan to revise as well as the reasons for any change.

Even if you develop a plan that is flexible, keep in mind that no straightforward answers exist with respect to what to change and when those changes should occur. Revisions to a change plan require a good understanding of both the problems being addressed and the interventions being used. More specifically, it is essential to have a well-developed understanding of the causal structure of the problem that is being targeted. This, again, speaks to the importance of comprehensive assessment and careful integration of the assessment data to fully understand the problems at hand. A strong understanding of the problems can give you insights into how long it might take to address a particular problem.

Having a strong understanding of the research is also very important. The research on interventions can outline the time it takes for an intervention to have an effect and the degree of the effect that you should expect, assuming the intervention was delivered in a manner consistent with the original study. Longitudinal research is particularly helpful to understand the decay in effects following the cessation of the intervention.

Change Plans Understood by and
Personally Meaningful to the Client

All aspects of the change process should be understood by the client to the extent that it is allowed by his or her cognitive capacity. It is often the case that social workers are required to follow specific administrative procedures when writing up change plans, including using standardized forms. Whenever necessary, consider creating an alternate set of forms that can be used along with the organizational forms. These alternate forms can be provided to the client and should communicate the critical information in a way that is readily understood by the client. Be sure to eliminate all jargon and pay careful attention to formatting and aesthetics to promote understanding of the change plan.

In addition to being understood by the client, it is essential that the change plan is personally meaningful to the client. This is where the change planning links back to the philosophy of evidence-based practice, where the client's goals and values are recognized as essential elements of the process. In particular, it is essential that social workers operate from a position of cultural competency—that is, recognizing and incorporating the specific cultural values or beliefs of the individual for whom a change plan is being developed. For example, is it important to the individual to involve other family members or friends to support the change process? Some individuals might welcome or want the involvement of a religious leader, but others may not. It is important that the social worker maintain this lens throughout the change planning process.

Change Goals

The assessment process helps us understand an individual's current state, particularly the specific problems that have resulted in the need for social work services. When we engage in change planning, we begin to think more actively about the desired state or target level of functioning that can be achieved through the provision of social work services. Change planning represents the development of a strategy that attempts to bridge the gap between the current level of functioning and the target level of functioning. In this section, we make a distinction between two different types of goals—*intermediary goals* and *ultimate goals*—and distinguish change *outcomes* from change *processes*.

Intermediary Goals Versus Ultimate Goals

Change often takes place in steps. That is, we may have a goal in mind, but a number of changes are required to achieve that goal. The final change or state that we are seeking is referred to as an *ultimate goal*, and the smaller changes that lead to the ultimate goal are referred to as *intermediary goals*. For example, if you are seeking a career in social work, then this can be considered an ultimate goal, and your completion of a social work degree would be considered an intermediary goal. In other words, the degree you are seeking is a necessary but not sufficient condition to achieving your ultimate goal.

The distinction between intermediary and ultimate goals is conceptual and is based on the viewpoint of the client. It is possible that two clients have the same goal, but the goal may be an intermediary goal for one client and an ultimate goal for another client. For example, consider two different clients who want to achieve an increased level of physical fitness. This might be an ultimate goal for one client who recognizes fitness is essential to maintaining good health. A number of other intermediary goals are then considered for achieving this ultimate goal—putting together an exercise plan, establishing an exercise schedule, finding an exercise partner, and so on. Another client might have the same goal of achieving an increased level of physical fitness, but it could be an intermediary goal that is directed toward an ultimate goal. For example, a client who suffered a serious car accident and is actively taking steps to return to work would view achieving an increase in the level of physical fitness as an intermediary goal toward the ultimate goal of returning to work. Other intermediary goals would likely also be necessary, such as exploring work modifications to accommodate any disability from the accident.

Proximal and Distal Goals

When thinking about ultimate goals, it is helpful to make a distinction between proximal and distal goals. Goals with a shorter causal chain are considered *proximal*, and those with a longer causal chain are considered *distal*. This is a general distinction for helping us think about how far out the goals are in a causal chain. It is often the case that the further out our goals are, the more important or significant they are. This is because a number of preceding changes must take place in order to achieve a more long-distance goal.

For example, if you are working with an individual with a serious mental illness, a distal goal for this individual might be an improved quality of life. This is a distal ultimate goal, as it is based on a fairly extensive causal chain that requires a number of intermediary goals. If this client is struggling with employment, then achieving sustained employment is a necessary (but not sufficient) condition for an improved quality of life. And achieving sustained employment may require additional training or education and possibly the improvement of core social skills. This causal chain is presented graphically in Figure 7.1.

The distinction between distal and proximal goals is important because it has practical implications for the provision of social work services. Although distal goals are important, they may not be practical in the context of providing social work services. It is important that social workers specify goals that are attainable within the context of social work services available—this is part of the *SMART* criteria for writing goals (reviewed later in this chapter). In other words, it is necessary to think about the causal chain of events that are required in order to achieve a given goal. Distal goals take a long time and are more difficult to achieve. Social work services can help put clients on a path toward the attainment of distal goals, but these goals are generally not practical for social workers to pursue as part of a change plan.

We recommend thinking carefully about which goals within a causal chain can be reasonably addressed by social work services. The goals beyond these limits are important and should not be ignored, but the efforts of the social worker need to target what can be reasonably accomplished with the resources at hand. Improving overall quality of life may take a very long time, perhaps years (depending on how it is

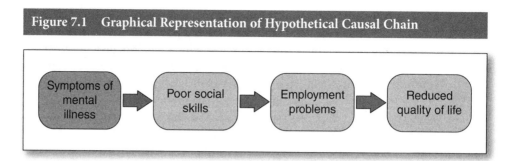

Figure 7.1   Graphical Representation of Hypothetical Causal Chain

defined), so it is better to focus on resolving those immediate needs that will result in the highest level of functioning possible given the resources at hand. Rather than specifying improved quality of life as an ultimate goal, therefore, it might be more effective to target an earlier point in the causal chain as the ultimate goal—for example, sustained employment. This still puts the client on a trajectory for improved quality of life and allows the social worker to bring greater focus to the change plan.

Outcomes and Processes

Many of the services provided by social workers have funding sources that require the monitoring and reporting of outcomes. While this will be the focus of Chapter 11, it is important to make a distinction at this point between outcomes and processes—sometimes the distinction is not immediately self-evident, so spending time working through the differences can lead to a deeper understanding.

Outcomes should be considered the achievement of goals or the actual changes in the client that occurred during the course of services and can be reasonably attributed to the services provided. As a side note, we cannot rule out the possibility that a decline in functioning may occur during the course of service and that this decline could possibly be the result of service. These negative changes in client functioning due to services are considered *iatrogenic effects*. Surprisingly, iatrogenic effects may result from the provision of social work services; therefore, it is important that consider the possibility of iatrogenic effects when you consider client service options. Dishion, McCord, and Poulin (1999) provide an excellent overview of iatrogenic effects that is highly relevant to social work practice.

Processes, on the other hand, are the various factors that provide the context for achieving outcomes. For example, satisfaction with services and the therapeutic relationship are essential aspects of social work services, and it makes sense for us to measure and systematically track these processes. This chapter and Chapter 11 focus on outcomes while making clear distinctions for processes. We do this to coincide with the technical aspects that are involved with change planning, especially since many different social work organizations and respective funding agencies require the reporting of outcomes. We do not want this distinction to suggest that treatment processes are unimportant. In fact, treatment processes are essential to outcomes.

Whiston and Sexton (1993) reviewed over 50 years of psychotherapy research that shows the important role of therapeutic relationships and session characteristics and how they interact with the interventions that are provided. And over 1,000 studies have provided strong support for the therapeutic bond between the relationship and client (Simpson, 2004).

REFLECTIVE LEARNING ACTIVITY

Think of some changes you want to make in your own life. Consider different goals for different areas of your life—health behaviors, career goals, social or interpersonal goals, and so on. Identify possible intermediary goals that are necessary to achieving each particular goal. Then, extend the goal out further to see whether it can be part of a long-term or distal goal.

Goal Selection

This section reviews different types of change goals. Any given client can have a potentially large number of possible change goals, and it may be the case that only a subset of these goals can be addressed during the course of social work services. This naturally raises a number of questions:

- How many goals should a client have?
- If we can't address all the goals, then which ones do we address?
- How do we pick them?

These questions are easier to address in program-driven approaches because the goals for clients may have already been preselected. In tailored change planning, these questions are given serious consideration during the formulation of change plans. Similar to our strategies for managing questions without straightforward answers, we provide you with a set of key principles to consider when formulating responses to these questions. Attempt to apply each of the principles to the case situations presented at the beginning of the chapter.

Safety

Issues of safety must always be given immediate consideration when delivering social work services. When clients present a clear and imminent danger to themselves or others, they are not able to engage in the change process as described. The systematic change process is set aside to ensure that all efforts are focused on putting together a plan of safety for the individual. Aside from crisis situations, the idea of promoting the safety and well-being of the client should be a priority. For example, serious health issues that can be improved through lifestyle or behavior changes would likely take priority over other problems that do not directly impact the health and safety of the client.

Issues of safety can also give rise to very significant ethical issues that are deserving of immediate long-term attention in the provision of social work services. For example, self-determination is an explicit ethical standard of the National Association of Social Workers (NASW) Code of Ethics (1.02 Self-Determination). Assume a crisis situation in which the client has provided compelling evidence of being at risk of serious harm to self, such as expressing a plan to commit suicide. The client has a right to self-determination, although the code states that social workers may "limit clients' right to self-determination when, in the social workers' professional judgment, clients' actions or potential actions pose a serious, foreseeable, and imminent risk to themselves or others" (NASW, 2008). While expressions of suicide may appear to meet the provision for limiting the clients' right, these are professional judgment calls that must be clearly justified and documented.

Issues of safety are not just issues that pertain to clients but to social workers, too. Former NASW president James Kelly offered an insightful viewpoint on the issue of job-related violence (Kelly, 2010). As described by Kelly, social workers are often asked to enter risky situations, similar to the duties of police officers. However, unlike police officers, social workers do not have partners or proper safety training, which necessarily increases the risk of harm to the social worker. Although social workers are expected to elevate service to others above self-interest (Kelly, 2010; NASW, 2008), social workers cannot reasonably perform their duties if they are put in harm's way. Further research and policy is needed to help reduce the job-related risks that many social workers face on a regular basis.

Importance to the Client

As stated numerous times throughout this chapter, the most effective change plans are established through a collaborative relationship between the social worker and client. The social worker helps to clarify the goals that are most important to the client, and while the social worker may express a professional opinion, the client has the final authority in determining which goals are most important and should be the focus of the change plan.

The social worker will face a number of difficulties when the change goals are not appropriate for services. In these situations, the social worker needs to be tactful but direct in bringing clarity to the type of services and the range of services that can be provided. If the social worker does not agree with the importance of a goal, the social worker should still recognize it as an important opportunity to help encourage change. Social workers can focus on a goal the client thinks is meaningful to leverage important processes (such as motivation, engagement, and satisfaction) that are critical to achieving this and other goals.

Highest Level of Generalizability

The generalizability of goals—the ways certain goals might generalize or apply to other problems—is a very important concept when attempting to promote the highest level of functioning and independence among our clients.

For example, we may be working with a client who regularly encounters challenges in social relationships due to poor social skills. One possible goal would be the improvement of a specific relationship that has been tarnished by poor social skills. Another possibility, and perhaps a more generalizable strategy, would be the improvement of social skills and development of problem-solving strategies that could be applied to a wide range of social encounters. Of course, the improvement of a single relationship may be more meaningful to the client—and perhaps in one's professional opinion, depending on the circumstances—but this can be used to generalize the strategy to other situations. The spirit of this principle is to remain cognizant of the opportunities that can lead to the development of skills that can be generalized and can lead to increased functioning and independence.

Most Impairing

Another important criterion for selecting goals is by focusing on the problems that are most problematic to the client. This should be consistent with the viewpoint of the client. Which problems are the most impairing or are creating the most significant barriers to meaningful change? Problems that are most impairing should be considered as a priority for any given change plan.

Easiest to Address

While selecting the problems that are most impairing is important, be sure that you don't overlook the opportunities that are relatively easy to address. Easy goals should not be selected at the expense of other problems, but selecting goals that are easy to address is important for a number of reasons.

Selecting goals based on the ease of addressing the issue can be highly motivating for a client and help spark initial progress in treatment planning. It is a way to build early success in the change process, which can then be used to leverage later successes around more difficult goals. Achieving these initial goals can help build the client's confidence early in the change process, which may promote motivation and higher levels of client engagement and satisfaction.

Goal Specification: A SMART Approach

At this point, you should be clear on the core principles of change planning, how to differentiate between different types of change goals, and the process of selecting goals. Throughout this process, we have been talking about goals at a conceptual level—that is, bringing to light the different nuances among the various concepts used in the change process. While many social work settings use different language and terminology in change planning, it is important to keep in mind that the framework we are presenting is intended to be highly generalizable, even if modifications to language and terminology are required.

In this section, we move from a conceptual discussion of change to an examination of the more technical aspects of change. In particular, we focus on the specification of goals and the various criteria that should be applied to that specification. Our approach is based on the acronym *SMART,* which stands for *specific, measurable, attainable, relevant,* and *time-bound.* While we use the SMART approach for goal specification with our clients, keep in mind that this approach is highly generalizable and is applied in many other fields, including (but not limited to) education (O'Neill, 2000), business (Cross & Lynch, 1988), organizational management in health care (Lazarus, 2004), and team development (DuFour & Burnette, 2002).

Specific

When writing a change goal, it is important that goals are specific—there should be no ambiguities in any of the concepts being used. Specific goals are free from jargon and use the most concrete language possible to delineate the change that will be achieved. A goal of *improving mental health* is not specific because the concept of *mental health* can mean many different things. A more specific goal would be to specify the specific mental health problems that are the target of change, such as the symptoms of anxiety or depression.

You can bring greater specification to a change goal by breaking it down even further into its specific components. For example, if you are working with a person with a developmental disability and the improvement of social skills was identified as an ultimate goal, you can break this down further into intermediary goals, such as increasing eye contact, initiating conversations, and giving and receiving negative feedback. Keep in mind that the degree of goal specificity can be informed by comprehensive assessments. However, be cautious in the assumption that more assessments produce more specificity. It is more important to focus on proper integration of high-quality assessment data than to seek as much data as possible.

Measurable

Measurable goals refer to goals that can be quantified. Specifying measurable goals helps to provide a way to monitor progress toward the attainment of these goals and clarifies whether or not a goal was achieved. It helps us to move beyond simply sensing or getting an impression of whether the goal was achieved. Measurable goals also provide the basis for outcome evaluation. This is covered in Chapter 11 in more detail, but we are providing preliminary coverage of this important topic to help you gain a big-picture understanding of goal specification.

One of the challenges of goal specification is that sometimes our goals are not directly measurable. Educational goals, for example, often have very specific measurements, such as a grade in a course or a GPA, although these may not necessarily be perfect measurements. Educational goals can be measured at different levels, such as the simple completion of a specific task, completion of a course, or completion of the school year. Now, consider depression—what is the level of depression? This becomes much more complicated and might require the use of a scale looking at a variety of factors, such as frequency, intensity, latency, and severity.

Keep in mind that the more behavioral your goals, the easier it will be to write measurable or SMART goals. *Behavioral goals* involve goals that look for changes in behavior, preferably increasing desirable behaviors that are incompatible with undesirable behaviors. For example, a goal for a child with serious behavioral problems might be to increase the number of positive interactions with her or his peers. This is a behavior change that isn't incompatible with negative interactions, and the framing of the goal is in a positive direction. But keep in mind that this goal does not yet meet the criterion of specificity or of being measurable. Take a moment and think about how you might further develop this goal to be consistent with these criteria.

Also, the specific process of measuring or monitoring the progress toward the goal must not place any unreasonable or excessive burdens on the client or another individual. The system must be easy to use while generating good data to inform decision making. We will talk more about the process of monitoring in Chapter 11 on outcome evaluation.

Attainable

Attainable goals are those that can be reasonably achieved, given the resources and capacity of the client with whom you are working. Keep in mind that you should expect goal achievement to fall within a range of performance. You should always target the minimum expected level of achievement that would result in meaningful movement toward the goal. If you are helping the client acquire a specific skill, this doesn't necessarily mean perfecting the skill but instead setting the target at a level that is reasonable in relation to the functional capacity of the individual.

Relevant

All ultimate goals specified within a change plan must reflect the needs and values of the client. All intermediary goals must be directly supportive of at least one ultimate goal. The overall set of goals must also be coherent. A good way to check the relevance of each goal is to describe the rationale for each goal along with the causal process of how the achievement of the goal will lead to functional improvement, independence, or capacity to change. Your inability to clearly describe the rationale will raise questions about the relevance of the goal.

Time Bound

The specification of a goal should be time bound. There should be a specified date when the goal is to be achieved. This typically requires sequential ordering of goals, since intermediary goals need to be achieved in order to reach ultimate goals. Building time boundaries around your goals helps ensure that you are making meaningful progress during the course of services. Again, similar to other parts of the change plan, the time boundary around a goal can be flexible, but it must be clearly stated. Any changes to the target completion date should coincide with a strong rationale for why the changes were made.

REFLECTIVE LEARNING ACTIVITY

Revisit some of the goals you specified for yourself earlier in the chapter. Restate these goals using the SMART criteria. Ensure that each goal applies each criterion.

Intervention Selection

Having clear goals is a necessary step before interventions can be selected. In other words, it involves specifying the end or desired state of functioning and working backward. Once we clarify the goals that are to be pursued in the course of services, we can explore specific ways to achieve those goals. Similar to the specification of goals, we want to ensure that we have a strong rationale for why specific interventions are selected, and they should have a logical fit within the overall structure of the change plan. Be sure to keep in mind the core principles of change planning, particularly the principle of collaboration with the client, when choosing appropriate interventions. While a social worker may have a preferred intervention approach, this approach may not align with the interest and needs of the client.

Skill Focused

Skill-focused interventions should be a priority, as they promote the functional capacity of the individual. Skill development gives the client resources that can be used following the termination of services. Certain skills can help clients achieve proximal goals, and over time, these can lead to the achievement of more distal goals. For example, a client who has severe problems with social anxiety that has resulted in a limited amount of social interactions could develop skills to overcome this problem and expand the number of social interactions during the course of social work services. If successful, the skills acquired for managing social anxiety can result in fundamental changes in the client's life. The client may consider other activities that have been previously thwarted by social anxiety, such as completion of a college degree, pursuit of a different career, or participation in a community group. Thus it is always important to keep in mind the importance of skill development when selecting interventions for a change plan.

Simple Versus Complex

An intervention plan should never be overly complex, and simple plans are much preferred over complex plans, provided that the intended effects are roughly the same. Complexity can result in barriers to implementation and engagement. Be cautious of putting together an intervention plan that has an excessive number of working parts. An easy way to check the complexity of the plan is to ask the client to reflect on her or his understanding of each part of the plan and the rationale behind the plan. If the plan is not understood by the client, it is unlikely that it can actually be implemented with fidelity or in a manner consistent with the original intentions of the plan.

Generalizable

Generalizable interventions relate to intervention approaches that may help a client achieve more than one goal or help address a range of problems. For example, teaching a client systematic problem solving can, potentially, be used in many different areas of a client's life. This is a highly generalizable intervention strategy. This is not the same as helping the client work on addressing a single problem that is occurring in her or his life. Keep in mind that generalizability is not always the priority, as it may be important for the client to work on a very specific problem. The idea behind this principle is to look for opportunities that will allow a single intervention to help address multiple problems.

Resource Sensitive

As social workers, it is necessary to remain cognizant of the resources required to implement a given intervention. This is in response to the limited number of resources available to certain client populations. Many years ago, resources may have been available to deliver psychotherapy for extended periods of time, even years. This is certainly not feasible in most cases, given the current funding environment, which has given rise to brief and time-limited approaches to interventions. While this change to the service delivery system is often viewed negatively, it is important to keep in mind that many of the brief interventions do show the same positive effects compared to more lengthy approaches. This change in the system also has value to the client, since it is important that clients are not dependent upon services for lengthy periods of time. We want to help clients achieve as much functional capacity and independence as possible in the shortest time frame possible. Having a menu of time-limited and focused interventions is essential to this value.

Evidence Based

An entire chapter has been devoted to the concept of empirically supported treatments. This does not imply that we do exactly what the research says; rather, we are seeking an integration of the best available research knowledge with client values and professional experience. The principle behind selecting evidence-based interventions is to ensure that social workers are aware of intervention approaches that have been systematically tested and found to be effective for a specific client population. Doing so can help the social worker avoid possible iatrogenic (negative) effects of services. Again, evidence-based interventions may not fit exactly, but it is essential that the social worker be aware of the best available research and be able to clearly articulate how the research does and does not apply.

Adaptable

All intervention efforts to promote change should be adaptable to the cognitive and functional capacity of the client, since some interventions require the client to have a certain level of cognitive or functional capacity. For example, certain modalities of psychotherapy may require the client to write down negative thoughts that are experienced in the course of a given day. This may be particularly challenging for a client with a severe brain injury or a developmental disability. Thus, the selection of any given intervention needs to be appropriately adapted to ensure that it can be implemented in a way that helps achieve the desired intervention effects. Think about ways an intervention can be simplified or ways certain cues can be incorporated to promote effective implementation.

Active

Change can rarely, if ever, take place in an office area or during some other meeting time with a social worker. Your job as a social worker is to create a context that will help promote change. And everything you do is focused on simply increasing the likelihood or probability of change. One common way of promoting change is to focus on interventions that have clients apply skills or engage in certain activities in between meetings with the social worker. This is typically referred to as *homework*, but this is a concept that is usually more problematic than beneficial. The concept of homework is obviously a carryover from school settings, where activities are assigned by the teacher and turned in at a later time by the student. This has been used for years by social workers and other providers who seek to promote change. Unfortunately, the use has been unsuccessful and for very good reason: it is usually created in a way that is burdensome and unhelpful to the client.

These activities should be negotiated with the client and should directly support the change plan. In fact, each activity should be structured in a way that meets the SMART goals. The activities could be formulated as micro-goals that are intended to promote the acquisition of the intermediary goals, which then support the acquisition of ultimate goals. For example, a social worker may provide the client with social skills training during a scheduled meeting time, focusing on different ways to initiate a conversation. A related therapeutic task could be for the individual to attempt to initiate at least one conversation per day. But keep in mind what is needed to help remind the client of this plan. Is it good enough for the client to simply remember to do so when awareness is actually part of the problem? You might ask the client to write down or journal about the experience, but how well would that work with the individual? Is it reasonable to carry around writing implements and make notes in community settings? Is there a way to help minimize all writing burdens to make this useful?

> **REFLECTIVE LEARNING ACTIVITY**
>
> Again, revisit the goals that you specified for yourself earlier in the chapter. Consider different strategies or interventions that you could select that would help you achieve these goals. Consider the extent to which each of the interventions are based on the general principles of goal selection.

The Written Change Plan

At this point, we have covered the essential ingredients of the change planning process. This includes knowing the core principles of change planning, differentiating between different types of change goals, specifying change goals, and selecting interventions. These efforts need to be summarized in a written change plan, which exists as a hard copy or an electronic document. Many service organizations require some type of written plan, often referred to as a *treatment plan*, and the forms and structure differ significantly across organizations. Thus there is no standard template or set language that represents all the different plans that you might encounter.

Having a written change plan is important for a number of reasons. Foremost, it provides a way to organize and communicate the change plan. It would likely be very difficult to remember all the different aspects of a change plan. The change plan also serves as an accountability tool for both the social worker and the client. More specifically, the written change plan spells out exactly who is responsible for doing what in addition to dates for expected completion.

It is essential that all written change plans exhibit professional writing. Social workers are often burdened by extraordinary amounts of paperwork, and a common coping strategy is to use abbreviations and incomplete sentences. We strongly urge you to avoid this practice, particularly when writing a change plan. The change plans are the basis of effective change, so they must be written using complete sentences while minimizing the use of technical language and jargon. Conveying your ideas in concrete language is essential to reducing ambiguities and improving the clarity of the plan for the client and other providers involved in the change planning process.

Although you should expect to see significant heterogeneity in change plans across organizations and different social service sectors, we think it is important that change plans have the following components. If you are writing change plans that are different in either structure or language, consider how they align with the following principles. If any aspect is missing, you can always create a supplemental record to ensure all the essential ingredients are contained.

1. Problem statement: These are statements that define the specific need for services. Problem statements are a direct product of the assessment process and should reflect the client's point of view. Clarity of the problem statement is essential, as the problem statement is the basis for goal selection.

2. Ultimate goals: Each ultimate goal should be clearly stated and should address some aspect of the problem statement.

3. Intermediary goals: Intermediary goals should be clearly linked to the ultimate goals. The written intermediary goals should conform to the SMART criteria.

4. Interventions: Interventions should be clearly described. Be sure to identify specifically who is responsible for doing what. This includes specifying the specific responsibilities of the social worker (or other service providers) and the specific responsibilities of the client. It is often helpful to use the SMART criteria for the specification of tasks.

5. Narrative: Many change plans contain a narrative that provides a rationale or strong justification as well as further explanation for the various components of the change plan. The narrative is a good place for clarifying aspects of the change plan that contain possible ambiguities. The narrative is an excellent place for documenting your reason for the intervention and any evidence supporting that decision.

CHAPTER REVIEW QUESTIONS

1. Describe some of the core principles of change planning.

2. What is the difference between program-driven and tailored change plans?

3. What are advantages of tailored change plans compared to program-driven plans?

4. What is the difference between intermediary and ultimate goals?

5. What is the difference between proximal and distal goals?

6. What is the difference between outcomes and processes?

7. What are some core principles for selecting goals?

8. What does the acronym *SMART* represent in SMART goals?

REFERENCES

Clarke, S., Oades, L., Crowe, T., & Deane, S. (2006). Collaborative goal technology: Theory and practice. *Psychiatric Rehabilitation Journal, 2*(9), 129–136.

Cowger, C. D. (1994). Assessing client strengths: Clinical assessment for client empowerment. *Social Work, 39*(3), 262–268.

Cross, K. F., & Lynch, R. L. (1988). The "SMART" way to define and sustain success. *National Productivity Review, 8*(1), 23–33.

Dishion, T. J., McCord, J., & Poulin, F. (1999). When interventions harm: Peer groups and problem behavior. *American Psychologist, 54*(9), 755.

DuFour, R., & Burnette, B. (2002). Pull out negativity by its roots. *Journal of Staff Development, 23*(3), 27–30.

Graham, J. R., & Barter, K. (1999). Collaboration: A social work practice method. *Families in Society: The Journal of Contemporary Social Services, 80*(1), 6–13.

Karver, M. S., Handelsman, J. B., Fields, S., & Bickman, L. (2006). Meta-analysis of therapeutic relationship variables in youth and family therapy: The evidence for different relationship variables in the child and adolescent treatment outcome literature. *Clinical Psychology Review, 26*(1), 50–65.

Kelly, J. J. (2010). *The urgency of social worker safety.* Retrieved June 18, 2014 from http://www.socialworkers.org/pubs/news/2010/10/social-worker-safety.asp

Kessler, R. C., Nelson, C. B., McGonagle, K. A., Edlund, M. J., Frank, R. G., & Leaf, P. J. (1996). The epidemiology of co-occurring addictive and mental disorders: Implications for prevention and service utilization. *American Journal of Orthopsychiatry, 66*(1), 17–31.

Lazarus, A. (2004). Reality check: Is your behavior aligned with organizational goals? *Physician Executive, 30,* 50–52.

National Association of Social Workers (NASW). (1996). *Code of Ethics of the National Association of Social Workers* (Revised in 2008). Washington, DC: Author. Retrieved July 25, 2014 from http://www.naswdc.org/pubs/code/code.asp

O'Neill, J. (2000). SMART goals, SMART schools. *Educational Leadership, 57*(5), 46–50.

Simpson, D. D. (2004). A conceptual framework for drug treatment process and outcomes. *Journal of Substance Abuse Treatment, 27*(2), 99–121.

Tryon, G. S., & Winograd, G. (2001). Goal consensus and collaboration. *Psychotherapy, 38*(4), 385–388.

Vongxaiburana, E., Thomas, K. S., Frahm, K. A., & Hyer, K. (2011). The social worker in interdisciplinary care planning. *Clinical Gerontologist, 34*(5), 367–378.

Whiston, S. C., & Sexton, T. L. (1993). An overview of psychotherapy outcome research: Implications for practice. *Professional Psychology: Research and Practice, 24*(1), 43.

Workers, N.A. (2008) NASW Code of Ethics. Washington, DC.

Core Intervention Skills: Using Cognitive and Behavioral Approaches in Social Work Practice With Individuals, Families, and Groups

C ognitive behavioral therapy (CBT) represents one of the most widely recognized and empirically supported approaches available to social workers. Unfortunately, this approach is also often misunderstood. CBT could, and perhaps should, be referred to as *cognitive and behavioral therapies,* as it is based on two distinct yet complementary theories—cognitive theory and behavioral theory. CBT is an integration of these theories, and through this integration, we can make informed decisions in our work with individuals and families.

In this chapter, we provide an overview of CBT. We discuss cognitive and behavioral theory separately to help you understand the unique elements of each approach, followed by their integration. Given the lengthy and rich history of CBT, it should come as no surprise that the amount of information on CBT is vast. You are strongly encouraged to review the recommended readings in the Ongoing Professional Development section at the end of the chapter as a point of departure in the pursuit of advanced knowledge and skills.

CHAPTER LEARNING OBJECTIVES

By the end of this chapter, you should

- know the major components and applications of cognitive theory,
- know the major components of behavioral theory,
- understand how cognitive theory and behavioral theory serve as the essential building blocks of CBT, and
- describe basic interventions that can be informed by the CBT framework.

The Council on Social Work Education Educational Policy and Accreditation Standards (CSWE-EPAS) Competencies that are highlighted in more depth in this chapter include the following:

2.1.3 Apply critical thinking to inform and communicate professional judgments.

2.1.4 Engage diversity and difference in practice.

2.1.6 Engage in research-informed practice and practice-informed research.

2.1.9 Respond to contexts that shape practice.

2.1.10 (a–d) Engage, assess, intervene, and evaluate with individuals, families, groups, organizations, and communities.

CASE SITUATION A: MELISSA

Melissa is a 28-year-old female who was diagnosed with paranoid schizophrenia in her early 20s. This is a chronic disorder that is characterized by significant functional impairments. Thus, she has many difficulties maintaining employment, stable housing, and interpersonal relationships. Some of the specific symptoms she experiences include auditory hallucinations (i.e., hearing things in absence of auditory stimuli) and delusions (i.e., holding beliefs that are not consistent with reality). Melissa's primary treatment goals include improving her social skills and her ability to cope with her serious and persistent mental health symptoms. Melissa also has a history of forgetting to take her psychiatric medication, which is necessary for maintaining her psychiatric stability. Thus, the social worker at the treatment center has helped develop a system that reinforces or rewards her when she takes the medication as prescribed.

The Cognitive Aspect of CBT

Cognitive theory, generally speaking, is built on the assumption that our cognitions (i.e., thoughts, beliefs, and other mental processes) influence how we respond and behave in everyday life. This is best represented by a causal chain commonly referred to as the *ABC model* (see Figure 8.1). More specifically, we have a particular event or antecedent (A) that cues a belief (B) that results in a particular consequence (C). Sometimes we have an opportunity to make modifications to a person's environment to reduce the specific cues. For example, we may help persons with substance use disorders avoid certain situations that may cue thoughts about drinking. Unfortunately, we can never entirely eliminate such antecedent events or cues, which necessarily requires us to focus attention on changing *cognitions*, which are the basis for emotional responding. Let's first cover the major classes of cognitions we hold, making distinctions between automatic thoughts and core beliefs. Then we will review specific strategies for changing these belief systems.

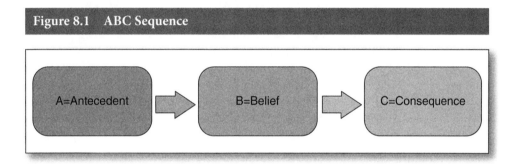

Figure 8.1   ABC Sequence

Belief Structure

A person's belief structure is based on different types of cognitions. From a cognitive perspective, it is helpful to distinguish between automatic thoughts and core beliefs. Provided below is a summary of different types of cognitions.

Automatic Thoughts

In everyday life, we continually have thoughts going through our mind. When an antecedent event triggers a thought, we typically have what are referred to as *automatic thoughts*. These are the thoughts that emerge immediately following an antecedent. For example, think about driving a car on a busy day, paying careful attention to the road and your surroundings, and then being cut off by another driver. Immediately after being cut off, a thought may suddenly emerge (e.g., "That person is so rude!"). It would be entirely reasonable for you to feel a sense of anger or frustration, which could be expressed in a variety of ways. For example, you might choose to let the emotion pass. You might feel compelled to say something out loud about the driver, even if the driver cannot hear you. Or you might try to get the attention of the driver by making an explicative gesture. Hopefully, you would not let the anger escalate to a degree that would be considered aggressive behavior on the road, although this type of response is not uncommon in light of the recent attention to road rage.

From a cognitive perspective, thoughts that suddenly come to mind following the antecedent event are considered automatic thoughts. There are a few important characteristics of automatic thoughts that should be considered. First, automatic thoughts are constructed. We can readily see this when people have different reactions to or interpretations of the same event. That is, some people can experience the exact same event but have fundamentally different automatic thoughts that give rise to different behaviors. Second, automatic thoughts do not need to be in response to external events or events occurring in our environment. Memories, flashbacks, images, or internal states (e.g., sleep deprivation, hunger, physical pain) can also be events that cue automatic thoughts.

A third point about automatic thoughts is that they are not inherently good or bad. In fact, in many ways, they are functional and even necessary. Imagine what life would be like if we had to carefully assess and select our response to every situation. We rely on our automatic thoughts for making rapid assessments and taking action to common events in our life. It is only when our automatic thoughts are not in line with what we want or are intending to achieve that they become troublesome.

Finally, automatic thoughts are not haphazard or random thought processes. Rather, automatic thoughts tend to exhibit certain themes or trends that are a reflection of our underlying core beliefs. Thus, part of the process of cognitively based interventions is first assessing and managing our automatic thoughts and then working on changing our core beliefs. Before talking about the intervention strategies, let's first explore core beliefs in greater detail.

Core Beliefs

Our core beliefs are the views we hold about ourselves, our world, and our future. They serve as a lens or filter for interpreting events and rules for our own actions. Core beliefs are generally firmly held beliefs that are resistant to change, even in the face of evidence that might suggest otherwise. For example, drawing upon the example provided in the foregoing section, we considered a person's automatic thought after being cut off in traffic by another driver. This was an automatic thought that was likely grounded in a core belief about driving behavior and etiquette. More specifically, it is reasonable for a driver to hold a rule or core belief that all drivers must be respectful and safe. So people who hold this core belief may rightfully feel angered or frustrated when cut off by another driver; this frustration manifests as a result of their core beliefs.

As another example, a student may struggle with social anxiety and be particularly self-critical as it relates to public speaking. Even if the student has a good performance— for example, successfully making a presentation in a classroom setting—that student's core beliefs will likely cause the person to focus on all the aspects that might suggest a bad performance as opposed to receiving and believing the evidence or feedback that the performance was good. Similarly, a person may hold particularly negative views about her or his physical appearance. Compliments that the person receives about her or his appearance may be dismissed or even misinterpreted—for example, "That person isn't really being honest with me."

Core beliefs are stable over time and fairly resistant to change. They tend to be of this nature because they are established over time through many experiences of interacting with the world and making interpretations of events and experiences. Core beliefs can also be influenced by the broader social context. For example, persons with a mental illness may come to view themselves as deficient or flawed in some way, given the negative views that much of broader society holds about mental illness. Racial discrimination and homophobia can also give rise to core beliefs that impact a person's perception of his or her capabilities and opportunities.

Core beliefs serve as the wellspring of our automatic thoughts, and we come to discover our core beliefs through a careful and systematic review of our automatic thoughts. It is important to emphasize that no single automatic thought is considered representative of our core beliefs. Rather, it is best to consider the various themes and trends that occur among a set of automatic thoughts. From these themes and trends, one can more accurately determine one's underlying core beliefs. It should also be noted that core beliefs are neither good nor bad but should be evaluated in the context of how they are helping the individual maximize functioning or meet particular goals.

Now that we have reviewed the difference between automatic thoughts and core beliefs, we can look more closely at methods of assessing these types of cognitions. Once we have identified these cognitions, we can then select one of a variety of strategies to change them. We will first review methods of assessment and then discuss intervention strategies.

Cognitive Restructuring

So far, we have discussed different types of cognitions, emphasizing the role of automatic thoughts, the relationship of automatic thoughts with core beliefs, and the role they all play in affecting our emotions and subsequent behavior. We also situated these beliefs within the ABC model as a way to help us understand the causal associations among our cognitions, emotions, and behaviors. Having an understanding of these cognitive principles is fundamental to the major therapeutic activity involved in CBT: *cognitive restructuring*. Cognitive restructuring is a technique used to help individuals change the way they think to reduce stress associated with unrealistic or inaccurate thoughts.

Cognitive restructuring can be conceptualized as a process of four different steps (Andrews et al., 2003; see Figure 8.2).

Step 1. Identifying Thoughts and Interpretations

The first part of cognitive restructuring involves identifying thoughts and interpretations in response to specific events. In particular, we are interested in

Figure 8.2 Cognitive Restructuring Process Steps

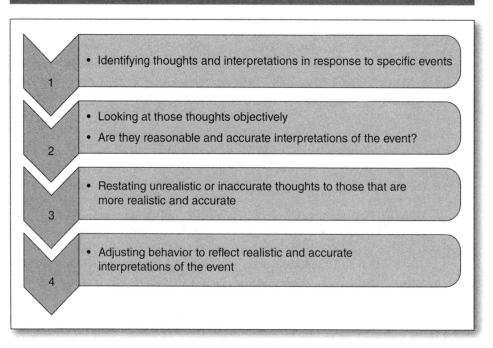

helping clients identify automatic thoughts that create some degree of distress or problems (e.g., cognitive distortions). It is important that individuals have a good understanding of what automatic thoughts are, know from where they emerge (i.e., core beliefs), and are able to effectively name the specific patterns of dysfunctional thinking (i.e., cognitive distortions and biases). Again, while your role is to help individuals identify these thoughts and interpretations, your objective is to advance the individual's capacity to do this independently. Thus, to achieve this, you need to help individuals identify these automatic thoughts as well as the themes of the thoughts. We recommend the use of thought records and standardized questionnaires as part of the process.

Thought Records

A thought record is a data collection tool that clients use for systematically record-ing information about their thoughts in their everyday life. Figure 8.3 is an example of a thought record. A fully formatted version is available at the end of this chapter, which can be modified to meet the specific needs of the client. In this example, we have a three-column event that is often referred to as the *ABC model*. That is, the client is to record information about the antecedent event (A), the belief that was triggered by the antecedent event (B), and the consequences (C) of the belief, which are the specific emotions and behaviors that followed.

Figure 8.3   Example Thought Record

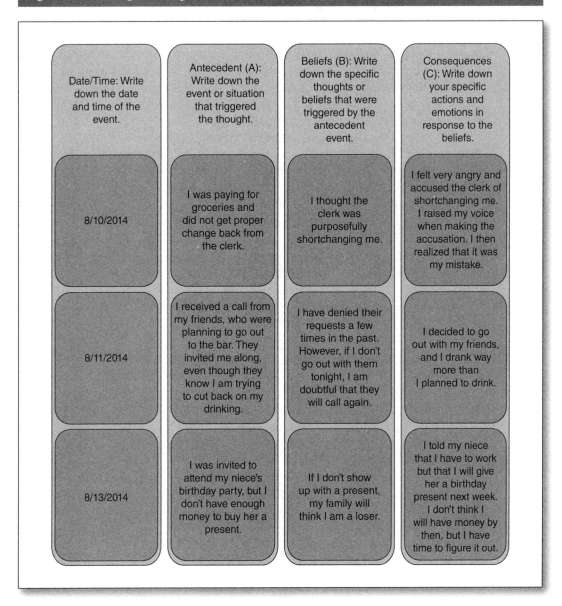

The thought record serves a number of important purposes. First, it helps the individual become aware of automatic thoughts—and having an awareness of a given problem is fundamental to changing the problem. The thought record also becomes an important source of data for making inferences and monitoring changes. More specifically, a thought record helps to provide data for identifying specific cognitive biases or distortions that are used by the individual.

Many of our automatic thoughts show particular patterns that replicate across many situations. For example, consider a college student with a fear of speaking in front of large groups. This student gives a presentation as part of a course requirement. The student receives a B+ for the presentation but considers the experience a complete failure. The student focuses on how much he tripped over his words during the presentation and on how he forgot to make a few important points. Although the presentation wasn't perfect, it is very likely that the student had a number of successes in the experience, which earned him a good grade. This student exhibited a cognitive distortion or bias referred to as *selective abstraction,* which involves making judgments based on certain information (i.e., the negative aspects of the presentation) while ignoring other information (i.e., the successes of the presentation). Selective abstraction is one of many different kinds of cognitive biases and distortions. This type of bias is often linked to the core beliefs of the individual. That is, the individual applies a particular lens that frames how she or he receives and interprets evidence. Other biases are described in Table 8.1. In reviewing these biases, it is important to think about how they are related to core beliefs.

Table 8.1   Examples of Common Cognitive Errors and Distortions

Cognitive Error or Distortion	Description
Self-centered	Preoccupied with oneself and one's own desires, often disregarding others
Minimizing	Downplaying a thought and/or behavior to a degree that no longer reflects reality
Assuming the worst	Expecting the worst possible outcome, usually without investigation
Blaming others	Placing responsibility for one's own behavior and/or situation onto outside sources, often another person
Selective abstraction	Forming a judgment based on particular information while disregarding the remaining information
Magnification	Exaggerating a thought and/or behavior to a degree that no longer reflects reality
Dichotomous thinking	Categorizing thoughts into one of two extremes, such as always or never
Confirmation bias	Interpreting or seeking information in a way that confirms one's own perception
Fortune telling	Predicting negative and inflexible outcomes before they happen
Mind reading	Concluding negative intentions or thoughts of others

Thought records can be of significant value to the change process. For example, a thought record can help individuals see the specific type and frequency of their automatic thoughts. Simply raising awareness of the presence of these thoughts is an important step in the change process. A thought record can also provide the basis for identifying common cognitive biases and distortions. You can then educate the individual on various strategies to challenge their biases and distortions in order for the thoughts to be more adaptive and realistic. The thought record can also reveal various core beliefs that are the basis of many automatic thoughts. These core beliefs can then be considered a target for change.

The use of thought records with clients who have low levels of literacy needs to be constructed carefully. It is essential that the social worker constructing such records ensures that all aspects are clearly understood by the individual using the record. The individual must have the skills to reliably complete a thought record. In some cases of very low levels of literacy, the thought record may not be an appropriate tool. It is possible to adapt the actual exercise, whereby the client makes audio recordings (as opposed to a written record). Fortunately, the CBT toolbox is large and flexible, so many other opportunities exist for using CBT with clients if a monitoring record is not suitable.

Standardized Questionnaires

Standardized questionnaires are structured surveys that can be used to elicit various types of information. A variety of questionnaires are available to facilitate the collection of information on the client's cognitions and beliefs. As a developing social worker, it is important that you become familiar with the scientific literature in order to identify and appraise questionnaires that could be useful for planning and evaluating the services you provide. We recommend that you use established questionnaires contained in the scientific literature, as these questionnaires typically have information available regarding their validity and reliability.

As a starting point, we recommend a scale that is referred to as the *Dysfunctional Attitude Scale* (*DAS*; Weissman, 1979). The original version contained 100 items and was subsequently reduced to two 40-item forms (Versions A and B) and then even further reduced to nine-item forms (Beevers, Strong, Meyer, Pilkonis, & Miller, 2007). The short form of the DAS is ideal for direct service. Example items from the short form of the DAS and other standardized instruments are provided at the end of this chapter.

The DAS was developed to measure dysfunctional attitudes among adults. Each short form version comprises nine items, which are based on a four-point Likert-type response scale (1 = totally agree, 4 = totally disagree). It is only necessary to administer one version of the questionnaire to the client, as they are both considered equivalent questionnaires, even though the content is different. If you choose to administer the questionnaire multiple times in order to measure change over time, then you might consider alternating versions.

This type of questionnaire is typically administered in a paper-pencil format, although it can be administered in an interview format if necessary. When administering questionnaires to clients, it is important that you give them specific instructions on how to complete the questionnaire as well as an interpretation of the results. To score the DAS, be sure to follow the specific scoring instructions for the respective version of the DAS. The DAS contains reverse-coded items, which requires you to subtract certain items from five before creating an overall summed score. The possible score range is from four to 36, with higher scores representing higher levels of dysfunctional attitudes. This measurement is useful as it provides a quantitative estimate of the extent to which clients have dysfunctional attitudes, which is a risk factor for various psychosocial and clinical problems—namely depression (see Beevers et al., 2007).

REFLECTIVE LEARNING ACTIVITY

Every client you encounter has a set of core beliefs that are the foundation of automatic thoughts. It shouldn't come as a surprise that you also have core beliefs and automatic thoughts. Construct a monitoring record to identify various automatic thoughts that relate to your social work education or your field training. Also, complete one version of the DAS provided in this book. Can you identify any core beliefs or automatic thoughts that may be a barrier in your professional development as a social worker?

Step 2. Looking at Thoughts Objectively

The second step of cognitive restructuring involves looking at thoughts objectively to determine whether or not they are reasonable and accurate interpretations of the event. This is most commonly done through a process called *Socratic questioning*. Socratic questioning helps clients clarify their thinking, consider alternative explanations, examine the likelihood of certain events, and evaluate the implications and consequences of their cognitions. Table 8.2 provides a framework of the different types of Socratic questions that can be utilized to help your clients consider alternative explanations of events. By doing so, you are elaborating on the ABC model to include D: *disputation of cognitions*. In other words, you are preparing your client to dispute their dysfunctional or problematic beliefs in order to respond more effectively.

A few important points should be kept in mind when engaging your clients in Socratic questioning. The first point is to try and promote objectivity, which requires you to help the client carefully assess the evidence for and against the belief. Asking questions to elicit only refuting evidence can be problematic to the engagement process, since you are not validating the significance of what they are currently experiencing. Thus it is often helpful to first ask questions that elicit supporting evidence, and then ask transition questions that elicit refuting evidence. Once all of the evidence has been elicited, you are in a better position to help the client dispute irrational beliefs.

The second point is to be sure that you don't move too quickly from asking questions and considering the evidence to disputation of thoughts. Your objective is not to ask questions to convince your client to change her or his beliefs. Rather, you want your

Table 8.2 Major Types and Examples of Socratic Questions

Questions for Clarification
Can you explain what _____ means to you?
How else could you define that?
Why is the event significant?
You seem to be saying _____. Is that correct?
How does this relate to what we've been discussing?
Questions that Probe Assumptions
Are there different ways of looking at this situation?
Why do you think you are making that assumption?
What do you think the person is assuming?
How could we challenge that assumption?
Questions that Probe Reasons and Evidence
How do you know that is true?
What evidence supports that belief?
What causes _____ to happen?
What led you to believe _____?
Questions about Viewpoints and Perspectives
What are the benefits of having that point of view? And the challenges or problems?
What might be alternate interpretations?
Questions that Probe Implications and Consequences
How would _____ affect _____?
What are other possible outcomes you might envision?
When you say _____, what are you implying?
What would happen after _____ occurred?

client to develop the skills to look broadly at the full range of supporting and refuting evidence. If you do not consider the full range of evidence and then attempt to help the client dispute her or his beliefs, you may find that you are actually strengthening rather than weakening the dysfunctional thoughts. Focusing only on the refuting evidence may result in a debate rather than an assessment about the full range of evidence.

Step 3. Restating Unrealistic or Inaccurate Thoughts

The third step of the process is restating unrealistic or inaccurate thoughts. This should be a natural outgrowth of the earlier step that was involved with a careful weighing of the evidence. That is, the process of Socratic questioning (with an emphasis on weighing the supporting and refuting evidence) should lead to a new thought that is incompatible with the original thought that was considered unrealistic or inaccurate. In this step, the new thought should be clearly articulated and accurately reflect the evidence that was reviewed. It is important that the new thought is clearly and explicitly articulated. By doing so, you can help the client assess whether the reformulation is accurate. You may also help guide the client in refining the new thought in order to make them clearer. Be sure that the client actively engages in any process of refining, as this is the thought that is to be accepted by the client. If the client does not believe in the new thought, it is very unlikely you will see any meaningful change in behavior and emotions.

Step 4. Adjusting Behavior

The fourth step involves adjusting behavior to be consistent with the modified thoughts. This may sound rather simple, as though an individual will automatically start acting accordingly. However, remaining cognizant of the new thoughts and deliberate actions is necessary to promote a change in emotions, behavior, and subsequent behavior. Thus, it is important to help the client consider the range of emotions and behaviors that are in accordance with the new thoughts. For example, it can be helpful to have the client describe which emotions and behaviors reasonably reflect the new thoughts and systematically compare the new thoughts with the original cognitions that were changed.

REFLECTIVE LEARNING ACTIVITY

Based on the information provided thus far about CBT, you should infer that this treatment approach involves the changes of beliefs and thoughts. The field of social work places high value on self-determination and enhancement of functioning. Does this mean that people are free to believe and think what they want to? If a social worker sees that a particular belief or thought is particularly problematic to that client's functioning but the client doesn't see it as a problem, how do we achieve a balance between self-determination and enhancement of functioning?

Behavioral Aspects of CBT

Thus far, we have focused on the cognitive aspects of CBT, emphasizing the important role of how our beliefs and belief structures influence our interpretations and responses to events. By breaking down problems into causal chains and fitting these causal chains into an ABC model, the social worker is equipped to identify potential targets for intervention. In this section, we will redefine the meaning of the ABC model as it is understood from the perspective of behavioral theory. If you have a background in psychology, the notion of *behavioral theory* may give rise to the famous experiments of Pavlov training his dog to salivate following the ringing of a bell. This early behavioral theory focuses on reflex behavior and is typically referred to as *classical conditioning*. This is an important history but represents only part of behavioral theory. Another major system of thought that better characterizes the behavioral aspect of CBT is *operant conditioning*. From the perspective of operant conditioning, behavior change occurs within three major processes: reinforcement, punishment, and extinction.

Before talking about these different processes, it is first important to define *behavior* within the context of operant conditioning. Behavior is anything that a living organism can do, including thinking, feeling, and acting. Behavior has different dimensions, which are important considerations with respect to planning services and treatment. It is important to have clarity on these dimensions, as certain behaviors are often better understood in the context of one dimension over another. These dimensions serve as a measurement of a behavior, which is essential for understanding the extent of the behavior before services are provided. This initial measurement is often referred to as *baseline*. By having a specific measure of behavior, we can then be more precise in our assessment of whether the services we provide are effective.

Below are the dimensions of behavior that are typically considered when working to change a behavior from a behavioral perspective. It should be noted that certain dimensions of behavior may be more relevant than others, depending on the behavior under consideration. Table 8.3 provides various examples of behavior and the different dimensions.

- Frequency: the number of times the behavior is exhibited
- Magnitude: the intensity of the behavior
- Duration: the amount of time the behavior is exhibited
- Latency: the amount of time between an antecedent event and the behavior

ABC from a Behavioral Standpoint

In the first part of the chapter, we discussed the ABC model from a cognitive standpoint—that is, an antecedent event (A) cues beliefs or automatic thoughts (B) that lead to specific consequences (C) associated with emotions and behaviors. The ABC model is relevant from a behavioral standpoint, but the causal chain is a bit different. We still have an antecedent event (A) that serves as a cue to the individual. This antecedent event cues a behavior (B) that is followed by a consequence (C) of either a reinforcer or a punisher. The consequence ultimately strengthens or weakens any given dimension of the behavior. For example, consider a smoker who experiences a stressful event, such as an argument with another individual. The stressful event and the associated state of anxiety serve as cues for a behavioral response. A plausible behavioral response might be to escape the stressful event and smoke a cigarette.

Table 8.3	Examples of Different Dimensions of Behavior			
Behavior	**Frequency**	**Magnitude**	**Duration**	**Latency**
Cigarette smoking	Number of cigarettes smoked in a given week	N/A	Number of years smoking	Time to the first cigarette smoked upon waking
Anger	Number of times the emotion of anger is experienced in a given week	The intensity of the emotion of anger	Length of time anger was experienced following the antecedent event	The amount of time lapsed from the antecedent event to the expression of anger
Homework completion	Rate of homework completed in a given week	Amount of effort exhibited during a homework task	Amount of time devoted to homework	Amount of time lapsed from when homework was assigned until engaging in the homework task
Use of relaxation strategy for coping	Number of times relaxation strategy was used in a given week	Amount of effort exhibited in using the coping strategy	Amount of time devoted to use of the coping strategy	Amount of time lapsed from stressful event to the use of the coping strategy

In this situation, we have two separate mechanisms that strengthen two different behaviors. Let's first consider the act of escaping or leaving the stressful event. This is an anxiety reduction strategy because the individual is attempting to lessen the exposure to the event—that is, the argument. The argument itself can be regarded as an aversive or unpleasant stimulus, so leaving is a way of removing or avoiding this stimulus. The act of smoking also serves to calm the individual, which further lessens the stress associated with the event. The consequence of these behaviors is stress reduction.

This example shows a basic causal chain from a behavioral standpoint. It is important to emphasize that from a behavioral standpoint, we are interested in the behaviors that are cued by the antecedent event and the consequences that follow. This causal chain helps us understand how behaviors are established, strengthened, maintained, and weakened. In order to understand these causal processes, it is necessary to have a refined understanding of the consequences.

Before reviewing the various consequences of a particular behavior, an important point on terminology needs to be made. More specifically, many of the terms used in behavioral theory (and other theories that inform social work) match terms used in everyday language. For example, the term *consequence* is generally understood as the result of a particular behavior. In everyday language, we sometimes use this term to suggest a form of punishment. It would not be uncommon to hear of a parent describing the consequences of misbehaving to a young child. In behavioral theory, consequences are the results of a particular behavior and should not be confused with the everyday use of the term. More important distinctions will need to be made with respect to the terms *positive* and *negative,* as everyday language considers them to be synonymous with *good* and *bad.* However, as you will see, the definitions embedded within behavioral theory are fundamentally different from everyday language. The following discussion will cover this in more detail.

Reinforcement

When a specific consequence strengthens a particular dimension of behavior, that consequence is considered a *reinforcer.* For example, a person who does a kind gesture for another person may be reinforcing that other person's response. A kind response could strengthen the behavior (e.g., frequency) of making kind gestures. The consequence that strengthens behavior is called a *reinforcing stimulus* or, more simply, a *reinforcer.*

It is important to keep in mind that a reinforcer is only a reinforcer under the very strict definitions of the theory. First, the reinforcer must come after the behavior, which logically follows the ABC model since *B* is the behavior and *C* is the consequence. Second, the reinforcer is only a reinforcer if it strengthens the behavior. If it doesn't strengthen the behavior, then it isn't a reinforcer. This is to emphasize the difference between *intended* reinforcers and *actual* reinforcers. In common-day language, we may praise a child for good behavior and consider it positive reinforcement. However, if the praise doesn't actually strengthen good behavior, then it is not a reinforcer.

There are two different types of reinforcers—*positive* reinforcers and *negative* reinforcers. Based on our definition of a reinforcer, it follows that both types come after the behavior and strengthen behavior. Positive reinforcement involves presenting a desirable stimulus, and negative reinforcement involves removing an aversive stimulus. The essential part of these definitions actually relates to the presentation or removal of the stimulus. The concepts of a desirable stimulus and a negative stimulus is understood only from the viewpoint of the individual. Keep in mind that some stimuli might be considered desirable to one person, negative to another person, and neutral to a third person. Thus, in determining whether a stimulus are a positive or negative reinforcer, you must first assess the action on the behavior (i.e., Does it strengthen behavior?) and whether it is desirable or aversive from the viewpoint of the individual.

Let's consider another example to bring specificity to our understanding of positive and negative reinforcement. Let's start with cigarette smoking, as this is a good example to show a number of principles of behavioral theory. Let's assume that an individual is cued to smoke a cigarette. The cue might be a stressful event. So the stressful event (A) leads to smoking a cigarette (B). The cigarette produces a sense of relaxation (C). This would be positive reinforcement because the sense of relaxation that the individual experiences strengthens the behavior—that is, the frequency or the overall number of cigarettes smoked.

Smoking behavior can also be conceptualized in the form of negative reinforcement. For example, a person who smokes cigarettes may be cued to smoke when feeling anxious. The individual smokes a cigarette and subsequently feels a sense of anxiety release. The feeling of anxiety is considered aversive, so the individual continues the smoking behavior, which subsequently reduces the anxiety. This consequence (i.e., reduction in anxiety) strengthens the smoking behavior. Again, keep in mind that behavior change can refer to its frequency, magnitude, duration, or latency. By definition, a reinforcer is only a reinforcer if it is a consequence of the behavior—that is, it comes immediately after the behavior. The consequences must follow the expression of the behavior as opposed to occurring before the behavior. Moreover, the consequences, which are generally considered a reinforcing stimulus, are only considered a reinforcer if the behavior is strengthened. If the behavior isn't strengthened by the stimulus, then the stimulus is not a reinforcer but a neutral stimulus.

Examples of positive reinforcement can be found in virtually every aspect of social work. Positive reinforcement occurs when a parent provides desirable attention to a child for desirable behavior. At the same time, a parent may scold a child for undesirable behavior only to see the behavior worsen. In this situation, the act of scolding may be serving as a positive reinforcer, even though it was intended to be a punisher (described in more detail in a later section).

Two types of reinforcement are used in behavioral theory—*positive reinforcement* and *negative reinforcement*. Again, the terms *positive* and *negative* are not to be confused with *good* and *bad* but whether a stimulus is added or removed (respectively). More specifically, if a behavior is strengthened when a pleasant or appetitive stimulus follows the behavior, it is considered positive reinforcement. Examples of positive reinforcement can be tangible (e.g., money or food) or intangible (e.g., attention or special privileges). Negative reinforcement strengthens behavior by the removal of an aversive stimulus. It is important to emphasize that reinforcers are unique to the individual. Again, using smoking as an example, typically only a smoker would find a cigarette to be reinforcing, and nonsmokers would experience it as a form of punishment—a concept covered later in this chapter.

Schedules of Reinforcement

Many times, we can observe reinforcement processes occurring naturally—that is, we aren't intentionally administering and removing reinforcers. In fact, our behaviors are continually being shaped by various reinforcements in our own environment.

We can also construct plans to shape certain behaviors, and we do this through the use of reinforcement schedules. These schedules indicate the timing at which the reinforcer is to be implemented. There are two different types of reinforcement schedules: continuous and intermittent.

Continuous Reinforcement. *Continuous reinforcement* refers to a 1:1 correspondence between the target behavior and the reinforcing stimulus. For example, medication compliance is of significant concern in programs that provide services to persons with serious mental illnesses. In institutional settings, it is not uncommon to see some type of reinforcement given when medications are received. If the reinforcer is provided every time the behavior is emitted, then it is on a continuous schedule of reinforcement.

Continuous reinforcement is well suited for establishing new behaviors or starting the change process of existing behaviors. It does promote behavior change, although the target behavior often quickly weakens upon cessation of the reinforcement system. Additionally, this reinforcement system can lead to a sense of *satiation* for the individual—that is, their need becomes satisfied, so the strength of the reinforcer weakens. This is especially true when food is used as a reinforcer. Finally, while this reinforcement schedule is quite straightforward, it may not be very economical over time, particularly when the target behavior exhibits a significant increase in its frequency. The economics relate to the cost of the reinforcer as well as the resources required in delivering the reinforcer.

Intermittent Reinforcement. Many of the limitations of a continuous reinforcement schedule can be overcome through the use of an intermittent schedule of reinforcement. An intermittent schedule varies the delivery of the reinforcer using either an event-based or time-based definition. A *fixed-ratio* schedule is an event-based schedule of reinforcement. It involves the delivery of a reinforcer after a specified number of times a target behavior is emitted. Building on the earlier example of medication compliance, we may change the continuous schedule of reinforcement to a fixed interval, which could be illustrated by giving the reinforcer after three full days of medication compliance as opposed to after every scheduled occurrence.

The other type of event-based intermittent schedule is a *variable ratio*. This involves a variation in the number of behaviors emitted before the reinforcer is given. An easy example to remember is gambling. Consider a slot machine—it doesn't pay off every single pull, but it might give a small payout after the eighth pull. However, it wouldn't really be gambling if the payout happened on a fixed ratio (i.e., one payout to every eight pulls). Instead, there is variability around an average number of pulls. This type of reinforcement schedule has been applied in substance use disorder treatment for adults. For example, participants in such a program may receive a urinalysis every week and be provided with a highly desirable reinforcer (e.g., money) for not testing positive for drug use. When their urinalysis is negative, they are given a die to roll, and rolling a six (or any other prespecified number) would result in a reinforcer. This would be a variable ratio, with the reinforcement provided (on average) one out of six rolls of the die. Both fixed- and variable-ratio intervals are effective in producing behavior changes, although the variable-ratio tends to produce the most durable effects among all the different schedules. Despite these desirable properties of variable-ratio reinforcement, they can be difficult to administer.

Fixed-interval reinforcement schedules follow a time-based definition. More specifically, the reinforcer is administered when the target behavior is emitted within a specified amount of time. Unlike the event-based schedules, the reinforcer is actually withheld until the end of the interval. For example, consider an after-school program for inner-city children. The counselors who are guiding the children in activities may give special privileges (e.g., time on playground) to children who have exhibited good behavior throughout a one-hour block of time. It is a fixed interval if all the reinforcements are delivered in this same fashion.

Variable interval reinforcement schedules are also time-based. Similar to a fixed-interval ratio, a variable-interval ratio involves a set duration or block of time. However, the fixed interval remains consistent over time. The variable interval has an average amount of time, but there is some variation around the average. Using the after-school program as the example, the interval may start at one hour of good behavior, but some days, it will be a lesser amount of time and other days, it may be a bit more. It is only a variable interval schedule if the participants are unable to determine whether or not the reinforcement will be given on a specific occasion. Similar to the variable ratio, the variable interval tends to produce more durable changes in behavior but can be difficult to administer.

Punishment

Punishment is another primary mechanism that is associated with the reduction or suppression of a target behavior. Similar to reinforcement, two different types of punishers exist: positive and negative. Positive and negative do not refer to desirable or undesirable but to the action of the punisher. That is, a *positive punisher* would introduce an aversive stimulus to the individual. For example, going back to the example of medication compliance, a positive punisher might be some sort of reprimand when compliance was not observed. A *negative punisher* involves the removal of a desirable or pleasant stimulus, such as the loss of privileges. Negative punishers are also sometimes referred to as *response costs*.

It is important to emphasize that we do not endorse the use of punishment. While we can make an argument on ethical grounds, the science of behavior clearly shows that punishers are not effective in suppressing behaviors over the long term. In fact, punishers generally require a continuous punishment schedule (akin to the continuous reinforcement schedule), and the target behavior returns to baseline in absence of the punisher. Before considering any type of punisher, it is recommended that you identify specific incompatible behaviors you can target using principles of reinforcement. For example, in the after-school program, it would be more effective to provide reinforcers for good behavior as opposed to punishment for bad behavior.

With respect to punishers, social workers should consider examining policies and practices in the environments in which they are working to identify whether punishers are being used and how. Punishers are very common in institutional and large group settings, such as schools, mental health and addiction treatment programs, and juvenile detention centers. Social workers have an excellent opportunity to help administrators and other program managers think about and make the best use of the science of reinforcements. In doing so, it is important that the various stakeholders are provided the necessary background on reinforcements and punishers. It is often the case that certain policies and practices have been guided by good intentions, although the intentions may not necessarily align with the best available evidence.

Extinction

Extinction is the third primary mechanism that accounts for behavioral change within the framework of operant conditioning. Extinction occurs when no consequence occurs after a behavior is emitted. For example, in parent training, parents are often taught how to systematically extinguish certain behaviors that have been previously reinforced. A tantrum may have resulted in the parent providing a lot of focused attention, which was considered positive reinforcement from the viewpoint of the child. However, after parent training, the parent learns to actively ignore the tantrum-like behavior. Because this behavior no longer produces any form of a consequence, it is likely to weaken over time. This can be an important tool for change, although with extinction plans, it is possible to see a sudden spike in the target behavior before it lessens. Additionally, whenever extinction plans are not working, it is a good idea to systematically consider possible sources of reinforcement that are maintaining the target behavior.

REFLECTIVE LEARNING ACTIVITY

What are the ethics on the use of punishment in social work settings? Are there any settings in which punishment may be used (e.g., extreme behavioral disorders among children, persons with developmental disabilities or mental illness)? Is it possible that some agency or program policies can be considered punishment? Provide a definition of what types of punishment, if any, are ethically acceptable in the delivery of social work interventions.

REFLECTIVE LEARNING ACTIVITY

Think about a behavior in your life that you would like to strengthen. Identify the specific dimensions of the behavior that would be most important to change. What types of reinforcers would be necessary to achieve this behavior change? Then think about a behavior in your life that you would like to decrease. What dimensions of that behavior are most important to consider? From a behavioral perspective, what would be necessary to facilitate that change?

CBT as an Integrative Framework

In this chapter, we have reviewed the core tenets of cognitive theory and behavioral theory. The current status of CBT in social work includes other theoretical modalities such as acceptance and commitment therapy and social cognitive theory. However, having a grounding in cognitive theory and operant conditioning is essential to understanding the basics of CBT. When we work from a CBT perspective, we are ultimately concerned with identifying the specific needs of clients and providing skills training that addresses those needs. You may formulate some interventions from a behavioral orientation, emphasizing observable antecedents and consequences of behavior. At other times, you may assume a cognitive orientation, taking into account the thoughts and beliefs that precede or maintain behavior. CBT offers the flexibility of drawing on both cognitive and behavioral approaches in order to provide the necessary skills training to achieve desired outcomes.

While CBT is heavily oriented toward skill development, this orientation does not take precedence over the therapeutic relationship. Rather, a major task of the social worker is to establish a balance between skills training and the development of the therapeutic relationship (Carroll, 1998). A positive therapeutic relationship is critical to establishing an environment that effectively engages the client in skills training processes.

A number of general principles unify the practice of CBT, which helps distinguish CBT from other therapies. For example, while psychodynamic and insight-oriented therapies work to uncover unconscious processes and explore early childhood experiences, CBT is problem-focused on the here and now. CBT is also a time-limited approach, meaning that a clear date of termination is expected, with the duration being relatively short compared to other approaches. For example, CBT may be a few sessions, perhaps 12–15, but it would not be characteristic of CBT to extend many months or a year in duration. CBT is also highly structured, with sessions usually broken down to meet the specification of the session agenda. Although CBT sessions provide opportunities to address acute problems that clients face, the overarching strategy is to facilitate the development of a generalizable skill set that minimizes problems as they arise.

Practice of CBT

CBT is an important evidence-based practice available to social workers. A number of CBT treatment manuals exist to help guide treatment. Social workers are strongly encouraged to use high-quality treatment manuals whenever possible, as they provide important guidance on the structure and content of treatment. However, a CBT treatment manual is hardly a "cookbook approach" to treatment. In fact, social workers retain considerable freedom in tailoring CBT to individual client needs. Through conscientious use of treatment manuals, we are confident that social workers will readily see that CBT treatment manuals provide guidelines, but the overall treatment must be tailored to the client's needs and values.

In this section, we provide an overview of how CBT is provided within the context of routine social work practice. We highlight characteristics of treatment that are common to many of the evidence-based treatment manuals that are freely available on the Internet. Specifically, we summarize the major tasks and structural features of treatment and then discuss intervention strategies with a particular focus on functional analysis and skills training. It should be noted that CBT is often perceived as an *office-based* intervention—that is, it is only applicable in an environment that is akin to traditional psychotherapy. This is hardly the reality with CBT. The social worker can apply many of the principles and CBT activities in the field. For example, even if a client isn't ready to commit to a change plan or engage in social work services, a number of CBT activities designed to foster motivation to change may be useful. Similarly, helping refine a client's social skills for a job interview might draw on the major principles of CBT, even though the social worker is not formally providing a series of CBT sessions for that client.

Major Treatment Tasks

A number of important treatment tasks provide the foundation for successful substance use disorder treatment. The work of Rounsaville and Carroll (1992) and Carroll (1998) proposes a set of major tasks that are generalizable to treating different treatment settings, client populations, and unique client needs. These major tasks, summarized in Table 8.4, are grounded in both behavioral and cognitive theories. Some tasks may be more relevant to certain clients than others. For example, clients may show different levels of treatment motivation or exhibit varying levels of social skills. Careful assessment is necessary in order to effectively tailor these treatment tasks to the unique needs of the client.

Structural Features of CBT

The length of CBT sessions are approximately one hour, although the length and number of sessions are determined by the treatment needs of the individual, payment mechanisms, and availability of social workers to provide treatment. CBT is commonly delivered in approximately 12 to 16 sessions, although this is a general guide, as the actual number of sessions will be determined by the treatment needs of the individual, policies of the agency providing treatment, and reimbursement mechanisms.

CBT is a highly structured form of treatment, with an agenda guiding each session. The development of an agenda should be a collaborative effort between the social worker and client. Session topics can be predetermined, although it is important that sessions are linked to any acute issues or problems raised by the client and have been selected according to her or his treatment needs. The agenda is intended to be a tool for assuring the client that her or his immediate needs are taken into account. When formulating an agenda, it is useful to divide the session into three different parts.

Table 8.4   Major Treatment Tasks in the Delivery of CBT-Oriented Interventions

Treatment Task	Description
Foster motivation for change	This task necessitates stopping or reducing problematic behaviors. This involves using decisional balances, matching interventions to the client's level of motivation, and fostering a sense of self-efficacy.
Develop a range of effective coping skills for managing difficult or stressful situations	Clients need to be equipped with a variety of strategies for managing difficult or stressful situations. Skill training may focus on enhancing existing skills or acquiring new skills.
Modify reinforcement contingencies	Clients will need to spend considerable time focusing on meaningful and rewarding activities that are incompatible with the situations that they typically find distressing.
Manage emotional responses	Strong emotional responses can serve as barriers to effective change. Clients should be equipped with the necessary skills to manage these responses. This may involve refining existing responses or developing new responses.
Improve social functioning	Problems are commonly embedded in social relationships. Thus, working to improve social functioning is key to meeting the ultimate treatment goals. Training in social skills is an important treatment activity.

Source: Adapted from Rounsaville and Carroll (1992) and Carroll (1998).

The first part of each session reviews skills that were taught during the previous session, with an emphasis on addressing barriers to successful implementation. For example, a client may have learned a set of drinking refusal skills that are effective with friends and family but that may not generalize to work-related social gatherings. This review allows the opportunity to further enhance skills when necessary. The second part of the session involves teaching new skills and information. The third part of the session involves planning for the use of the skills in real-world situations. This provides an opportunity to review potential barriers to successful implementation of skills, which is a critical and often under-recognized aspect of treatment.

Functional Analysis

As with most interventions, CBT includes an assessment in the beginning of treatment. However, unlike other treatment modalities, assessment is an ongoing and essential process in CBT with substance use disorders (SUDs). The particular type of assessment that plays a crucial role in CBT with SUDs is functional analysis. The purpose of functional analysis is to help the client identify and describe how a given behavior occurs in the real world. Functional analysis is driven by the ABC model. As previously described, the ABC model helps describe, explain, and even predict behavior through the linking of antecedents of either the beliefs (i.e., cognitive theory) or behaviors (i.e., behavioral theory) to the consequences.

In functional analysis, all three aspects of the ABC model are put forth as *clinical hypotheses* or working explanations of the function of behavior. Data are collected on the problem behavior in order to assess its response to treatment. Through this process, the functional analysis helps determine the target of treatment in addition to providing a framework for monitoring treatment outcomes.

Social workers must think carefully and creatively to help the client find the most reliable data to provide a valid summary of the function of behavior. One strategy involves the use of self-monitoring records, as described earlier in the chapter. Clients with higher levels of motivation and cognitive functioning can collect additional information that could be of potential value to the treatment process, including each aspect of the ABC model. Systematic data collection can improve the reliability of data to inform the treatment process, given that retrospective accounts are subject to a variety of biases. Self-monitoring records can also be an intervention, as such tools are often *reactive* (see Sobell, Bogardis, Schuller, Leo, & Sobell, 1989); that is, such tools can help clients become more aware of problematic behavior and make adjustments. In addition, by systematically monitoring specific behaviors over time, the social worker can use the data to monitor treatment progress and outcomes.

When using self-monitoring records, it is important that only data that are useful to treatment be collected. Social workers need to carefully think through how the data will specifically be used to inform treatment; otherwise requests for such data should not be made. Finally, a variety of existing self-monitoring records can be found through basic Internet searches, which may be immediately amenable for treatment or modified in some fashion to meet the unique treatment goals.

Skills Training

Another important feature of CBT is teaching clients practical skills that help minimize the distress or consequences of thoughts and behaviors. It is important that social workers remain fully aware of the importance of not only the acquisition of skills but the generalizability of the skills to various aspects of the client's life. Homework is an important way of promoting the development of skills learned in the treatment sessions and promoting their generalizability and utility to real-world situations. Social workers should construct assignments that are relevant to the information and skills taught in the session. Moreover, the assignments should be developed collaboratively with the client to ensure that they are relevant to her or his interests and needs. Completed assignments are then discussed at the beginning of each session as part of the review.

Structured Problem Solving

A general skill that can help clients respond more effectively to problems is learning how to alter the nature of the problem (e.g., overcoming obstacles to a goal) or change the distress reaction to the problem (e.g., acceptance that the goal cannot be reached) (Nezu & D'Zurilla, 2005). This process is known as *structured problem solving*. Clients are taught discrete steps that are involved in solving problems. These steps are considered highly generalizable to problems that are often encountered in social work settings.

Social Skills Training

From a CBT perspective, the maintenance of some problematic behaviors may be influenced, in part, by a client's social supports or network. For example, a client is at risk of using substances through exposure to substances within a social network and pressures to use. Negative interpersonal interactions can also be a trigger to maladaptive cognitions and behaviors. Thus, enhancement of social skills can help establish a more effective social support system. Social workers need to carefully assess different aspects of the client's social skills and determine what can be effectively altered to meet a given goal.

Social skills training is often done using role-play. Role-play incorporates the different aspects of the modeling sequence and is structured to allow for role reversals. If the client is practicing the expression of feelings, the social worker might assume the role of the client and the client would assume the role of an antagonist. This role reversal provides the opportunity for modeling the target behavior.

Revising Cognitive Errors and Distortions

A variety of cognitive errors and distortions (refer to Table 8.1) are commonly encountered among clients in various social work settings. As previously described, such errors and distortions contribute to the maintenance and severity of a variety of problems. CBT addresses these problems by helping the client identify these biases and errors. Treatment involves learning to see other sources of data that can be used to help support self-refutation dialogue.

Stress Management

Stress can serve as a powerful emotional or behavioral cue, especially for those behaviors or beliefs that are considered maladaptive or problematic. Thus, the development of stress management techniques becomes a focus of many social work interventions. Such strategies might involve diaphragmatic breathing, meditation practice, and progressive muscle relaxation. Social workers should work collaboratively with clients to find out whether they already have existing strategies that can be enhanced in the treatment setting.

Ongoing Professional Development

A historical review of CBT shows that the current system of treatment has evolved over many years, drawing on various strands of research, theory, and clinical experience. The overview of CBT provided in this chapter is merely a snapshot of its current place in social work. However, it is important to remain cognizant of the ongoing efforts to continually improve the effectiveness of CBT interventions for a wide range of problems. Thus, social workers face the challenge of acquiring expertise with the major tenets, tools, and techniques of this therapeutic system while updating their knowledge as new evidence becomes available. This is not easy, given the time constraints and limited resources that social workers commonly face in various treatment settings. Attending professional development trainings and seeking out high-quality supervision are important learning activities.

Social workers are strongly encouraged to follow the scientific literature regarding CBT. This includes CBT-related research specifically for SUDs as well as other disorders. A broad-based understanding of CBT can provide social workers with insights on how CBT may be tailored to meet the complex needs of persons with SUDs. Some journals that may be relevant include *Cognitive Behaviour Therapy, Cognitive and Behavior Practice, The Cognitive Behaviour Therapist,* and *The Journal of Cognitive and Behavioral Psychotherapies.* It is unlikely that social workers in routine practice settings will have subscriptions to these various journals. However, efforts are being made to increase access to articles and make them freely available, especially articles containing research that has been supported by federal organizations (see National Institutes of Health, 2014). Professional associations, such as the National Association of Cognitive-Behavioral Therapists and the ABCT Association for Behavioral and Cognitive Therapies, can provide further opportunities for social workers to develop their professional networks. These associations can be useful in helping social workers in training identify high-quality supervision and other training opportunities to ensure that their clients receive the best available treatment.

CHAPTER REVIEW QUESTIONS

1. Compare and contrast the ABC model as it is understood from behavioral theory and cognitive theory.

2. What is the relationship between core beliefs and automatic thoughts?

3. Provide at least five specific examples of different types of cognitive errors that a client may exhibit.

4. What are the major steps for changing belief structures in a cognitive framework?

5. What is the difference between negative reinforcement and positive punishment?

6. What are the different dimensions of behavior? Provide examples to show your understanding.

7. What is Socratic questioning and why is it used?

8. Give three different examples of how an intended punisher may actually be a reinforcer for a certain behavior.

10. Give at least three examples of problems that would be appropriate for cognitive restructuring.

THOUGHT RECORD

In the space provided, write down an event that triggered negative thoughts, feelings, or beliefs. Describe your initial thoughts or beliefs in response to that event or situation. Then describe the consequences (reactions or emotions) of those thoughts.

Date/Time	A: Antecedent Event	B: Beliefs/Thoughts	C: Consequences/ Outcome

SAMPLE ITEMS FROM STANDARDIZED QUESTIONNAIRES

Dysfunctional Attitudes Scale

My value as a person depends greatly on what others think of me.
(1 = Totally agree, 4 = Totally disagree)

I cannot be happy unless most people I know admire me.
(1 = Totally agree, 4 = Totally disagree)

It is best to give up your own interests in order to please other people.
(1 = Totally agree, 4 = Totally disagree)

Source: Beevers, Strong, Meyer, PIlkonis, Miller (2007).

Rosenberg Self-Esteem Scale

I feel that I am a person of worth, at least on an equal plane with others.
(0 = Strongly disagree, 3 = Strongly agree)

I feel that I have a number of good qualities.
(0 = Strongly disagree, 3 = Strongly agree)

I am able to do things as well as most other people.
(0 = Strongly disagree, 3 = Strongly agree)

Source: Rosenberg, 1965.

Beck Depression Inventory – II

Sadness

0   I do not feel sad.
1   I feel sad much of the time.
2   I am sad all the time.
3   I am so sad or unhappy that I can't stand it.

Loss of Pleasure

0   I get as much pleasure as I ever did from the things I enjoy.
1   I don't enjoy things as much as I used to.
2   I get very little pleasure from the things I used to enjoy.
3   I can't get any pleasure from the things I used to enjoy.

Self-Dislike

0   I feel the same about myself as ever.
1   I have lost confidence in myself.
2   I am disappointed in myself.
3   I dislike myself.

Source: Beck, Steer, & Carbin (1988).

Zung Self-Rating Anxiety Scale

I feel more nervous and anxious than usual.
(1 = None or a little of the time, 4 = Most or all of the time)

I feel like I'm falling apart and going to pieces.
(1 = None or a little of the time, 4 = Most or all of the time)

I get feelings of numbness and tingling in my fingers and toes.
(1 = None or a little of the time, 4 = Most or all of the time)

Source: Zung, 1965.

Drug Abuse Screening Test

Have you used drugs other than those required for medical reasons. YES   NO

Are you able to stop using drugs when you want to?   YES   NO

Have you engaged in illegal activities in order to obtain drugs?   YES   NO

Source: Skinner, 1982.

Michigan Alcohol Screening Test

Can you stop drinking without difficulty after one or two drinks?   YES   NO

Do you ever feel guilty about your drinking?   YES   NO

Have you ever attended a meeting of Alcoholics Anonymous (AA)?   YES   NO

World Health Organization Quality of Life

Do you get the kind of support from others that you need?
(1 = Not at all, 5 = Completely)

How would you rate your quality of life?
(1= Very poor, 5 = Very good)

How satisfied are you with your health?
(1 = Very dissatisfied, 5 = Very satisfied)

Source: WHOQOL Group (1994).

REFERENCES

Andrews, G., Creamer, M., Crino, R., Hunt, C., Lampe, L., & Page, A. (2003). *The treatment of anxiety disorders: Clinician guides and patient manuals.* Cambridge, UK: Cambridge University Press.

Beck, A. T., Steer, R. A., & Carbin, M. G. (1988). Psychometric properties of the Beck Depression Inventory: Twenty-five years of evaluation. *Clinical psychology review, 8*(1), 77–100.

Beevers, C. G., Strong, D. R., Meyer, B., Pilkonis, P. A., & Miller, I. W. (2007). Efficiently assessing negative cognition in depression: An item response theory analysis of the Dysfunctional Attitude Scale. *Psychological Assessment, 19*(2), 199–209.

Carroll, K. M. (1998). *A cognitive-behavioral approach: Treating cocaine addiction.* Rockville, MD: National Institute on Drug Abuse.

National Institutes of Health. (2014, March). *NIH Public Access Policy details.* Retrieved September 1, 2014 from http://publicaccess.nih.gov/policy.htm

Nezu, A. M., & D'Zurilla, T. J. (2005). Problem-solving therapy—General. In S. Felgoise, A. M. Nezu, C. M. Nezu, & M. A. Reinecke (Eds.), *Encyclopedia of cognitive behavior therapy* (pp. 301–304). New York, NY: Springer.

Rosenberg, M. (1965). *Society and the adolescent self-image.* Princeton, NJ: Princeton University Press.

Rounsaville, B. J., & Carroll, K. M. (1992). Individual psychotherapy for drug abusers. In J. H. Lowinsohn, P. Ruiz, & R. B. Millman (Eds.), *Comprehensive Textbook of Substance Abuse* (2nd ed.; pp. 496–508). New York, NY: Williams and Wilkins.

Selzer, M.L. (1971). The Michigan Alcoholism Screening Test (MAST): The quest for a new diagnostic instrument. American Journal of Psychiatry, 127, 1653–1658.

Skinner, H. A. (1982). The Drug Abuse Screening Test. *Addictive Behaviors,* 7, 363–371.

Sobell, M. B., Bogardis, J., Schuller, R., Leo, G. I., & Sobell, L. C. (1989). Is self-monitoring of alcohol consumption reactive? *Behavioral Assessment, 11,* 447–458.

Weissman, A. N. (1979). The Dysfunctional Attitudes Scale: A validation study. *Dissertation Abstracts International, 40,* 1389B–1390B.

WHOQOL Group. (1994). Development of the WHOQOL: Rationale and current status. International Journal of Mental Health, 23 (3), 24–56.

Zung, W. W. (1971). A rating instrument for anxiety disorders. *Psychosomatics,12*(6), 371–379.

Intervention Skills: Using Problem-Solving, Psychoeducation, and Multisystemic Intervention Approaches, and Case/Care Management Skills in Working With Individuals and Families

This chapter will highlight evidence-based intervention skills that use problem-solving approaches, psychoeducational approaches, and multisystemic intervention approaches. We will also examine the importance and relevance of integrating case/care management skills and the importance of using stress management strategies.

These evidence-based approaches are grounded in an understanding of person-in-environment concepts, with the goal of promoting individual and family participation in decision-making processes.

We will review core concepts and skills from each of these approaches and highlight specialized applications of these approaches in our work with individuals, families, and small groups. In particular, family psychoeducational groups in mental health care and multisystemic therapy with adolescents will be covered.

CHAPTER LEARNING OBJECTIVES

By the end of this chapter, you should be able to examine, understand, and apply

- the core skills and concepts of problem-solving approaches,
- the core skills and concepts of psychoeducational approaches,
- the core skills and concepts of multisystemic approaches, including understanding how to use the fit mapping tool, and
- the core case/care management skills critical to working with individuals and families and small groups.

The Council on Social Work Education Educational Policy and Accreditation Standards (CSWE-EPAS) Competencies that are highlighted in more depth in this chapter include the following:

2.1.3 Apply critical thinking to inform and communicate professional judgments.

2.1.4 Engage diversity and difference in practice.

2.1.6 Engage in research-informed practice and practice-informed research.

2.1.7 Apply knowledge of human behavior and the social environment.

2.1.9 Respond to contexts that shape practice.

2.1.10 (a–d) Engage, assess, intervene, and evaluate with individuals, families, groups, organizations, and communities.

CASE SITUATION A: SAIRA

Saira, a single 24-year-old Muslim female, comes to the Community Center due to sleep problems (insomnia) and ongoing problems with fatigue. She has gained over 30 pounds since her visit last year. She has a history of experiencing anxiety problems. The primary care physician has referred her to you to address her anxiety. She has been on medication in the past for anxiety issues. Saira tells you that she is afraid that she might have cancer, since her mother had cancer at her age. Her mother died of breast cancer at age 26, when Saira was two years old. Saira worries all the time about getting cancer, and this has interfered with completing tasks on time at her work. She has been put on probation at work and may lose her job. Saira is not in regular contact with her father, since he lives in Jordan and does not have easy access to the Internet in his small town. Her two sisters are also living in Jordan. Saira has lived in the United States for the past seven years. She came on a college scholarship to the U.S. Saira reports that she misses her family and often feels lonely and depressed, but she loves the work she does. Saira does have two close college friends whom she sees often during the week. Saira just wants to sleep better and not worry so much about getting cancer.

CASE SITUATION B: JOSE AND MARIA

Jose, a 35-year-old Mexican American male, is morbidly obese. He was diagnosed with schizophrenia when he was 17 years old. He has been on several different psychotropic medications over the years and has been hospitalized periodically due to this illness. Currently, Jose is participating in a supported employment program at the local community mental health center. He lives with his sister, Maria, and her family. Maria is finding it more difficult to care for Jose, and her husband wants Jose to move out of the home. Jose stays up late at night and keeps the TV on for hours when he is at home. Jose is usually good with Maria's three small children, but one day, she found him hitting the youngest child for taking away the TV remote control. Jose has asthma, and his physical mobility is limited due to his weight issues. Maria has called you at the mental health center to see what can be done about Jose. Recently Jose stopped taking his psychotropic medications and tells her he doesn't need them anymore. Maria's husband has threatened to leave her and the children if Jose is not out of the home soon, but Maria feels obligated to provide a home for Jose. She promised her mother that she would always take care of Jose. Her mother is living with her sister in another state, and her father died over five years ago.

CASE SITUATION C: CALLIE, LINDA, AND BRIAN

Callie is a 14-year-old Caucasian female referred to your youth center by her family due to her depression, drug use, and contacts with the juvenile justice system. Accompanying Callie to the intake assessment were her mother, Linda, and stepfather, Brian. Callie also has two stepbrothers who are ages two and five years old. Callie has a history of running away (e.g., more than five episodes in the last six months). The last time Callie ran away, she was found in a youth homeless shelter in a city 200 miles away. Callie uses alcohol and marijuana, especially when she hangs out with her friends from the neighborhood. She has been picked up by the police and referred to juvenile court for running away and her marijuana use. Linda is worried that Callie is depressed because for the past month,

(Continued)

(Continued)

she has stopped going to school and sleeps all the time. During the intake assessment, Brian expressed concern that Callie's behavior had become increasingly more difficult to manage. For example, Callie has become verbally and physically aggressive toward her mother, yells at her stepbrothers, refuses to do any chores, and will not attend school. Brian states that he has not been involved in the parenting of Callie for the past two years since she does not respect him. Callie tells you that she hates school and living at home but refuses to elaborate further. Linda shares that before she married Brian (five years ago), she and Callie lived with her parents in another state. Linda tells you she has no energy to deal with Callie's behavior. Brian has recently been laid off from work and Linda works part time at a hair salon to help cover the bills. Brian and Linda worry that they will lose their home if he does not find work soon.

Problem-Solving Approach

According to Nezu, Nezu, and D'Zurilla (2013, p. 20), "problem solving refers to the process of finding or developing solutions to specific problems, whereas solution implementation refers to the process of carrying out those solutions in the actual situation." Therefore, it is important for us to recognize that problem-solving skills and solution-implementation skills differ in their approach and use.

Let's define what we mean by *problem(s)*. Nezu et al. (2013, p. 20) describe a "problem as a life situation, present or anticipated, that requires an adaptive response" from the individual/family or small group or client/consumer. The problem(s), if not addressed, could result in negative consequences for the individual/family. For these individuals/families, a resolution that addresses the problem(s) is difficult for them to carry out due to their perceived obstacles or barriers. These perceived obstacles or barriers could surface due to many reasons that include the individual's or family's confusion about what to do, conflicting goals, a lack of control over the problem situation, or a lack of skills or resources to develop a resolution. As you will note from this definition, the problem must not only be viewed as it exists within an individual or family system, but it also must include an emphasis on the person-environment balance. Many clients and families experience problems due to environmental conditions (e.g., poverty, unemployment) or due to discriminatory or oppressive conditions. These types of problems require not only helping clients and families to cope with the current problem situation but also involve advocacy to change policies and practices that contribute to the problem situation. It is critical that we learn to address the imbalance between individuals and their environments created by their life situations/problem(s) in order to be effective in our practice.

Nezu et al. (2013, p. 21) define a *solution* as "a situation-specific coping response or response pattern that is the product or outcome of the problem-solving process when it is applied to a specific problem situation." Individuals or families may approach a problem or problem situation using a rational approach that involves defining the problem, generating alternatives, engaging in a decision-making process to determine the best alternative, and putting the plan or solution into play. This is often called the *constructive approach* to solving problems or coping with problem situations. When individuals or families use less constructive approaches, they may engage in actions that avoid the problem(s) or they may react to the problem(s) in an impulsive manner. When an *avoidant* or *impulsive* approach is used, the individuals or families usually experience negative consequences and/or problem resolution is not achieved.

According to Nezu et al. (2013, p. 25), the objectives of a problem-solving approach include the following:

- Enhancing positive problem orientation
- Decreasing negative problem orientation
- Fostering problem solving
- Minimizing avoidant problem solving
- Minimizing impulsive/careless problem solving

The goal of using this intervention approach is to enhance the individual's or family's ability to cope with life stressors and to enhance their well-being. When you use the problem-solving approach, your focus is on helping individuals and families to address their experience with cognitive overload, emotional regulation issues, and feelings of hopelessness/helplessness; their ineffective problem-solving skills; and problems they may be experiencing in cognitive processing (Nezu et al., 2013).

The SSTA model of problem solving is based on extensive research and clinical trials completed by Nezu et al. in 2013. The acronym SSTA stands for S=Stop, S=Slow down, T=Think, A=Act. *Stopping* involves a client becoming aware that he or she is experiencing a problem. *Slowing down* means taking a moment to be in the present, becoming more aware of the problem or situation, and letting the client explore his or her feelings, thoughts, and actions related to the problem or situation. *Thinking* is where we engage the individual or family in exploring and examining alternatives to the situation and understanding what the possible consequences are for each alternative action that is developed. *Acting* is the actual carrying out of a solution or action plan. Figure 9.1 highlights the SSTA steps that are used in this approach to problem solving.

Another model that can be used to when applying a problem-solving process is captured by the acronym SOLVE. Table 9.1 outlines the steps to take when using the SOLVE model.

While the problem-solving steps may appear to be easy for us to implement, the challenge lies in how we effectively engage individuals and families in the actual process. The work of Otto, Simon, Olatunji, Sung, and Pollack (2011) helps us to clarify another method we could use to implement an effective problem-solving process with individuals/families (Table 9.2). There are several steps involved when you use this

Figure 9.1   The SSTA Approach to Problem Solving

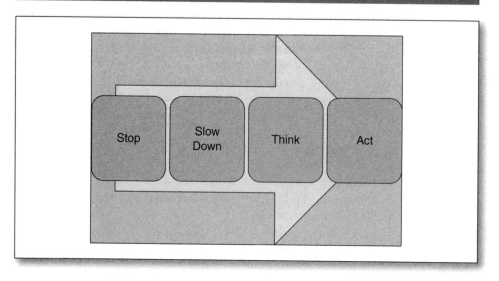

Table 9.1   Problem-Solving Skills

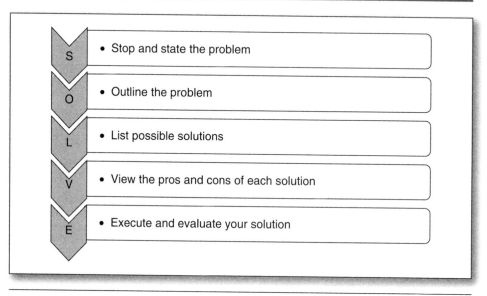

Source: Khatri and Mays, 2011.

process. The first is to identify the problem. The second is to clearly define the problem, which is a critical step and is often the step that many of us who are new to the problem-solving process overlook. It is therefore important for us to make sure the problem is identified and defined in clear terms. This includes highlighting examples of *what* the problem looks like, *how* the problem is present in day-to-day life, *where* the problem is most noticeable, *who* is involved in the problem situation, and *when* the problem is most distressing to the individual or family members. These *what, how, where, who,* and *when* questions will help you and the individual and family members clearly define and clarify the problem so that a plan to address the issues can be created. For example, when a child engages in outbursts that result in the physical throwing of objects, we should look at each outburst and determine what was happening *before* the outburst, what happened *during* the outburst, *who* was involved in the outburst, *how* long the outburst lasted, and what happened *after* the outburst to see if we can discover patterns or other opportunities wherein if a different action had been taken, perhaps a different outcome might have resulted. Clarifying and defining the problem at the start will help you more effectively engage in applying the steps involved in the problem-solving process. Most problems that involve communication issues, relationships, or emotional regulation issues or those that focus on feelings can benefit from using the problem-solving steps found in this model.

The third step when using the active problem-solving approach is to encourage the individual or family members to brainstorm possible solutions. When you brainstorm solutions, it is important that you encourage individuals and family members to not focus on evaluating the solutions they might come up with during this phase, because it is important that every solution is explored and discussed further. During the brainstorming phase, it is typical to identify at least five or six potential solutions. The fourth step in this approach is to evaluate each potential solution that has been

Table 9.2   Components of Active Problem Solving

Identifying the Problem	Clearly Defining the Problem	Brainstorming a List of Possible Solutions	Evaluating the Solutions	Selecting a Solution or a Combination of Solutions	Implementing the Solution	Evaluating the Effectiveness of the Solution

Source: Adapted from Otto, Simon, Olatunji, Sung, and Pollack, 2011.

identified. During the evaluation phase, you need to engage the individual or family member in sorting out the pros and cons of each potential solution they have identified. Once all the solutions have been evaluated, the fifth step involves having a discussion that focuses on determining which solution is the best. This solution or a combination of the solutions is selected for them to implement. The sixth step involves the individual or family actually carrying out the agreed-upon solution(s); and then, in the next visit/meeting, the seventh and final step involves you and the individual or family evaluating how the solution(s) worked (or didn't work), what parts of the solution(s) worked (or not), and what might need to be reevaluated in order to effect the changes they want to see.

REFLECTIVE LEARNING ACTIVITY

Use Case Situation A (Saira), presented at the beginning of this chapter, and make a list of the potential problems you think are present in this case. Clearly articulate the definitions of these problems and then make a list of the possible solutions you might develop.

The problem-solving process is one that might take a brief time or it could take an entire session or more with an individual or family. The key in using the problem-solving approach effectively is to make sure you help individuals and families learn the skills they will need, which will assist them in carrying out effective problem solving. This will ensure that they become skilled and confident and that they will be equipped to use the problem-solving approach in the future. In addition, it is important to note that throughout this entire process, you have had to collaborate/partner with the individual and/or family, thus jointly ensuring that you have identified the problem(s) to work on as well as that the solutions that have emerged have built upon the individual's/ family's strengths, reflected an understanding of the person-in-environment situation, and taken into account the diversity factors that were present.

REFLECTIVE LEARNING ACTIVITY

Explore and examine your own problem-solving style. Discuss how difficult it might be for you to use the rational/constructive approach to problem solving in your own life.

Think of a current problem or challenge that you have experienced in the past few weeks. Use the problem-solving steps to examine this situation/problem, develop a solution, and implement it. In a week, evaluate the solution and examine why it did or didn't work and determine what needs to happen next.

Find a classmate or colleague whom you can work with to role-play carrying out the problem-solving approach with Case Situation A (Saira) while using this process in an interview format.

Psychoeducational Approach

Psychoeducational approaches are used in a range of social work settings where social workers with people who have identified physical and behavioral health related issues. You may be able to use the psychoeducational approach when working with individuals or groups, depending on the needs of those individuals and families who are engaging in the change process.

The evidence-based psychoeducational approaches that have been developed use a professionally delivered intervention format that integrates and synergizes psychotherapeutic and educational interventions. There are three elements involved when you use a psychoeducational approach. These include an educational component, which focuses on understanding and learning about the illness or problem area; a cross-cutting knowledge and skills component, which is required to effectively address the illness or problem area; and a support component, which is necessary in order to implement changes. According to Lukens and McFarlane (2004), a psychoeducational approach is based on a strengths perspective and is focused on the present. The individual and/or family are considered your partners when facilitating change and, therefore, their outcomes are improved. One of the central notions of this approach assumes that the more knowledge the individuals and/or family members have about the challenges/problems they are experiencing, the more positive the outcomes will be related to their identified behavioral and physical health issues. You will often find it useful to use this approach in a small group setting, and many times, this will involve the use of *peer advocates* (individuals who have lived through the experience that the group members face and who have received additional training that will allow them to effectively share their own experiences) or *parent leaders* (parents who have children who have had similar challenges and who have received additional training in order to equip them to share their own experiences). The peer advocates or parent leaders function as co-facilitators in the group setting. One example involves individuals living with schizophrenia or mood disorders and their family members and/or caregiving/support persons, who may join a psychoeducational group that focuses on helping these individuals to understand the illness, assisting them in problem solving day-to-day challenges, enhancing their communication skills, and helping them build and access support networks and resources. As the group leader, you would be working with a peer advocate to co-facilitate this group in focusing on the issues listed. A second example might include hosting a group for individuals who have chronic health conditions (such as diabetes, coronary heart disease, or cancer) or those who are experiencing depression, anxiety, or a mood disorder. The focus of this psychoeducational group would be on helping the participants gain a better understanding of their physical illness and/or the behavioral health challenges, developing problem-solving skills to assist them in coping with their current challenges, and allowing them an opportunity to receive support from other group members who are experiencing similar issues, which will result in them learning how to more easily cope with their own respective physical/behavioral health challenges. Again, you might consider working closely with a peer advocate who has learned to live with the physical illness/behavioral health challenges that the group members are experiencing. A third example might be when you are working with parents of children living with a bipolar disorder. Your parent psychoeducational group might include sessions that focus on education regarding the illness, assisting the parents in understanding medications, helping them learn how to more effectively communicate with their children, assisting them in developing problem-solving strategies and skills, and providing them networking opportunities. Co-facilitation with a parent leader has the inherent ability to help parents feel comfortable enough to open up more easily, offers opportunities to connect with other group members who share their struggles and challenges, and provides a venue to more easily establish rapport with other group members and the facilitators.

The cross-cutting key skills that have been identified in order for the psychoeducational approach to be effective require that you become knowledgeable about and proficient in the use of effective education and learning strategies; in problem-solving approaches that are useful in addressing challenges found in day-to-day life; and in facilitating, developing, and building the skill sets of the individuals and/or family members/caregiving support persons, with the goal of improving their coping strategies.

The use of effective education and learning strategies involves preparing materials that are understandable, comprehensive, age and stage appropriate, and easy to use and that reflect a wide range of learning approaches that will adequately meet the needs of the diverse individuals and/or family members/caregiving support persons who are in your psychoeducational group, thus allowing them to engage more effectively in the change process. For example, we know that having individuals and/or family members/caregiving support persons sit in a lecture-style room for several hours while we provide them with information is not the most effective way to engage the participants in understanding and learning about the identified illness. You will have greater success if you segment the information to include active exercises that engage the participants in reflecting on what they are learning and why it is important in order to achieve better outcomes. The problem-solving activities that will be beneficial in these approaches use and apply the steps previously identified in the earlier section of this chapter on problem solving.

The building of cross-cutting knowledge and skills requires that you engage the group's participants in learning new skills that will assist them in developing better coping mechanisms to deal with their challenges (e.g., how to pay attention and actively listen; ways to approach and deal with conflict; and how to understand and apply the thinking/doing/feeling triad). It is important to remember that the goal of the psychoeducational approach is to enhance the individual's/family member's/caregiving support person's understanding of the illness and to facilitate the development of core skills that will help them to more easily cope with the challenges of living with the illness. In Case Situation B (Jose and Maria), participating in psychoeducational intervention may help Maria, her husband, and Jose to better address the challenges of living together and understanding the illness of schizophrenia. There are several psychoeducational models that we will explore that focus on helping people cope with a range of issues. Some of these examples include individuals living with a mental illness, living with a physical health problem, learning to quit smoking, learning how to better manage stress, learning better ways to make healthy food choices, and developing ways to better communicate with family members and peers.

REFLECTIVE LEARNING ACTIVITY

After reading Case Situation B (Jose and Maria), presented at the beginning of this chapter, discuss how using psychoeducational approaches might benefit this family.

In Case Situation A (Saira), would psychoeducational approaches help her situation? Explain.

The Substance Abuse and Mental Health Service Administration (SAMHSA) Evidence-Based Toolkit

The Substance Abuse and Mental Health Service Administration (SAMHSA) has identified family psychoeducation as an evidence-based model that is effective when working with adults living with schizophrenia or mood disorders and their families. If you go to the SAMHSA website, you can find their toolkit, which was developed in order to assist workers in gaining the skills they will need in order to effectively deliver this evidence-based intervention with fidelity (consistent with the evidence-based research). The model has three major components (see Figure 9.2). The three components include the following:

Joining—a process that focuses on engaging the individuals and family members

An *educational workshop* where participants learn about schizophrenia/mood disorders and medications

Ongoing multiple family/caregiver group (MFG) sessions that provide ongoing problem-solving sessions using a problem-solving approach where individuals and families work together to identify and address the challenges of daily living

The joining process involves you meeting with the individual and the family members/caregiving support persons to explain how the group model works, answer questions the participants may have about the aspects of the illness, and identify strengths and positive coping skills. During this process, the focus is on building a trusting relationship between the individual/family members/caregiving support persons and the group leader prior to the start of the individual group sessions.

The goals of the educational workshop include helping the family members/caregiving support persons get to know each other better, understand and learn more about the illness, become more knowledgeable about and better understand the medications used in treatment, and become more knowledgeable about and better understand the course of the illness.

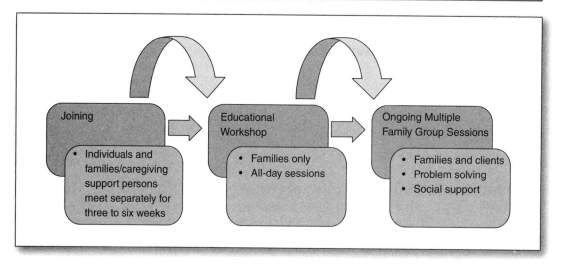

Figure 9.2 **Stages of a Multiple Family/Caregiver Group (MFG) for Adults/Families Living with Schizophrenia**

The focus of the ongoing MFG sessions is to facilitate and develop the skills to assist these individuals in developing problem-solving strategies so they are able to cope more effectively. The ongoing problem-solving group sessions are 45 minutes long and involve all group members (individuals living with schizophrenia/mood disorders and their family members/caregiving support persons) in working together to identify current issues, select a single problem to focus on, and generate solutions using a problem-solving approach (see Table 9.3). These groups typically meet every two weeks over a two-year time period. When you use this approach, you are simultaneously promoting the ongoing building of social support networks among the participants while at the same time improving communication between individuals living with schizophrenia/mood disorders and their family members/caregiving support persons. The SAMHSA toolkit is a very valuable resource, as it will provide you with information about how to develop and implement a MFG group and the skills you will need to facilitate the individual group sessions, and it provides you with core resources that will assist you in becoming an effective group leader.

Table 9.3 **MFG Sessions (Ongoing) Structure (90 Minutes)**

Socialize	15 minutes
Go around and identify current issues	20 minutes
Select a single problem	5 minutes
Use structured problem solving	45 minutes
Socialize	5 minutes

Online Psychoeducational Modules

Another way to deliver services using the psychoeducational approach is by accessing the Internet to seek out and deliver the psychoeducation using online modules. For example, there have been interventions that are Internet-based that have been developed that use the psychoeducational approach for individuals living with anxiety and depressive disorders. One such program that has been developed is by THIS WAY UP™ Clinic (previously CRUfAD Clinic), a nonprofit organization at St Vincent's Hospital, Sydney, Australia. Preliminary outcome data related to this Internet-based psychoeducational approach have demonstrated positive outcomes for individuals who successfully complete the online modules. This Internet-based program provides a focused, clinician-guided learning program that has the capacity to assist in the treatment of identified anxiety- and depression-related. Each THIS WAY UP™ course includes the following:

- Online questionnaires that are completed after each session and sent to the primary care site where the individual is being monitored
- Lessons in the form of comic-based stories
- Homework
- Extra resources
- Recovery stories
- Online calendar to set up the next session

Table 9.4 provides us with a sample outline of one of the online programs that has been designed for a 30-something female client who is a chronic worrier and suffers from Generalized Anxiety Disorder (GAD). Another promising feature of Internet-based psychoeducation is that it can be delivered to large numbers of individuals at any time. Online services may also prove to be cost effective, and they have the potential to allow access to these interventions by geographically diverse individuals and groups. Online services that use a psychoeducational approach may also prove to be more suitable for younger consumers/individuals and diverse cultural groups due to the fact that technology is more acceptable in their everyday lives.

The problem-solving approach and the psychoeducational approaches (in-person or web-based) are being integrated into primary care and other health settings as part of routine care. There is increasing evidence that in addition to individuals with a primary mental health diagnosis, many individuals who experience chronic health conditions such as heart disease, diabetes, and obesity would benefit from psychoeducational interventions.

Multiple-Family Psychoeducation Program (MF-PEP)

Another example of a psychoeducational model that was developed for youth living with bipolar disorders and their families (Fristad, Goldberg Arnold, & Leffler, 2011) is called the Multiple-Family Psychoeducation Program (MF-PEP). This model can be

Table 9.4   Online Psychoeducation GAD Program Example

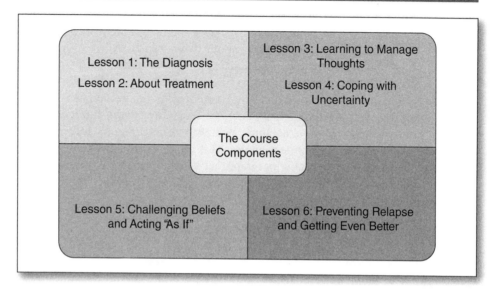

Lesson 1: The Diagnosis

Lesson 2: About Treatment

Lesson 3: Learning to Manage Thoughts

Lesson 4: Coping with Uncertainty

The Course Components

Lesson 5: Challenging Beliefs and Acting "As If"

Lesson 6: Preventing Relapse and Getting Even Better

delivered in either individual sessions or by using a group model. This model is also continuing to demonstrate positive outcomes for participants. The model involves a total of eight sessions where youth and parents/caregivers join together at the beginning and at the end of each group session but are separated for the majority of the individual group session in order to allow each set of participants to address their unique needs and focus on specialized education and skill development. Each group participant receives a workbook that contains an outline for each session and exercises that they can use in each session that will support the work that needs to be completed in between sessions by participants. Figure 9.3 provides the outline for the eight specialized sessions when delivered in a group format.

The MF-PEP has established a group motto: "It is not your fault, but it is your challenge." This motto captures the importance of learning to understand the illness and how critical it is to find new ways to cope with the illness.

REFLECTIVE LEARNING ACTIVITY

Go to the SAMHSA website and review the frontline training module for family psychoeducation. List 4–5 strengths of this model in working with individuals and families. List 3–4 challenges you would anticipate when starting an MFG group.

Conduct a literature search on psychoeducational models used for different physical and behavioral problems relevant to an area you are interested in.

List three pros and three cons that you have identified when using Internet-based psychoeducational interventions.

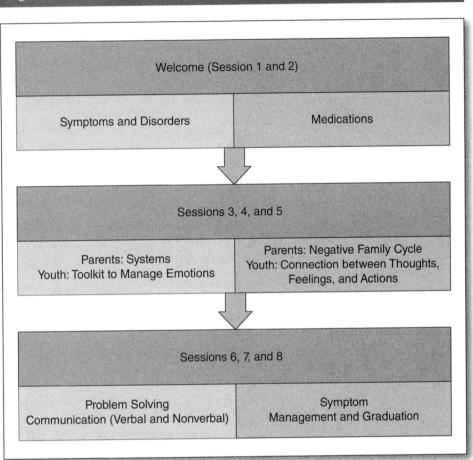

Figure 9.3   MF-PEP Session Themes

Welcome (Session 1 and 2)

| Symptoms and Disorders | Medications |

Sessions 3, 4, and 5

| Parents: Systems
Youth: Toolkit to Manage Emotions | Parents: Negative Family Cycle
Youth: Connection between Thoughts,
Feelings, and Actions |

Sessions 6, 7, and 8

| Problem Solving
Communication (Verbal and Nonverbal) | Symptom
Management and Graduation |

Multisystem Intervention Approaches

When you are working with youth and families, it is important for you to consider using intervention approaches that address multiple systems (e.g., schools, families, peers, neighborhoods) simultaneously. One particular evidence-based practice approach that has been identified is called *multisystemic therapy* (Henggeler, Schoenwald, Borduin, Rowland, & Cunningham, 2009). This approach has been studied in working with youth in the juvenile justice system, with youth who experience behavioral health problems, and with youth who demonstrate antisocial behavior. The overarching goals of this approach are to empower parents/caregivers with skills and resources needed to address parenting/caregiving challenges and to empower youth to be able to more effectively cope with family, peer, school, and neighborhood/community problems. The model requires that you spend intensive time (two to 15 hours per week) with youth and family members/caregivers in their home and community over a several-month period of time (approximately four months). The multisystemic therapy model pinpoints the following key principles:

- The purpose of assessment is to understand the fit between identified problems and the broader systemic context.
- Therapeutic contacts should emphasize the positive and use systemic strengths as levers for change.
- Interventions should

  - promote responsible behavior and decrease irresponsible behavior among family members;
  - be present-focused and action-oriented and target specific, well-defined problems;
  - target sequences of behaviors within and between multiple systems that maintain identified problems;
  - be developmentally appropriate and fit the developmental needs of the youth; and
  - require daily and weekly efforts by family members.

- Efficacy should be continuously evaluated and providers should assume accountability for overcoming barriers to success.
- Providers should promote treatment generalization and long-term maintenance of therapeutic change.
- Providers should empower caregivers to address needs across systems.

One of the unique features of this approach is the concept that you will be working as part of a team and that you need to do whatever it takes to help youth and their family members/caregivers reach the established goals. When interventions are not successful, the failure belongs to the team rather than being the responsibility of the family/caregiver (Henggeler et al., 2009, p. 18).

The cross-cutting core skills that are central to using this approach will require you to demonstrate the ability to do the following:

- Conduct strengths and needs assessments of the youth and family members/caregivers

This skill involves looking at systemic strengths and weaknesses/needs at the individual, family, school, peer, and community levels. You will need to learn how to engage the youth and family members/caregivers in identifying systemic strengths and weaknesses related to their overall goals/desired outcomes. This is a collaborative process and the team must engage the youth and family members/caregivers in leveraging strengths to facilitate positive changes throughout all system levels.

- Apply partnership-building skills with parents/family members/caregivers

This partnership-building skill set focuses on establishing a relationship with the parents/family members/caregivers that recognizes the unique expertise and experience that you and each individual member of the team bring to the helping process. It also recognizes and respects the unique expertise and experiences that parents/family members/caregivers bring to the process based on their ongoing involvement with the youth.

- Actively engage the youth and family members/caregivers in change efforts

The intervention plans you will be identifying and implementing using this approach require that the youth and family members/caregivers actively carry out tasks in between established sessions. The team's overall goal is to empower the youth and family members/caregivers to initiate change in their environments.

- Apply problem-solving skills

The problem-solving approaches we have discussed in the earlier section of this chapter will be helpful to you and are also critical to the success of this approach.

- Apply conflict management and negotiation skills

Conflict management and negotiation skills are important to ensure that you establish new boundaries between the family members/caregivers and other systems that may interact with the youth and family members/caregivers.

- Involve and facilitate multiple systems in the resolving of the identified problem(s)

You will be working directly with the youth and family/caregivers and all of the systems that are directly impacting the youth and family members/caregivers, such as schools and neighborhood/community organizations. Your role is often to act as coordinator or facilitator of the meetings or discussions among the different systems in order to help bridge the gaps in the systems in ways that will positively impact the youth and their family members/caregivers.

- Explore ways to improve the fit among the youth, family members/caregivers, and other system environments

This skill involves the use of the person-in-environment fit mapping tool (Figure 9.4), whereby you and the youth/family members/caregivers identify a problem situation. One example might be that the youth is not getting up in time to catch the bus in the morning and is missing/not attending school. Using fit mapping, you and the youth/family members/caregivers examine this problem situation using a range of perspectives

Figure 9.4   Fit Factor Mapping Tool

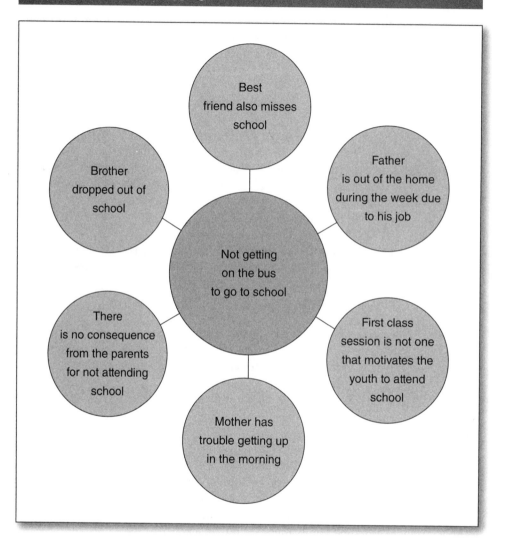

while ensuring that you include multiple system levels. When using the fit mapping tool, the goal is for you to receive greater clarity about the problem situation and to determine possible action steps.

In this example, we find out the following things:

- The mother has difficulty getting up in the morning, too, because she takes medications for depression in the later evening.
- The youth's older brother dropped out of school and stays home all day watching TV.

- The first set of classes that the youth takes in the morning are classes where he has conflicts with his teachers.
- When the youth stays home, there are no consequences for not going to school from the mother or father. The father is often gone during the week because of his job driving trucks long distances, and the youth's best friend also misses the bus/school frequently and hangs out with the youth at home.

By using this fit map, you and the team can begin to work with the youth and family members/caregivers to identify and develop solutions and action steps to address and impact the problem situations/conditions that have been identified. Several solutions that you might consider include working with the mother to alter when she takes her medications, the school to change the youth's schedule, the best friend and the youth to explore and develop incentives that would reward them both for attending school, the father and his work schedule to explore whether he is able to support the youth in getting to school on time by calling him daily, and the parents to collaboratively develop a plan to establish and enforce a set of consequences for the youth when school is not attended.

As you can see, when you use the fit mapping process, it will allow you to gather many more details about the problem/situation, to gain clarity about a particular problem/situation, and to easily uncover several possible factors that could be leveraged to address the problem/situation; any of these could result in a resolution of the identified concerns/issues. It is critical that you learn to apply your collaboration and facilitation skills when using a multisystemic intervention approach. Maintaining a focus on creating positive change for the individuals/family members/caregivers is important, but it is also critical that all the systems involved in the problem(s)/situation(s) are subsequently empowered to participate in the change process as well.

REFLECTIVE LEARNING ACTIVITY

Using Case Situation C (Callie, Linda, and Brian), presented at the beginning of this chapter, find a classmate to role play with. Develop a set of at least five questions that will provide enough information for you to be able to create a fit map for the family in the case.

Identify at least five problems/situations stemming from the case and from your role-play interview.

After you have completed your interview, complete a fit map in conjunction with your classmate.

Identify at least five possible action steps/solutions based on the map you both have created.

Switch roles and start this activity again. Identify new questions to use, new problems/situations that may not have been uncovered, and new action steps to create another fit map.

Case/Care Management Approaches

When working with individuals and families, we often find that the challenges they are experiencing are due to situations or problems that surface that are related to service delivery systems and/or the lack of access to resources/services that are required in order to effectively resolve the identified problems/situations. In the current behavioral/health systems, with the implementation of the Affordable Care Act, we often hear the phrases *care navigator, managed care coordinator, care manager,* or *case manager* as functions that are involved in some way, shape, or form in delivering case or care management services to our clients. In social work practice, we must view the role that case or care management plays as central to all the work we do with individuals and families. It is important that we recognize how to adopt a person-in-environment approach, which requires us to look beyond what is happening in the individual/family unit. In order to be effective, we must learn to engage in a process that allows us to understand how other systems might also be impacting the problems/situations that have been identified. According to Frankel and Gelman (2012, pp. 3–4), case/care management goals focus on ensuring that we learn how to improve the quality of care we provide to vulnerable populations while at the same time assist in controlling the costs of this care. These two tasks may often conflict in real practice situations, when advocating for improving the quality of care for vulnerable populations actually results in increasing the cost of that care.

Roberts-DeGennaro (2008) identify the following functions of case management:

- Developing a resource network
- Assessing the client's needs and strengths
- Developing the care plan
- Establishing a written contract
- Implementing the care plan
- Monitoring the services
- Evaluation
- Closing the case
- Follow-up

To effectively implement appropriate and ethical case/care management functions, your role should include the following (Frankel & Gelman, 2012):

- Providing direct support
- Engaging in crisis management
- Providing short-term treatment
- Brokering or facilitating access to services
- Enabling, teaching, or mediating situations
- Advocating for the client
- Coordinating services
- Tracking implementation

These cross-cutting knowledge, skills, and abilities will enable you to implement effective case/care management functions in a range of service settings (e.g., school, health, juvenile justice, behavioral health, public/child welfare). As you will note, case/care management involves many of the elements we have already covered in this book. A few of these include using our skills by demonstrating active listening, empathetic responses, and ethical boundary setting when we enter into the helping process. This allows our work to then move through the stages identified below, during which we must remember to apply a social justice lens to ensure that we are reflecting on issues of diversity and social and economic justice and that we are cognizant of relevant research to inform our practice.

- Engagement
- Assessment
- Intervention
- Evaluation

In addition, it is critical that we develop additional skills that may be necessary to implement sound case/care management functions. These include

- understanding and addressing service delivery systems,
- determining eligibility/access to services,
- advocating for eligibility/access to service,
- securing needed resources/services, and
- coordinating eligible services over time.

It is necessary that you take the time to identify and learn about all the service systems that may impact the individuals/families/clients/consumers you serve, with the goal of being able to develop a network of resources/services that you are subsequently able to link individuals/families with when needed. The case/care coordination role can be critically important in empowering individuals and families in reaching their hoped-for outcomes. Assisting your clients and demanding that different systems work more effectively in order to better serve your clients is going to be time consuming and will require that you participate in active outreach in order to ensure that the services your clients are entitled to and will benefit from are being delivered. It is not enough to just provide clients with a phone number and/or contact information. Many times, you will also need to play an active role in the change process by calling, as an example, the resources/services for your client and following up on plans to ensure that the referral connection has in fact been activated.

In the current social work practice environment, social workers are not the only ones who perform case management functions. In some settings, such as in health care/behavioral health settings, nurses are actively engaged in the delivery of case/care management services. The evidenced-based argument in favor of case/care management services varies, but the strongest evidence has emerged from programs that have manualized their case/care management functions and established fidelity checks (e.g., Wraparound Services).

One area that needs a special mention when engaging in case/care management is that of multidisciplinary teams, especially in the behavioral health and health care systems. With the implementation of the Affordable Health Care Act, social workers need to work effectively as contributing members of multidisciplinary teams. The focus of the multidisciplinary collaborations is to ensure that individuals who receive case/care management services demonstrate improvement in key physical and behavioral health domains over time.

Finally, it should be noted that the profession of social work strives to maintain a focus on all the bio-psycho-social-spiritual elements that influence and impact people's lives while *simultaneously* evaluating the context within which these individuals exist (person-in-environment concept). This is why social work practice has proven to be effective when working with multiple diverse groups of individuals, families, small groups, and communities.

CHAPTER REVIEW QUESTIONS

1. Review the problem-solving approaches presented in this chapter. List the key elements that should be included when using a problem-solving approach.

2. List and discuss 3–4 reasons why it is important to collaborate/partner with the individuals/families when using the problem-solving approach.

3. List the core components of the psychoeducational approach. Discuss how you might apply this approach in working with individuals who are living with anxiety and who also have been diagnosed with coronary heart disease.

4. List the steps that you would use to create a fit map.

5. Discuss your reaction to the philosophy that in multisystemic therapy, if things don't go well in the intervention work, this is the team's responsibility and not the responsibility of the individual/family members/caregivers.

6. Discuss three ways you would use your case/care management skills in service coordination in your current field placement or work/volunteer setting.

REFERENCES

Frankel, A., & Gelman, S. (2012). *Case management: An introduction to concepts and skills.* Chicago, IL: Lyceum.

Fristad, M., Goldberg Arnold, J., & Leffler, J. (2011). *Psychotherapy for children with bipolar and depressive disorders.* New York, NY: Guilford.

Henggeler, S., Schoenwald, S., Borduin, C., Rowland, M., & Cunningham, P. (2009). *Multisystemic therapy for antisocial behavior in children and adolescents* (2nd ed.). New York, NY: Guilford.

Khatri, P., & Mays, K. (2011). SAMHSA-HRSA Center for Integrated Health Solutions: Brief interventions in primary care. Retrieved August 25, 2014 from http://www.integration .samhsa.gov/Brief_Intervention_in_PC,_pdf.pdf

Lukens, E. P., & McFarlane, W. R. (2004). Psychoeducation as evidence-based practice: Considerations for practice, research, and policy. *Brief Treatment and Crisis Intervention, 4*, 205–225.

Nezu, A. M., Nezu, C. M., & D'Zurilla, T. (2013). *Problem-solving therapy: A treatment manual.* New York, NY: Springer.

Otto, M., Simon, N., Olatunji, B., Sung, S., & Pollack, M. (2011). *10 Minute CBT: Integrating cognitive behavioral strategies into your practice.* New York, NY: Oxford.

Roberts-DeGennaro, M. (2008). Case management. In T. Mizrahi & L.E. Davis (Eds.), *Encyclopedia of social work* (20th ed., pp. 222–227). Washington, DC: National Association of Social Workers.

Additional Skills for Working With Families and Groups

In the earlier chapters, we have included core assessment and intervention skills that focus not only on individuals but also families and groups. In this chapter, we will highlight some additional skills needed when working with families and groups. The primary focus of this chapter is to address the special skills needed when working with more than one individual at a time in family and group interventions.

CASE SITUATION A: JOHN, RICO, SOPHIA, LILA, AND LISA

John is a 16-year-old male who attends a small private all-male Catholic high school. He is an honor student and plans to attend an Ivy League college. John has two older sisters. John was born in the United States. His parents emigrated from Colombia due to his father's job eighteen years ago. His family is very involved in their local Catholic church, which has special services for Spanish-speaking families. John attends the youth group at his church. John was referred to you at the local mental health center for family intervention after a serious suicide attempt. John had tried to hang himself. John's suicide attempt occurred after his parents found alcohol in his car. John was ashamed to have disappointed his parents. His parents, Rico and Sophia, are worried about John and see him not respecting their rules. John has been breaking curfew and getting into verbal fights with his father for the past two years. Sometimes, John takes off after one of the verbal fights and goes to his paternal grandmother's apartment (two blocks away). John says that his grandmother understands him. His mother says that she is scared that the family is falling apart. John's two sisters are away at college but want to be involved in the family sessions. John's oldest sister, Lila, reports that she has problems with her father, too. She finds him too controlling. John's other sister, Lisa, says that she does not understand why John doesn't just follow the rules at home. Lisa is upset that John is making their mother anxious all the time and she worries about her.

CASE SITUATION B: PETER, SALLY, TREY, TINA, AND RICH

You co-facilitate a group with another colleague that focuses on helping veterans who have recently returned from overseas deployments. The purpose of the group is to provide support and to help group members to address challenges they are having in their day-to-day lives since their return to the U.S. The group is a closed group with only five members. The group meets once a week for two hours, and each group session involves using problem-solving skills to address challenges. Peter, a Mexican American male, is 26 years old. He has been back in the U.S. for one month. He is having difficulty relating to his children, ages two and four years old. His wife reports that he also has anger issues. Sally is a 22-year old Caucasian female. She is single and lives alone. She finds that she is often lonely and has no one to share her life with. She is depressed most days and stays at home. Trey, an African American male, is 24 years old. He was wounded and only recently returned to his family's home. He is now in a wheelchair and is actively engaged in physical rehab most days. He joined the group because he doesn't know how to relate to his family anymore and he feels frustrated with all their helpfulness. Tina is a Native American female and is 30 years old. She joined the group because she found herself drinking too much most days and getting into disagreements with coworkers, which resulted in her being fired from her job. She recently broke up with her partner, Cindi. They had been in a relationship for over eight years. Rich, a Caucasian male who is 21 years old, joined the group after completing his physical rehab program. He has lost the use of his right arm, and he limps with his right leg due to war injuries. He is a new father and is worried that he will not be a good father and that no one will want to hire him. He uses several pain medications on a daily basis to cope with his pain.

Introducing the Core Skills Needed When Working With Families and Helping Families to Change

In addition to the core skills that we have presented in the earlier assessment and intervention skills chapters, we want to expand our discussion to highlight some of the unique aspects of working with families. The first area that we need to consider involves the many different family forms and structures. We need to conceptualize *family* based on how the individuals who are seeking family interventions define their family. For example, in some cases, this may be a heterosexual couple and their biological children, a gay couple and their children, a single-parent family, a blended (step) family with their children, a foster family, or all of the adults and children who live in the same household (including extended family members or unrelated children/ adults). The key when working with families is to be sure to take the time to understand how individuals define their family and to recognize that some individuals who are key members of the family may not live in the same household or may not be easily identified using traditional definitions of family. One definition of family when working with children that is often used in child welfare (based on the family group conferencing approach to intervention) is anyone in the child's life who cares about the child and wants to work to assist the child in dealing with the life challenges the child faces. It is important to note that you may need to define *family* differently than how the individuals who are seeking help define *family*, based on your agency's or organization's definition, especially as it relates to legal issues. It is important to learn about the legal responsibilities you have when working with families. For example, in many situations when working with children in medical emergency departments, schools, or child welfare, you will need to determine who has legal authority to make decisions about the child or to be involved in interventions addressing the child's needs.

Social Work's Mission in Working With Families

Social work's mission in working with families can be captured in the five beliefs summarized by Seabury, Seabury, and Garvin (2011):

1. To support the empowerment of the family to seek the changes that will enhance well-being

2. To enhance the ways families interact with their environments so that families are more likely to obtain the resources they need to meet the needs of the family as well as meet the needs of its members

3. To assist the family in identifying aspects of the environment—such as sexism, racism, heterosexism, ageism, and other forms of discrimination—that limit the family and its members' access to opportunities

4. To advocate for changes in agencies, communities, and society that enhance the healthy functioning of families

5. To help families address internal strains and conflicts within the family that can be changed by interpersonal practice interventions (p. 365)

We will work with the family when the reasons for referral to us or the nature of the problems presented indicate that involving the family in the change process is central to achieving positive outcomes. Sometimes we will find ourselves helping families learn better ways to communicate with each other or helping families deal with the stresses in day-to-day life related to conflict within the family or as a result of experiencing various forms of discrimination. In Case Situation A, engaging John, his parents, and his sisters in family work may improve the relationships in the family and open up communication related to sensitive issues so that family members can better support each other.

Using our multisystemic perspective on family assessment and intervention as defined in earlier chapters will help us to address the complex needs of each family we engage in change efforts. The family is a unique system with responsibilities and functions, and any change for one family member affects all family members. We want to build on the strengths and resiliencies that families bring to the change efforts and to understand the best ways to promote positive family functioning. It is important, especially when working with diverse family systems, to examine how our own cultural, family, and personal life maps influence the ways we engage and work with families toward hoped-for outcomes. Falicov (2014), in her work with Latino families, suggests that we consider taking a knowing and not-knowing stance when exploring the multidimensional aspects of families we work with and that we use a strengths-based orientation to capture what is working for families. The knowing and not-knowing stance involves sharing with the family members that while you understand some aspects of their lives, they are the experts on their family and you are open to learning from them and hearing their stories. It is also important to use a both/and stance in your work with families, which means actively avoiding the trap of either/or conceptualizations. For example, using a both/and stance, you might say that in Case Situation A, John's father, Rico, is protective toward his teenage son (e.g., having an early curfew, insisting that John participate in church activities) and he also wants him to be independent (e.g., encouraging him to make his own decisions and to go away to college). This both/and stance allows us as social workers to see how two seemingly opposing perspectives are intertwined and both contribute to what is happening in the family.

A Multidimensional Ecosystemic Comparative Approach (MECAmaps) to Assess Cultural and Contextual Sociopolitical Contexts

Falicov (2014, p. 38) has developed a tool called a multidimensional ecosystemic comparative approach map (MECAmap) to assess cultural and contextual sociopolitical maps of diverse family systems and those of the clinician. We are encouraged to use this map to better understand our own family's map and how our understanding of family may be influenced by our past. According to Falicov (2014, p. 34) by becoming aware of our own maps and those of the families we engage in change efforts, we can explore our similarities and differences and build cultural bridges of connectedness between families and ourselves. The information to complete the tool is collected through conversations with family members.

The MECAmap examines four domains (ecological context, migration/acculteration, family organization, and family life cycle). In the center of the MECAmap are circles representing the family seeking services, the clinician, or the supervisor. Figure 10.1 outlines the basic MECAmap components. The MECAmap offers a way for us to think about similarities and differences that are relevant to our work with diverse family systems. In examining the *ecological context* domain, we gain a greater understanding of stresses the family experiences related to community, work, school, and religion and how their beliefs and attitudes are related to the presenting issues. It is important in this domain to be sure to develop a greater understanding of the beliefs of the family members related to health, illness, and spirituality. The *migration/acculturation* domain allows us to explore the meanings family members make of their own history of migration/acculturation, separations and reunions, trauma, disorienting anxieties, and cultural identities experienced by the family. We explore these two domains using a social justice position that focuses attention on life conditions, power differentials, and contextual stressors that limit opportunities and affect the well-being of family members. The *family organization* domain explores the diversity of family structures and different family arrangements. In this domain, as a social worker, you want to get a greater sense of the family communication styles and ways that conflicts are handled. In Falicov's work, she highlights the fact that many immigrant Latino families are in a state of rapid cultural transformation and this affects communication styles and connectedness between family members. Families often are experiencing changes in family member roles, especially within the nuclear/extended family network. These role changes may impact how the family members stay connected and may alter the traditional hierarchies that families formerly relied on to communicate important cultural values. In the *family life cycle* domain, we explore with family members the ideals, meanings, timings, and transitions in their lives. The goal for you as the worker in this domain is to understand the similarities and differences of each family's life cycle values and experiences. The family organization and family life cycle domains explore the change process through a cultural diversity lens, where you will appreciate the experiences that the family brings to the helping process and the ways that this diversity can strengthen the helping process.

Figure 10.1   MECAmaps

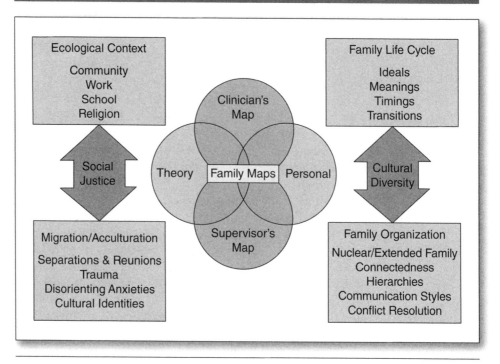

Source: Adapted from Falicov, C. J. (2014) *Latino Families in Therapy (2nd ed.)* Figure 1.1. NY: Guilford Press.

REFLECTIVE LEARNING ACTIVITY

1. Using the MECAmap, engage in an interview with a class member or colleague addressing the four domains. Switch roles. Once both interviews are completed, reflect on how your own MECAmap influences your work and the similarities or differences that you shared with your class member or colleague based on these interviews. How might you use this MECAmap in your own work with families?

2. In Case Situation A, what types of questions might you ask to gather information about the family related to the four domains in the MECAmap? How might your own MECAmap differ from the family in Case Situation A? Where might there be some similarities? How might your awareness of your own MECAmap influence your work with this family?

Establishing a Relationship With Each Family Member

One of the greatest challenges we face in working with families is learning ways to establish relationships with each family member. We need to incorporate the unique perspectives of each family member as we work to establish a plan for change that builds on areas where there is consensus or agreement about the challenges the family faces. It is important to establish guidelines for family interactions early in your work (i.e., during initial sessions) to promote participation from each family member and to foster respect and active listening. Establishing some basic guidelines or rules can facilitate hearing how each family member views the family's problems or challenges and what he or she hopes to have happen by participating in family work. Learning from the family members how they have experienced the problem(s) or challenge(s) and the ways it has affected and continues to affect their lives is critical to successfully engaging the family in change processes. Balancing the focus between the needs of individual family members and the needs of the family as a whole is often difficult and requires us to be active during the sessions to ensure that communication among family members is enhanced and that family members reflect new understanding of the family problems. For example, one technique that we might use to foster improved communication among family members is to have family members repeat what another family member has said before sharing their own views. This technique allows one to focus more on listening first and then adding to the discussion, based on having listened to the other family members. We need to remember that the focus of family work is the family system and not the individual, so we need to be vigilant that we do not fall into the trap of blaming an individual for the challenges the family faces. We will often hear family members say to us that if another family member would change or do something differently, then things would be better. Our task is to help family members become aware that the only person they can change is them-selves and that they should focus on how they handle the family challenges, not others. We will be engaging the family members in exploring family–environment transactions, family coping strategies, family problem solving, and solution-finding strategies. Sometimes our work with families will involve only a small part of the fam-ily system, since these individuals may be the only family members willing to work on change. In family work, the more family members that engage in family change efforts, the more likely the family will reach their goals or hoped-for outcomes. It only takes one person to make a change, and the other family members will be affected by that change. When engaging family members in change efforts, it is vital to remember to focus on strengths and resiliencies. Every family system is complex, but our task is to find the potential that they have to meet the challenges they face day to day and to promote the development of the skills they need to cope with these challenges as individuals and as members of the family.

Models of Family Work

There are many approaches to working with families that have evolved over the past several years. Some of the models of family therapy focus primarily on communication patterns and systems, some on structural issues and intergenerational dynamics, and some on the families as experts in their own lives. As noted earlier in the book, we know that multisystemic family therapy has a strong evidence base for working with adolescents and their families involved in the juvenile justice system. There are several other evidence-based family therapy approaches that target families at different stages of the life cycle and at different developmental phases. The Substance Abuse and Mental Health Services Administration (SAMHSA) National Registry of Evidence Based Practices and Programs (NREPP) (2014) lists over 160 family interventions that have demonstrated promising outcomes for a range of diverse family systems. It is important for us to review what is known from previous studies as we establish our own practice with families.

Special Note: Working With Couples

In addition to family interventions, social workers have a long tradition of working with couples who are experiencing relationship problems. The relationship problems can surface due to communication difficulties, power issues, conflicts around roles and responsibilities, trust or intimacy issues, sexual concerns, or a range of other interpersonal challenges. Couples interventions can effectively address some psychological disorders and enhance adjustments to physical health problems (Snyder & Halford, 2012). When couples are in relationship distress, it affects the physical health, parenting practices, and psychological health of the individuals in the relationship. It is important for us to consider the central role of the couple relationship in our work with individuals and families.

Many of the techniques and skills presented in Chapter 8 related to behavioral and cognitive behavioral approaches to change and in Chapter 9 related to problem-solving and psychoeducational skills will be useful in working with couples. The core relationship-building and engagement skills we discussed in Chapter 5 are critical in working effectively with a couple, too. In fact, Friedlander, Escudero, Heatherington, and Diamond (2011) found that—similar to individual therapy—when conducting a meta-analysis of couples interventions, a positive therapeutic alliance is associated with positive couple therapy outcomes.

One example of an evidence-based approach is behavioral couple therapy. It has been demonstrated to have positive outcomes for couples when compared to 72% of untreated couples (Shadish & Baldwin, 2003). Behavioral couple therapy involves focusing on behavior exchanges, communication training, and problem-solving training. When we work with couples in distress using the behavioral couple therapy model, we encourage each individual in the relationship to be committed to changing themselves in order to facilitate a better relationship with their partner. Interventions tend to increase specific positive behaviors and decrease negative behaviors. There are other approaches that have also demonstrated positive outcomes in working with couples, such as integrative couples therapy, couples enrichment programs, and relationship/communication enhancement programs.

We do need to pay special attention when working with couples to assess intimate partner violence issues, since our interventions will need to change to ensure that partners and family members are safe. Safety is the primary concern when working with individuals in relationships where intimate partner violence is present. At this time, most research does not support engaging couples in treatment when intimate partner violence is present.

Introducing the Core Skills Needed When Working With Groups

In an earlier chapter, we shared the multifamily psychoeducational approach to group work with families living with schizophrenia or with younger families living with bipolar disorders and depression. Let's look a little more closely at how we work with groups in social work. If we go to the International Association of Social Work with Groups, Inc. (IASWG) website, we find that they have developed core standards for group work practice in social work. IASWG (n.d.) states in their standards,

> Central to social work practice with groups is the concept of mutual aid. The group worker recognizes that the group, with its multiple helping relationships, is the primary source of change. The group worker's role is one primarily of helping members work together to achieve the goals that they have established for themselves.

For many of us, moving from working with only the individual to working with individuals in groups can be challenging. It is important for us to realize that the individuals are vital to helping other group members to address the challenges that bring them to the group. Individuals who participate in the group interventions will gain new skills and knowledge about their own situations through engagement with other group members. Your role is to help group members engage with each other to achieve their hoped-for outcomes. In Case Situation B, helping the group members to share their own challenges and problem solve together creates opportunities for each group member to learn from the others.

These standards further define the core knowledge, values, and competency-based assessment skills needed to facilitate positive outcomes through group interventions. Figure 10.2 lists the competency-based assessment skills for group work identified by IASWG. There are 20 different assessment competencies that address the key components and skills needed to intervene effectively in a group model. We know that there are several types of groups you might lead and each type of group has unique issues to address, but these core assessment competencies will guide you in the process of becoming an effective group leader.

Leading Groups and Understanding Group Development Stages

We know that groups are dynamic and that change is occurring at all times. As group leaders/facilitators, we need to take into account the different phases of group development. According to Seabury et al. (2011, p. 415), in reviewing the literature on stages of group development in closed groups (groups where membership is stable), there are five general stages. These stages include pre-group planning, formation, revision, maturity, and termination. Let's review briefly each stage and the focus of our work during that stage.

Figure 10.2 Competency-Based Assessment Skills for Group Work (IASWG Practice Standards)

There is an emphasis on member strengths and concerns.	The group functions as a source of mutual aid.	The group consists of multiple helping relationships.	The social worker's primary role is one of assisting members in helping one another.
The group is characterized by democratic process.	Members are helped to own the group.	The worth of the group members and the social worker is equal.	The social worker is not an all-powerful expert.
Social worker-to-groups and social worker-to-members relationships are characterized by egalitarianism and reciprocity.	There is an emphasis on empowerment.	Group goals emphasize individual member growth and social change.	Social workers promote individual and group autonomy.
Social worker's assessments and interventions are characterized by flexibility and eclecticism.	Small group behavior is the norm.	The group as an entity is separate and distinct from individual members.	The phases of group development foster change throughout the life of the group.
The social worker recognizes how the group process shapes and influences individual member behavior.	Groups are formed for different purposes and goals.	Group type (e.g., education, problem solving, social action) influences what the social worker does and how the group accomplishes its goals.	The monitoring and evaluation of the success of the group in achieving its objectives is accomplished through observation and measurements of outcomes and/or process.

In the pre-group planning phase, we need to consider the purpose of the group we want to initiate; the composition of the group (who will be the members); when, where, for how long, and how often the group will meet; and the structure of each group session. The pre-work you engage in prior to starting a group will increase the likelihood that the group will launch. As we noted when reviewing the multiple family psychoeducational groups in an earlier chapter, the joining sessions prior to the first group session were found to be important in facilitating individuals to take part in the group work sessions. During the pre-group phase, it is important to review the literature to find group models that have already demonstrated positive outcomes for individuals with similar problems/ challenges or issues. In Case Situation B, we might find that it is important to build a relationship with each group member first so that when they join the group, they understand the purpose of the group and have some initial trust established with you as a leader of the group.

Recruitment of group members can be challenging and is often the most frustrating aspect of starting a group intervention in many agencies/organizations. For example, you may have three families that are ready and prepared to join a parenting group, but you need at least five families for the group intervention to be successful. You, as the group leader, would need to keep the parents who are already set to start in a holding position while recruiting the additional parents. We also know that many families may indicate interest in joining the group, but on the actual day of the first group session, only a couple of the families may show for the session. It is important to address potential barriers for members to participate in groups. Some barriers for individuals with behavioral health challenges might include stigma, cultural differences, transportation, time of the group, child care issues, fear, and not being sure how the group will help. By addressing the barriers to group participation, we will have a greater chance of success in getting a group started.

In the formation phase, group members have an opportunity to get to know one another and to learn more about the leaders and the group focus. The formation phase is critical in closed group models, since ground rules are established and group members begin to identify the group as central to their own growth and development. In the revision phase, group members may challenge group rules, or conflicts may surface among group members or between group members and the group leaders around the group work to be done. This phase may result in modifications to the group structure and process to better meet the needs of the group members and to shape the group work for future phases. During the revision phase, some group members may leave or drop out of the group due to the increased tensions that may surface.

The maturity phase in closed groups occurs when the group members engage more directly with each other and provide support and opportunities to learn from the experiences of other members. The termination phase involves members reviewing the work that was done during the group, addressing loss issues related to the group ending, and looking ahead to ways that the learning from the group will continue.

There are several advantages for individuals who engage in group interventions. Some of these advantages for group members, identified by Toseland and Rivas (2012, p. 17), include

- receiving empathy from multiple sources,
- getting feedback from multiple points of view shared by group members,
- providing help and support to other group members,
- instilling hope from group members who have coped effectively with similar situations,
- socialization opportunities,
- normalization and removal of stigma, and
- connectedness among group members.

One of the biggest challenges for individuals who have never been a part of a group intervention is to trust that the group intervention will help them reach their own goals, not just the group goals. In Case Situation B, the group members each have unique issues but also share a common experience in having been in the military and deployed overseas. By participating in a group, the members in Case Situation B have the opportunity to experience many of the advantages of being a part of a group as they reach their own goals.

When we lead group interventions, we need to develop several core skills. In their book on group work, Alle-Corliss and Alle-Corliss (2009, pp. 50–52) identify the following core skills that group leaders need to demonstrate:

- active listening
- restating
- clarifying
- summarizing
- assessing
- questioning
- interpreting
- confronting
- reflecting feelings
- supporting
- empathizing
- facilitating
- initiating
- goal setting
- evaluating
- giving feedback
- suggesting
- protecting
- disclosing oneself
- modeling
- dealing with silence
- linking
- blocking
- terminating

We have discussed many of these skills in earlier chapters, since these skills are also critical to working with individuals and families.

REFLECTIVE LEARNING ACTIVITY

1. If you were to design a group intervention at your field internship site or with a special population, what type of group might you develop and what would your goals be for the group? Search the literature to find groups that have already been started to demonstrate positive outcomes for group members you are interested in serving.

2. Using Case Situation B, role play a group session using problem solving as your framework for the session. Start the group session with a go-round by having group members share a success and a challenge they experienced in the past week prior to moving into the problem-solving phase.

Many groups use a co-leadership model that allows group leaders to share and co-lead the group interventions. The co-leadership model provides leaders with a source of support when implementing groups. Some of the benefits of co-leadership are that members have two leaders to relate to early in the group process and to model different responses within the group session. It is important when you co-lead a group intervention that you work closely with your co-leader to be sure that the group focus is clear, that you regularly communicate about the group process, and that your roles are defined. Having a co-leader in Case Situation B might help group members to better engage with each other, since both co-leaders could share examples and provide support to different group members as needed.

REFLECTIVE LEARNING ACTIVITY

If you were to co-lead a group with another colleague, what might be some of your concerns? How would you address those concerns prior to the group getting underway, during the group, and after group sessions?

CHAPTER REVIEW QUESTIONS

1. Discuss different ways one might use to define *family* for intervention work.

2. List and discuss 3–4 reasons why it is important to engage in family interventions.

3. List the core components of the MECAmap. Discuss how you might apply this approach in working with families.

4. Identify five of the IASWG competency-based assessment skills.

5. List the five stages of group development.

6. Discuss the challenges of working with a co-facilitation model of group leadership.

7. Discuss three skills you need to develop to be an effective group leader.

REFERENCES

Alle-Corliss, L., & Alle-Corliss, R. (2009). *Group work: A practical guide to developing groups in agency settings.* Hoboken, NJ: John Wiley and Sons.

Falicov, C. J. (2014). *Latino families in therapy* (2nd ed.). New York, NY: Guilford.

Friedlander, M. L., Escudero, V., Heatherington, L., & Diamond, G. M. (2011). Alliance in couple and family therapy. *Psychotherapy, 48,* 25–35.

International Association for Social Work with Groups, Inc. (IASWG). (n.d.). *IASWG practice standards.* Retrieved August 18, 2014 from http://iaswg.org/Practice_Standards

Seabury, B. A., Seabury, B. H., & Garvin, C. D. (2011). *Foundations of interpersonal practice in social work: Promoting competence in generalist practice* (3rd ed.). Thousand Oaks, CA: SAGE.

Shadish, W. R., & Baldwin, S. A. (2003). Meta-analysis of MFT interventions. *Journal of Marriage and Family Therapy, 29,* 547–570.

Snyder, D. K., & Halford, W. K. (2012). Evidence-based couple therapy: Current status and future directions. *Journal of Family Therapy, 34,* 229–249.

Substance Abuse and Mental Health Services Administration (SAMHSA) National Registry of Evidence Based Practices and Programs (NREPP). (2014). [website]. Retrieved August 18, 2014 from http://www.nrepp.samhsa.gov/

Toseland, R., & Rivas, R. (2012). *An introduction to group work practice* (7th ed.). Boston, MA: Pearson Education.

11

Outcome Monitoring

So far, we have reviewed the process of assessment and how assessment data are used to inform the development of a change plan. The next step is outcome monitoring: the process of observing and measuring change that can be attributable to the services or interventions that are provided to the client. We use outcome monitoring to answer two very important questions: (1) Is the client making progress toward her or his change goals? and (2) Has the client reached or met each of the specified change goals? In outcome monitoring, the term *outcome* is a bit of a misnomer, because it implies an end state. For example, the Google dictionary definition of *outcome* is, in fact, "the way things turn out; a consequence." Outcome monitoring, however, actually begins when a change plan is implemented and involves measuring a client's progress toward her or his change goals throughout the duration of the intervention—not just at the end.

CHAPTER LEARNING OBJECTIVES

By the end of this chapter, you should know

- general principles of outcome monitoring,
- measurement strategies and sources of data, and
- methods of summarizing data and making inferences.

The Council on Social Work Education Educational Policy and Accreditation Standards (CSWE-EPAS) Competencies that are highlighted in more depth in this chapter include the following:

(Continued)

(Continued)

2.1.2 Apply social work ethical principles to guide professional practice.
2.1.6 Engage in research-informed practice and practice-informed research.
2.1.7 Apply knowledge of human behavior and the social environment.
2.1.10 (a–d) Engage, assess, intervene, and evaluate with individuals, families, groups, organizations, and communities.

CASE SITUATION A: TONY

Tony is an eight-year-old boy with problems regulating his emotions in his public school setting. Tony does not meet any diagnostic criteria for a mental disorder, but his emotions are concerning and disruptive to the classroom environment. Moreover, the teachers are concerned that his expressions of emotion are becoming increasingly intense and may result in long-term complications. His expressions of emotion are a problem at home, but they are not nearly as frequent or intense compared to the school environment. Provided below are a few representative examples of Tony's recent challenges with respect to managing his emotions, particularly his anger:

- screamed at a peer during recess because he was tagged out during a game they were playing
- raised his voice at the teacher during a classroom activity and then left the room without permission because he wasn't called on when his hand was raised
- made a threat of harm to another boy because he thought the other boy was trying to cut in front of him at the lunch line
- intentionally broke the pencil of a peer because she didn't want to work with him on a reading activity

CASE SITUATION B: MOLLY

Molly is a 24-year-old who was recently diagnosed with bipolar I disorder. This mental illness is characterized by extreme changes in mood and energy, which also affect many other aspects of life, including thinking and sleep. Molly tends to have more periods of high mood and energy (i.e., mania) compared to periods of low mood and energy (i.e., depression). Molly has reported a long history of having periods of mania, even though she was only recently diagnosed with the disorder. One of the triggers for a manic episode that Molly identifies is a lack of sleep. She reports that a few nights without sleeping makes her feel extremely energetic, and the increased energy further reduces her need for sleep. This relationship is somewhat paradoxical—that is, we often associate tiredness leading to less energy, not more. However, this is not uncommon among persons with bipolar I disorder.

Overview of Outcome Monitoring

Take a moment and think about what you might consider to be a fair and meaningful grading system in a college course. What specific features would you want and why? Like many students, you would probably want some type of regular feedback to know you are on the right track toward learning the information and receiving a good grade. Receiving the feedback at the end of the course is rarely helpful, because by then, it is too late—either you've learned the information and received the grade or you haven't. When you are being evaluated, you would probably prefer that the evaluation focus on what you have been assigned to learn, not material that is unrelated to the course. Finally, you probably want more than one opportunity to demonstrate your knowledge, because taking a single exam at the end of the course is difficult, stressful, and often doesn't accurately represent the progress.

The process of evaluating students in a college course has many similarities to monitoring outcomes for a change plan. Both systems are crucial for evaluating the effectiveness of the services that are being provided, whether those services are teaching or social work.

What Is the Purpose of Outcome Monitoring?

Outcome monitoring serves two primary purposes. The first purpose relates to service effectiveness. We have an obligation to provide our clients with services that work. Therefore, we want a system in place to make sure that the interventions we use are helping the client make meaningful progress (just as a grading system is necessary to evaluate whether students have successfully learned material in a college course). Furthermore, we want to have this knowledge during the course of treatment, so that if aspects of the change plan are proving ineffective, we can modify the plan immediately.

The second purpose of outcome monitoring is to ensure that clients have reached their change goals before services are terminated—just as a professor wants to ensure that students have achieved what is expected of them before the semester ends. As stated in the Code of Ethics laid out by the National Association of Social Workers ([NASW], 2008), we want to avoid abandoning clients who have not yet met their change goals, as these clients are still in need of social work services. Outcome monitoring gives us a systematic way to evaluate whether or not they have met their change goals so that we are not forced to depend upon our unreliable, often biased intuitions.

Are There Any Other Benefits to Outcome Monitoring?

Being able to adjust ineffective change plans and ensuring that clients have reached their change goals before terminating services are the primary reasons for outcome monitoring, but there are other benefits as well. One benefit is inherent to the nature of outcome monitoring: the process of measuring a client's progress can actually be considered an intervention itself, because the process of measuring is reactive. The process of measuring behaviors helps raise or maintain the client's awareness of the behaviors that they are trying to change, which is a necessary (but not sufficient) step toward changing the behaviors. In other words, ongoing measurement of behaviors can provide ongoing reminders to the client about the change direction being pursued.

Another benefit of outcome monitoring is that it provides a feedback mechanism to the client, which can be highly reinforcing. By measuring progress, outcome monitoring provides a measurement of the gap between an initial and target state. Thus, it communicates an amount of improvement, and when a client is committed to making a change, improvements can be highly motivating. For example, assume you are learning a new skill, but you have no way of knowing whether all the efforts you are investing are making a difference. Continuing to put forth all of that effort without any sense of whether you are actually learning the skill would be very difficult. Similarly, imagine you are taking a very difficult math class and you are working through numerous practice problems, but you have no way of knowing if you are getting the problems correct. This could result in significant levels of anxiety and frustration. By using a feedback mechanism—such as that provided by outcome monitoring—we help clients to see their own progress and, consequently, they are more motivated to keep putting effort into their change plan.

In summary, outcome monitoring provides a systematic way of determining whether interventions are being effective; it provides this feedback continuously throughout the duration of treatment; it ensures that we do not end treatment until the client reaches her or his change goal; and it confers other benefits, such as revealing problematic behaviors and motivating clients by highlighting improvements.

For example, in our current health and behavioral health system environment with the implementation of the Affordable Care Act, we are seeing an increased emphasis not just on outcome monitoring of individuals but also of population groups. Dashboards that capture core outcomes and inform individual practitioners and organizations on how they are meeting agreed-upon target goals for individuals with particular sets of physical or behavioral health challenges will be routine practice.

Is Outcome Monitoring Research?

Outcome monitoring draws upon essential principles and activities of research—that is, it involves measurement as well as the analysis and interpretation of data. Outcome monitoring is also systematic, which means it allows somebody else to independently review and replicate the monitoring strategy. As you become engaged in outcome monitoring, you will find many commonalities with empirical research. *Empirical research* is another way of referring to *scientific research*, which is a systematic way of gaining knowledge by direct and indirect observation. This is distinct from a more lay usage of the term *research*, whereby somebody might investigate a given topic by reviewing different sources of information on the Internet.

However, despite the commonalities and overlap with empirical research, it is important to emphasize that outcome monitoring is not research. Outcome monitoring measures different indicators of change to help determine whether the interventions provided are effective. Unlike empirical research, in outcome monitoring, we do not control for confounding factors (i.e., other factors that might also account for the observed treatment effects). This would require us to set up experiments and assign people to different types of treatment. In social work practice, this isn't possible; we want to give everybody the highest level of services, not randomly assign the services.

Therefore, while the results of an outcome monitoring system are used as evidence that the change plan for the client was effective, these inferences cannot be extended beyond this specific setting. The results of the outcomes we monitor may be suggestive that a particular intervention was effective, but we need to remain cautious with such claims—particularly when applying them more broadly—because we haven't controlled for many other factors that may have contributed to the client's success.

Is Outcome Monitoring a Type of Program Evaluation?

In the same way that outcome monitoring overlaps with empirical research, outcome monitoring also overlaps with program evaluation. For example, program evaluation uses various types of outcome data to make inferences about the effectiveness of different services. However, program evaluation is focused on a different unit of analysis; it looks at the effectiveness of a particular service, program, or organization by aggregating outcomes across clients. Alternatively, outcome monitoring focuses on the individual as the unit of analysis and only looks at results as they apply to that particular individual.

General Principles of Outcome Monitoring

Before delving into the technical aspects of outcome monitoring, we need to lay out some general principles. We use the term *general principles* here rather than *rules* because while these attributes need to be carefully considered when constructing an outcome monitoring system, they do not necessarily apply equally to every situation. That said, when it is necessary to deviate from these principles, you should have a clear rationale for doing so.

Systematic and Formal

Outcome monitoring systems are constructed so as to be systematic and formal— meaning that they are very different from the intuitive approach we use to glean more general impressions of the change process. The problem with using an intuitive and nonsystematic approach is that our impressions are subject to many serious biases that can distort our perceptions of what changes are actually occurring. For example, the research repeatedly shows that service providers of all types regularly make a confirmation bias—that is, we tend to consider evidence that supports our beliefs while rejecting evidence that refutes them. Therefore, if we believe our change plan is highly effective and have no way to systematically and formally judge its effectiveness, we will look only for evidences that show indicators of positive change and ignore any evidence that demonstrates otherwise.

Repeated Measurements

When we monitor outcomes, we need a minimum of two measurements at different points in time in order to make any inference or claim about change. The most basic approach is a pre-post design, also referred to as an *AB design*. This involves comparing baseline measurements or a measurement of a given condition before the intervention (A) with a measurement following the intervention (B). The idea behind the AB design is that we want to show a change in a particular outcome when the client receives an intervention. In other words, the *A* condition reflects the condition before the intervention, and we should expect to see a change in that condition when the intervention is delivered (*B* condition). This design is limited, because it doesn't provide any meaningful information about change over time. In other words, we don't want to wait until the end of the intervention to know whether our efforts were effective. Rather, we want to collect evidence along the way to ensure that if a change plan is not leading to the changes we are targeting, there is still enough time to make modifications to the plan.

An alternate approach involves repeated assessment before the intervention (e.g., AAA) along with repeated measures during and following the intervention (e.g., BBB). Each of the letters (A and B in the previous example) signifies a data collection time point. The actual number of time points you choose to collect data before, during, and after the intervention is a decision that you need to carefully consider. The repeated measures before the intervention are collected in order to fully understand the stability of the behavior or problem that the client is attempting to change.

Sometimes a single measurement will be sufficient, if there is good reason to believe that you have a good understanding of that particular level of behavior and know the limits of the fluctuations. For example, the health status of somebody who is particularly healthy would not require repeated measures of various physical health indicators. If he or she is physically healthy, it is unlikely we would see much change over the period of a couple weeks. However, some problems may be stable for a period and rapidly change. For example, in Case Situation B, Molly experiences episodes of mania. Some episodes can come abruptly and last a couple of weeks. In this example, we would want to have some measurements or indicators of energy levels to monitor possible fluctuations. A repeated-measures approach in this situation is much preferred to a single time point.

Consider Tony (Case Situation A), who might exhibit significant fluctuations in outbursts over time. In this situation, it would be especially important that behaviors are monitored and recorded closely throughout the provision of services. It can be difficult to sort out whether a sudden spike or drop in behavior is part of the natural fluctuations of that particular behavior or whether the behavior has been changed and is centering on a new average. The only way to understand this process is through careful, repeated measurements.

One last thing to consider is that while we want to use repeated measurements to best understand the change process, we want to be careful not to take these measurements too often. For example, if you had weekly meetings with a client and you were tracking levels of depressive symptoms, you may be inclined to have the client complete a depression inventory (e.g., Beck Depression Inventory) at each session. Doing so would meet the principle of repeated measurements. However, asking the client to complete the inventory at every session may create a burden on the client and take away valuable face-to-face time that could be used in other, more effective ways. This is why the social worker needs to carefully consider what type of behavior is being targeted and how it can best be measured.

It should be noted that many very sophisticated outcome monitoring designs exist that are formulated around the AB approach described here. This presentation should be considered a launchpad to more advanced techniques, which are often presented in stand-alone texts under the general rubric of single-subject designs.

Quality Over Quantity

In outcome monitoring, the quality of the data you collect is far more important than quantity of data. It is impossible to make good inferences from bad data. Therefore, while we emphasize the principle of repeated measurements, it is important that we pay attention to the measurement process to ensure that we can make accurate inferences about change from the data that are collected. Unfortunately, it is very difficult to know for sure whether our data have problems that might distort such inferences. Thus, it is essential to take care in setting up the measurement procedures and to consider any problems that might arise.

Whenever you see that the data collection process will be burdensome to the client, consider that an indicator of poor-quality data. For example, it can be very difficult for clients to take recordings of particular behaviors throughout a given day. If you are interested in monitoring change at a day-to-day level, a better strategy might be to have the client record information about the target behavior once a day, preferably at the same time every day. For example, in Case Situation B (Molly), the monitoring record could be completed one time every morning. The accuracy of the data could be enhanced by ensuring that the record is completed shortly after waking up, as the accuracy of recalling events diminishes over time and sometimes the client may forget to make the recording if it is put off too long. Be sure to always consider any possible barriers the client might encounter when asked to provide recordings that will be used for outcome monitoring, and look for ways that you might be able to overcome these barriers.

Another useful strategy is to think about what the data will actually look like and how they can be used to make an inference about change. In fact, it can be very useful to create some fictitious data in order to evaluate the measurement strategy that you are considering. Then consider different scenarios that may occur—what might the data look like if change goals are met or not met? Will you be able to make such inferences from the data?

Relevance to Change Goals

Outcome monitoring systems must measure results that are directly related to change goals set out for the client. Everything that we measure should be directly tied to the change goals being pursued. One easy mistake is confusing *process measures* with *outcome measures*. Process measures evaluate a client's engagement and satisfaction with our services. These are important factors in achieving goals, but they are merely the conditions that promote change—they aren't indicators that change has actually occurred. As an example, Molly (Case Situation B) may be very satisfied with the treatment she is receiving, but this certainly does not mean she is improving (e.g., fewer and less intense manic episodes). In order to successfully set up a system for outcome monitoring, we must use measures that reflect whether or not the change has actually occurred. Thus, we would want to have some evidence that Molly is having fewer and less intense manic episodes as a result of treatment. At minimum, we would need to have a baseline and follow-up measurement.

That being said, it is a very good idea to incorporate process measures into the services you provide, particularly if you are unsure about whether the client is remaining engaged and satisfied with those services. Be sure that the process measures do not overshadow the outcomes that you ultimately need to measure to evaluate a client's success or failure at achieving their change goal.

Accuracy of Measurement Tools

This may sound obvious, but it is important to make sure that the tool you have selected to measure change over time is designed to collect that particular measurement. For instance, you wouldn't use a ruler to measure how much liquid your water bottle can hold. Certain assessment tools gather information about how often behaviors occur over a lifetime, which are useful for baseline measures but not for measuring change over time. One example is the CAGE questionnaire, which is commonly used to assess alcohol-related problems (Mayfield, McLeod, & Hall, 1974). The questions include the following:

1. Have you ever felt you needed to **C**ut down on your drinking?

2. Have people **A**nnoyed you by criticizing your drinking?

3. Have you ever felt **G**uilty about drinking?

4. Have you ever felt you needed a drink first thing in the morning (**E**ye-opener) to steady your nerves or to get rid of a hangover?

These are *lifetime* questions, meaning that the questions capture a lifetime occurrence of a behavior. Thus, if a change goal was to reduce alcohol consumption, this would be an improper tool to use for outcome monitoring, because there is no way that the answers to these lifetime questions could reflect a reduction in alcohol use. To evaluate a measurement tool you are considering, it is helpful to think about the different ways the client might exhibit a particular change in behavior over time and to then consider whether or not the measurement strategy will be able to capture and accurately communicate data that would reflect their full range of behavior.

Measurement Types and Data Collection

The framework of the outcome monitoring system we have described is designed to answer two fundamental questions: (1) Is the client making progress toward the change goals? and (2) Has the client met or reached the change goals? To answer these questions, you need relevant, useful, reliable data as well as appropriate measurement types. Think carefully in advance about whether the data you are considering collecting and the measurements you intend to use can address these questions and whether they can capture the full range of behavior.

There are a number of different methods of data collection as well as measurement types. While research texts provide more extensive coverage on this topic, we will highlight only the aspects that are relevant to outcome monitoring in practice.

Measurement Types

Dichotomous Ratings

Dichotomous ratings are ratings that indicate a given condition when there are only two different states (e.g., yes/no, present/absent, complete/incomplete). Dichotomous ratings are useful to judge the completion of discrete tasks. For example, a dichotomous rating would be practical to determine whether or not somebody has completed a job application. Dichotomous ratings are also ideal to set out basic tasks that need to be completed, such as "Client will submit three job applications by November 13, 2014." Keep in mind that this type of rating provides only basic either/or information and cannot convey anything about quality. This may or may not be of concern but should be a consideration when using this type of rating.

Monitoring Records

Monitoring records are recordings that clients use in their day-to-day activities, typically in order to monitor a particular behavior. The benefit of monitoring records is that they can also serve as an intervention strategy. Because measurement is reactive, monitoring for a particular behavior can sometimes help a client become more aware of the behavior, and the awareness itself may lead to behavior change. Monitoring records can be created and used for almost any type of behavior. Although many different monitoring records already exist, you will likely have to tailor or create a new one for your client to ensure you are getting the proper measurements.

Take a moment and revisit the case situation (Melissa) that was presented in Chapter 8. Melissa is a 28-year-old female who struggles with symptoms of schizophrenia, particularly auditory hallucinations. Her treatment goals are to increase her capacity to effectively cope with these symptoms. The monitoring record presented in Figure 11.1 records information about various aspects of her hallucinations.

This monitoring record was used with a client who experienced periodic episodes over the course of a week, typically once a day. The client was encouraged to complete the record as close to the occurrence of voices as possible, but the client typically reported completing the record at night before going to bed. It is ideal—but not always possible—for monitoring records to be completed as close to the behavioral occurrence as possible so the data are not affected by any problems with recall. While this monitoring record is appropriate for the client who experienced periodic episodes over the course of a week, this record would not be particularly useful for somebody who experienced chronic voices over the course of a single day. It is formatted to capture one episode per day and therefore would not properly capture multiple occurrences of voices.

This particular monitoring record could be useful throughout the treatment process. For example, at the beginning of treatment, it can be used to develop a better understanding of the factors that give rise to hallucinations (e.g., triggering events). The monitoring record can also reveal how much the client actively uses a given coping strategy as well as the effectiveness of each given coping strategy. Collecting these data can be extremely useful for helping determine whether the services provided are effective. In absence of these data (or other systematically collected data), the social worker is limited to unsystematic appraisals that may or may not be accurate. A data-driven systematic approach certainly reduces possible biases and allows for independent verification of results.

Figure 11.1   Monitoring Record Example

	Mon	Tues	Wed	Thurs	Fri	Sat	Sun
What situation triggered the voices?							
How distressing were the voices? (1 = Not distressing, 10 = Very distressing)							
What coping strategy did you use?							
How well did the coping strategy work? (1 = Extremely well, 10 = Not at all)							

Adapted from Perron and Munson, 2006.

REFLECTIVE LEARNING ACTIVITY

Let's look back to Case Situation B, presented at the beginning of the chapter. Assume that you and Molly have worked together to put together a change plan. One mutually agreed-upon goal of Molly's treatment is establishing a sleep-wake cycle, aimed at achieving at least eight hours of sleep each night. Construct a monitoring record for Molly that would be used to collect the best information for monitoring her sleep routines. Such a monitoring record should be applicable before, during, and after the intervention to show change over time. Use the following bullets to help guide the construction of your record:

- Will the client be able to easily understand and complete the record?
- When should the client complete it?
- Should other behaviors that may be relevant to sleep also be monitored as part of this record (e.g., time and amount of caffeine consumed)?
- Will the monitoring record provide all the essential information? Will the data show whether the intervention is changing behavior or whether the goal has been achieved?

Behavioral Counts

Behavioral counts are closely associated with monitoring records. They involve operationalizing a particular behavior and recording the frequency of the behavior. *Operationalizing* means to specifically define the behavior that is to be counted in order to identify exactly what that behavior is and what it isn't. This might seem straightforward, but it is actually quite a complex task. For example, let's consider Case Situation A (Tony), which was presented at the beginning of the chapter. Tony is a young boy who is having challenges managing his emotions in the classroom environment, particularly his anger. Part of the job of the social worker would be to help Tony reduce the frequency and intensity of anger outbursts.

In this example, let's focus on the frequency. One way of doing this would be to perform a count of the number of anger outbursts that Tony has in a given timeframe. In order to count the anger outbursts, you first need to define exactly what an anger outburst is. The anger outburst must be defined in a way that will allow many people to apply the definition and reliably collect the same information. This would mean answering the following questions: What is the particular threshold that would constitute an expression of anger? What constitutes the beginning and end of an anger outburst—in other words, when has one outburst ended and a new one begun? These questions may seem straightforward, but they are very complex.

One way to tackle this problem is to begin with a set of representative examples of the target behavior (i.e., anger outbursts). More specifically, this would involve creating a list of specific incidents involving that particular individual (see the case situation for examples). It is important to think about *representative* behaviors or common patterns of the behavior. The idea is to establish a definition that can be used to determine what is and is not considered an anger outburst. Using this list, we can try to find some commonalities across the examples that would help us establish an explicit working definition of an anger outburst. From this, we see that a raised voice, intentionally breaking rules (e.g., leaving the classroom without permission), threats or acts of physical violence, and destruction of property are part of the set of micro-behaviors that can be used to define what an anger outburst is for Tony. It is important to emphasize that definitions must be tailored to the individual, as another individual might have a fundamentally different expression of anger outbursts that would necessarily warrant a different definition.

REFLECTIVE LEARNING ACTIVITY

Go back to earlier chapters in this book and select a case situation where you think a specific behavior change might be the focus of treatment. Provide an operational definition that could be used to provide a specific count of the behavior. Add sufficient detail to the definition to ensure that it is clear what behavior is counted and what is not counted.

Standardized Measures

Standardized measures are found in the research literature and go by many different names, including *inventories*, *assessments*, and *instruments*. We use the term *standardized scale* to refer broadly to an existing instrument that is used for collecting data in a standardized fashion. By *standardized*, we mean that the method for collecting and summarizing the data is done according to a fixed set of rules. For example, the Beck Depression Inventory (Beck, Steer, & Brown, 1996) is considered a standardized scale, because the questions listed in the questionnaire are asked every time the questionnaire is administered. Each item has corresponding response options, requiring the respondent (i.e., the client) to select the option that most accurately reflects her or his experience. The following item is an example from the Beck Depression Inventory:

Punishment Feelings

0   I don't feel I am being punished.

1   I feel I may be punished.

2   I expect to be punished.

3   I feel I am being punished.

The questionnaire also has a fixed scoring method. That is, a set of instructions are provided to exactly describe how to compute the scores based on the responses, along with guidelines for interpreting the overall score.

Standardized measures often have evidences of validity and reliability, which are very important in establishing the quality of a measure. *Validity* refers to the types of inferences that can be made from a measure. For example, validity evidence for the Beck Depression Inventory would support its use as a measure of depressive symptoms. *Reliability*, on the other hand, describes the consistency of the measurements. Again, using the Beck Depression Inventory as an example, it is said to be a reliable measure because it can be administered by different people or on different occasions (within a relatively short interval) and the scores will be approximately the same. Validity and reliability evidence helps to build our confidence in the measure and, consequently, our interpretation of the data that are collected. For example, assume a social worker is conducting a rating of a client's social skills. The ratings would be considered reliable if they were consistent with another social worker's assessment of those same skills. This is a form of inter-rater reliability, which is one of many different kinds of reliability. The topics of validity and reliability are important with respect to assessment and monitoring of outcomes. At the same time, validity and reliability are complex issues that are covered in much greater detail in research courses. Students are strongly encouraged to review this content, which is contained in nearly every social work research methods text.

An unstandardized method of assessing depression would involve asking different kinds of questions (often open-ended questions) to understand depression. Open-ended questions are very useful for gathering contextual data to better understand the experience of the client and to confirm a diagnosis. However, this unstandardized approach does not lend itself well to monitoring outcomes, because we are relying on our impressions for assessing change as opposed to objective indicators. The impressionistic approach is subject to various biases that can distort your assessment of the change process. One such bias, which was mentioned earlier in this chapter, is the *confirmation bias*. This bias involves looking for or accepting evidence that supports one's beliefs while discarding contradictory evidence. Thus, if you believe that the client is making progress toward her or his goals, you might look for evidence that supports your belief and unconsciously ignore evidence that may speak against the belief. Standardized measures are important to ensure systematic assessment of the change process.

Standardized scales can be found in professional journals such as *Research on Social Work Practice, Social Work,* and *Social Work Research.* Databases also exist exclusively for measures, such as *Mental Measures Yearbook* and *Health and Psychosocial Instruments.* Keep in mind that most of these sources can be accessed only with a subscription, typically through a university library system.

Constructed Scales

Constructed scales are measures that are constructed by the social worker and tailored for a given client's change plan. For example, the monitoring record shown in Figure 11.1 includes two constructed scales:

How distressing were the voices? (1 = Not distressing, 10 = Very distressing)

How well did the coping strategy work? (1 = Extremely well, 10 = Not at all)

Scales can be constructed for any change goals, and a notable advantage is that they are tailored specifically to the client's individual change plan—which supports the core principle of tailoring change plans to each client's needs.

Despite this important benefit, it is important to be aware of the limitations of constructed scales. Foremost, scale construction may appear rather straightforward, but it is actually a complicated process. Even small changes to response options can yield different results, thus leading to fundamentally different interpretations of the change process. For this reason, numerous texts are devoted specifically to the practice of scale construction. Ultimately with constructed scales, we do not have any information about their validity and reliability, so we can never be quite certain whether they are measuring the change process that we think we are measuring.

The foregoing limitations of constructed scales are quite significant, but these limitations do not mean that you should completely avoid constructing scales. Rather, it is much better to thoroughly examine other options, particularly the scientific literature, and see whether a standardized scale already exists. If you do use constructed scales, be sure that they are used in a consistent fashion, the same way as you would if they were standardized. It is also a good idea to avoid creating measures that involve asking multiple questions and then adding the responses together, as there are very specific procedures and rules that must be followed when doing so. If such procedures and rules are not followed, the data you collect will be inaccurate and will result in ineffective outcome monitoring.

Data Collection

There are two primary methods of collecting data during outcome monitoring. One method is self-reporting, which involves the client recording information about themselves. The other method is observation, which involves someone else recording information about the client. One modality is not necessarily better than the other; the usefulness of each depends upon what is being measured.

Self-Reports

Self-reports refer to the client as the source of information. For example, any questionnaire or measurement strategy that asks the client to provide a response or a particular piece of information is considered a self-report. A monitoring record is also an example of a self-report. Self-reports are ubiquitous in both social work research and practice. It is important to be aware of the strengths and limitations of self-report measurement strategies.

Self-reports have many advantages over other data sources. Most importantly, a self-report recognizes the importance of the client's perspective of the change process and ensures that this perspective is used to inform decision making. Self-report measures are also quick and easy to administer, which adds efficiency to the process of monitoring outcomes.

Despite these strengths, it is important to recognize a few important limitations. For example, self-reports of behaviors should occur close in time to the actual behavior. In other words, if we are attempting to monitor alcohol consumption, it is important that we minimize the time between the consumption and the recording of the amount of behavior. The more time that occurs between the behavior and the recordings, the more likely there will be errors in recall. Also, social desirability may affect the self-reported behavior of a client. Social desirability refers to persons responding in a way consistent with the expectations that others have of them, even though it might not be consistent with the actual behavior. For example, continuing with the example of alcohol consumption, a client may feel a sense to respond in a socially desirable manner and underreport the amount of alcohol she or he actually consumed.

The limitations of social desirability certainly do not preclude the use of self-report measures. In fact, you will likely use them quite often in your outcome monitoring efforts. The limitations of self-reports suggest the need to look for other data sources to triangulate the assessment of the change process—that is, to find other sources of data that can help reveal the actual changes that are or are not being made. It is also important to create an environment that minimizes social desirability. For example, normalizing setbacks in the change process is probably the most helpful step in accomplishing this.

Observation

Observational methods involve someone else making systematic observations or recordings of an individual. This method of data collection is appropriate for behaviorally oriented goals as opposed to changes involving specific thoughts or emotions. For example, referring to the case situations at the beginning of the chapter, it would be more feasible to measure Tony's behavior using observational methods, given that he is in a classroom setting and already being monitored. However, it would not be feasible to monitor Molly's behavior with observational methods. When relying on observers, it is important that if the client is an adult, you have full consent and agreement from the adult. Likewise, a parent or guardian should provide authorization for a minor.

When using observational methods, it is crucial that the observer has a very clear operational definition of what behavior is to be recorded and, ideally, some sort of training to help clarify what does and does not constitute the target behavior. For example, imagine that you are performing your behavioral count for Tony (Case Situation A), who was having anger outbursts in the classroom. In this instance, you might ask the teacher to provide recordings of Tony's anger outbursts. However, as was mentioned before, it is very important that the teacher is able to accurately identify an anger outburst as you have defined it. Under your definition, Tony's foot stomping does not count as an anger outburst, but if the teacher does not fully understand your definition of an anger outburst, she or he may record the foot-stomping incident, ultimately leaving you with inaccurate data.

In situations such as these, where you have a third-party observer, it can some-times be helpful to ask the observer to help you to precisely define the behavior. However, this definition still needs to be understandable to others apart from that specific observer. (Consider our example again: What if the teacher got sick and a substitute teacher needed to record Tony's anger outbursts? She or he would need to be able to identify the anger outbursts in exactly the same way as the original teacher for the data to be accurate.) When you have a definition of a behavior that allows different observers to yield the same data in a consistent manner, this measure is said to have good evidence of reliability.

Administrative Records

In some situations, administrative records may be available for the purposes of outcome monitoring. Most likely, these sorts of records would be reports from an insti-tutional setting, such as a school (e.g., truancy reports) or the legal system (e.g., arrest records), where behaviors that reach a particular level receive formal documentation. However, the use of administrative records as a data source is more the exception than the norm. There are two primary reasons for this. Firstly, many of the behaviors that social workers address cannot be understood very well through administrative records. The records are typically not developed to support social work services, so they often contain limited useful information. Secondly, social workers can encounter many bar-riers when attempting to access these records, which further limits their usefulness.

REFLECTIVE LEARNING ACTIVITY

Consider a skill in your own life that you would like to acquire. Be sure this is a skill that requires some type of practice in order to gain mastery of it. What would be indicators or measures of improvement that could be used to demonstrate acquisition of the skill? Consider the advantages and disadvantages of the various measurement strategies. In other words, what types of data would provide you with the best evidence that you are acquiring the target skill?

REFLECTIVE LEARNING ACTIVITY

Review some of the case situations presented earlier in the chapter. Identify multiple out-come monitoring strategies and sources of data that you think would be most appropriate for a given goal. Consider the relative strengths and weaknesses of each approach, and then select the strategy that you think would be the best approach. Provide an explicit rationale for your decision.

Summarizing Data and Making Inferences

As we collect and measure data, it is important that we have a mechanism in place to help us summarize our findings so that we can make inferences. Whenever possible, try to summarize data using a graphical display. This is not only one of the most straightforward ways to display data, it is also one of the easiest ways to facilitate the client's understanding of the data.

Constructing graphs involves plotting time on the x-axis (horizontal) and then plotting the measure of behavior on the y-axis (vertical). Figure 11.2 provides a possible graphical display of Tony's anger outbursts (Case Situation A). This particular figure includes the baseline assessment phase and a point at which the intervention was implemented.

After we summarize the data, we want to look for trends from which we can draw inferences—in particular, patterns of behavior or functioning that have some level of consistency. Be cautious of making inferences from data that are highly variable, as this type of pattern is difficult to use when attempting to predict future behavior. Also keep in mind that there will always be some natural variability in all behaviors. Fluctuations (incremental increases or decreases) in any particular dimension of a behavior—such as frequency, intensity, or latency—are expected; these are essentially random variations that will average out over time. Therefore, what we are really looking for is an understanding of the client's average level of behavior or functioning and whether that average level changes.

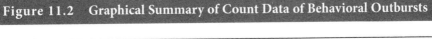

Figure 11.2   Graphical Summary of Count Data of Behavioral Outbursts

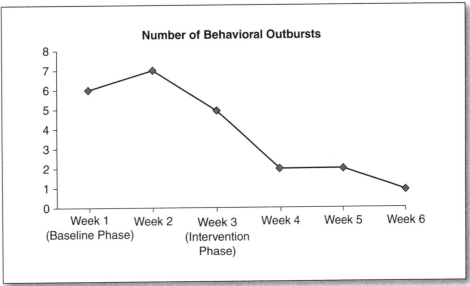

Common Measurement Questions

Do I measure everything?

No. It is not possible to measure everything; therefore, choosing what to measure is very important. Foremost, you are looking for measurement opportunities with the highest levels of validity—that is, those measurable aspects of the change plan that are essential to communicating whether change has occurred.

If I select an outcome measure and find that it isn't working well, can I change it?

This is a difficult question for a couple reasons. Foremost, we want to ensure we have the best data to inform our decisions, which ultimately includes asking questions: Should a goal be revised because we aren't seeing the expected changes? Did the client meet the target goal, and can we therefore terminate treatment? If we don't have good data, it is very difficult to make good decisions, so if you find that you aren't collecting good data, this suggests the need to make a change. However, it is important to keep in mind that the data you are collecting with the new measure won't be comparable to the old measure. There is no straightforward conversion, similar to what we have from kilometers to miles or kilograms to pounds; the measurement process is essentially starting over again the moment you switch to a different measure. The best approach is to avoid this situation by being very thoughtful and careful when you are selecting a measure initially. As you gain experience monitoring outcomes, you will acquire greater insight into the measurement strategy that will be most appropriate for the goals you choose to formally monitor.

If I find a standardized measure—that is, a questionnaire or inventory—that already exists, can I change it to fit my needs?

It is not recommended that you change or adapt an existing standardized measure to meet your needs. This is because a measure that is published in the scientific field has (presumably) been systematically tested to establish evidence for its validity and reliability. When you make changes or adaptations, it is really considered a *new* measure, and the validity and reliability are unknown.

How do I find standardized measures?

As previously stated, standardized measures are found in the scientific literature. As a student at a college or university, you have library resources that give you access to a wide range of journals. Social workers in the community, on the other hand, typically don't have the same level of access, given that subscriptions to journals are typically cost prohibitive to individuals. However, a new kind of publishing model referred to as *open access* makes journal articles freely available, so you can look in these journals to find published standardized scales. Additionally, recent policies of the National Institutes of Health have mandated that research that is funded by the federal government should be made freely available one year following publication (U.S. Department of Health and Human Services, National Institutes of Health Public Access, 2008). If you are interested in issues of health, mental health, and addictions, these freely available articles can be found using the advanced search features on PubMed, which is a database governed by the U.S. National Library of Medicine and the National Institutes of Health.

My outcome measures for a client involve self-reports. I'm not sure if my client is being truthful in reporting. What should I do?

This is a tricky situation, because good data are essential to determining whether or not the client is making meaningful progress toward her or his goals. It is difficult, if not impossible, to accurately assess change without good data. Your objective is to create a context that will encourage a client to remain actively engaged in the change process and to provide reliable self-reports. This is best accomplished by using the various strategies outlined in the earlier chapter on engagement (Chapter 5). To reiterate a few key points, it is important to emphasize that setbacks or relapses of undesirable behaviors are a normal part of the change process.

It can also be helpful to talk with the client about setbacks early in the change process in order to help the client recognize that change takes time and that perfection is not realistic with any goal. Then, when setbacks do occur, it is important that you have a heightened sense of awareness of how you respond. Expressing disappointment of any sort will almost always result in more harm than benefit to the therapeutic relationship. Ultimately, you have an obligation to respect the client's self-determination and to recognize that your efforts as a social worker are to create conditions that will increase their likelihood of reaching change goals.

CHAPTER REVIEW QUESTIONS

1. What is the purpose of outcome monitoring?

2. How is outcome monitoring similar to research? How is outcome monitoring different than research?

3. What are some of the general principles of outcome monitoring?

4. What are some of the different types of measurements that can be taken as part of an outcome monitoring system?

5. What are some of the advantages and limitations of the different measurement types?

REFERENCES

Beck, A. T., Steer, R. A., & Brown, G. K. (1996). *Manual for the Beck Depression Inventory-II.* San Antonio, TX: Psychological Corporation.

Mayfield, D., McLeod, G., & Hall, P. (1974). The CAGE questionnaire: Validation of a new alcoholism screening instrument. *American Journal of Psychiatry, 131*(10), 1121–1123.

National Association of Social Workers (NASW). (2008). *Code of Ethics of the National Association of Social Workers.* Washington, DC: NASW Press.

Perron, B., & Munson, M. (2006). Coping with voices: A group approach for managing auditory hallucinations. *American Journal of Psychiatric Rehabilitation, 9*(3), 241–258.

U.S. Department of Health and Human Services, National Institutes of Health Public Access. (2008). *NIH Public Access Policy.* Retrieved December 15, 2013 from http://publicaccess .nih.gov/

Lifelong Learning and Professional Development Over the Life Course

Lifelong learning is the process of self-directed and individualized education throughout the life span. It may seem premature to talk about lifelong learning, considering that you are still a social work student, but it is important to give the topic serious attention at this point for a number of reasons. Foremost, our knowledge of the various systems in which we provide social work services and the persons for whom we provide services are continually changing. Even though you will be acquiring professional practice experience, your knowledge can quickly become outdated if you fail to remain current with the best available knowledge. This will undoubtedly have very serious negative implications for both your career and your clients.

Your social work training represents the point of departure for a process of lifelong learning. Having an understanding of what lifelong learning is can ensure a seamless transition from your formal and structured training to one that is self-directed and individualized. Although it may seem as if there are really no wrong turns you can take when pursuing advanced educational opportunities, all opportunities involve some type of opportunity cost. More specifically, the time and money spent on any given opportunity will preclude the pursuit of some other opportunity. And, given the range of opportunities available following graduation and a finite amount of time to participate in them, it is critical that you select those activities that will be of maximum benefit to your career and your clients.

In this chapter, we provide you with a framework to help you think about the concept of lifelong learning. We do this by talking about your current identity and your future identity as a social worker. Although the focus of this chapter is on a professional identity, we do not refrain from talking about your personal identity, interests, and aspirations. In fact, the distinction between a professional and personal identity is much more arbitrary than distinct. That is, you will soon discover that career-related decisions (representing your professional identity) often have influence on your personal life—and vice versa. For example, the type of work you do and the money you earn influences the freedoms you have in your personal life. And the freedoms you seek in your personal life will influence the manner in which you shape your career. Thus, we think that a broad conceptualization of identity is necessary in the context of lifelong learning.

In this chapter, we begin by engaging you in an activity to help you define your current identity and envision what you want in your future identity. We then offer a number of different strategies and activities that can help you establish a trajectory to move you toward this future identity. We consider lifelong learning to be necessary in continually shaping and revising your future identity. The specific strategies we cover as part of the lifelong learning process include the use of supervision and mentorship, remaining current with the best available research, creating professional resource libraries, selecting continuing education activities, and building and using professional networks.

Your Professional Identity

We define a professional identity as the integration of your knowledge, skills, experiences, and values that ultimately determine your practice of social work. It is influenced by the various life experiences that have preceded your social work training as well as all the knowledge and experiences you are acquiring as a social work student. Your future identity can be viewed in a similar way, integrating knowledge, skills, experiences, and values. However, the future identity is one that you envision for yourself in the future—Who do you want to be? The future identity can be projected out as near or as far as you like, and the concept of lifelong learning is the bridge between these two identities. The greater the clarity you have on who you currently are (i.e., current identity) and who you want to be (i.e., future identity), the better prepared you are to select activities to bridge this gap.

Defining Your Current Professional Identity

As previously stated, your current identity represents the integration of your knowledge, skills, experiences, and values that ultimately determine your practice of social work. An understanding of your current identity requires ongoing critical self-reflection and assessment, as it is dynamic—that is, continually evolving. One of the most practical ways of defining your current identity is through your resume and an electronic portfolio, also referred to as an *e-portfolio*. E-portfolios are not as common as resumes, but they are becoming more relevant with the ongoing development of technology. E-portfolios are a collection of electronic evidences related to your knowledge acquisition and practice experiences (often projects/examples of your work) and include specific reflections on the tasks completed, the skills demonstrated, and lessons learned. They articulate the importance of your work/experience and how this experience impacted you and those involved. E-portfolios also include an "About Me" section, which requires that you reflect and develop your professional philosophy statement that will help others to see what has motivated you to become a social worker. Because this type of portfolio uses an electronic format—manuscripts, blogs, photos, videos, and so on—this further exhibits an individual's skills, knowledge, and other achievements beyond what can be reasonably contained in a resume. If you are unfamiliar with e-portfolios, we encourage you to review the companion website for this book to further orient you to this important tool.

Although your resume and e-portfolio create an incomplete picture of your professional identity, they are very important. In fact, they can be considered a public definition of your identity, as these are the primary tools for conveying to others who you are in the context of employment and promotion. From a practical standpoint, your resume and e-portfolio can serve as an assessment tool to help identify the critical gaps in knowledge and skills—that is, the gaps that are necessary to achieving your future identity. As described later in this chapter, we encourage you to utilize your supervisors and mentors to help identify critical gaps and select learning opportunities that can be of maximum benefit. The value of these tools can be realized only when they are regularly updated and critically evaluated and measured against our future identity. Let's now turn our attention to defining our future identity.

Defining Your Future Professional Identity

As previously described, your future identity represents your aspirations as a social worker at a future point in time. Similar to your current identity, your future identity is continually changing. As a starting point for defining your future identity, we encourage you to project yourself five to ten years into the future, as this is a point of time following graduation when you will have established yourself in a career as a professional social worker. We encourage you to define your future identify with both breadth and depth. With respect to breadth, you should think about your life as a social worker and the interplay between the personal and professional aspects of your life. Then, bring as much detail to this definition as you can. The reflective learning activity below contains various questions to help promote this type of thinking. As your current identity evolves, so will your future identity, so neither identity should be considered a static or unchangeable definition. The ultimate goal is to clarify who you want to be at this future point in time in order to select the proper activities to effectively bridge your current and future identity.

REFLECTIVE LEARNING ACTIVITY

This activity presents a series of questions to help you think critically about the definition of your future identity as a social worker. We encourage you to project yourself five to ten years into the future, thinking broadly about the type of life you want to have as a social worker. Try to incorporate as many details as possible, recognizing that the identity you foresee is one that will evolve over time. By incorporating as much detail as possible, you are better positioned to engage in the lifelong learning activities that will help ensure a trajectory from your current identity to the one you ultimately want to achieve.

1. Where do you want to be employed? Is there a particular geographic area? Urban, suburban, or rural?

2. What type of social work do you want to practice?

3. What populations do you want to serve?

4. What is your desired level of autonomy or flexibility in your work? Do you want to work completely independently (e.g., private practice)? Or do you want to be part of a community agency?

5. What is your target annual income?

6. Where do you want to live relative to the work you do?

7. How much stability in your employment do you want?

8. What is your understanding of family and work life balance?

9. Are you considering the possibility of doctoral level education?

Identity Development and Lifelong Learning

Thus far, this chapter has focused on defining your current and future identities. The idea is to help you gain a better understanding of where you currently are in your professional development and to purposefully select learning activities that will help you achieve your professional goals. We consider lifelong learning as the critical bridge between your current identity and future identity. In this section, we review a number of different lifelong learning strategies that can be used to create this bridge. We encourage you to explore how the strategies described can be used together in creating a comprehensive lifelong learning plan.

Supervision and Mentorship

Supervisors and mentors can be important assets to your immediate professional development needs, helping to shape and clarify your current identity. They can also make meaningful contributions to your future identity, provided that the discussions and activities you participate in with them are purposefully directed toward lifelong learning. One of the potential challenges that you may encounter with respect to receiving supervision and mentorship is that the quality can be highly variable. Therefore, in order to maximize the potential learning opportunities within the context of supervision and mentorship, it is necessary for you to have a firm understanding of what your supervisors and mentors can offer as well as how you can help shape both the structure and content of the supervision and mentorship sessions. Within this section, we provide an overview of the different yet overlapping roles of supervisors and mentors. We offer various suggestions that can help you maximize supervision and mentorship sessions in ways that will be of benefit to both your current identity and future identity.

Supervision

Social work supervision involves some type of fixed-schedule meetings with another professional who has more experience and a higher degree of responsibility within your organization. The purpose of supervision is to ensure that you are acquiring the necessary skills to deliver competent and ethical social work services. The supervisory process also includes evaluating your performance when you are demonstrating your skills, which typically involves the completion of an annual performance appraisal/evaluation. You will be introduced to the concept of supervision early in your social work training, and it will extend far into your period of professional development after you graduate. The type and amount of supervision you receive will be dependent on a variety of factors, including (but not limited to) your social work program, the agency in which you are working, and various licensing or accreditation bodies. There is an absence of guidelines that dictate the content and structure of supervision, which can result in significant variability in the quality of supervision provided. However, the absence of guidelines also means you have the opportunity to help influence the content and structure in a way that is maximally beneficial to your needs. Thus, it is important that your role as a supervisee is active, thoughtful, and deliberate. By taking a passive role in guiding the process, you are at significant risk of losing important learning opportunities.

It is often the case that you will be assigned a supervisor simply due to resource constraints provided by the agency in which you are employed. However, if you are given the opportunity to select a supervisor, it is important to carefully consider the fit of your supervision needs with the style of your supervisor. Think about her or his professional background, areas of expertise, expectations of supervisees, and overall style. These characteristics should be considered vis-à-vis your current and future identity.

The lack of choice in supervisors should not be regarded as a problem or barrier in your lifelong learning. In fact, having a supervisor with a style other than what you are seeking can have important advantages. That is, such a person can add diversity in beliefs and knowledge, ultimately expanding your own way of thinking. In this case, it is important to spend the necessary time with the assigned supervisor to better understand what she or he can offer.

Throughout your career, you will have many opportunities to consult others about your practice. This consultation can take several forms that may include interdisciplinary consultation and peer consultation. Interdisciplinary consultation occurs when you are discussing cases with various members of your organization who have different education, training, and perspectives than you (e.g., nurses, psychologists, physicians). This form of consultation can provide you with an appreciation of the scope of practice involved when working with a client and also is a vehicle for you to share your social work expertise. It also provides a means of ensuring that the client's change plan is an open process whereby all disciplines involved are on the same page and work to assist the client in achieving their change goals, many which could have an interdisciplinary focus (e.g., hypertension, obesity).

Another popular form of consultation involves establishing a peer consultation group whereby you meet on a regular basis with a small group of trusted social work colleagues to share and discuss cases. These groups typically meet every couple of weeks, and supervisory-level staff are not involved because the goal is for you to feel comfortable to share challenges you are experiencing and solutions you may have implemented that you would like feedback on that is non-performance-based. This type of group is particularly helpful and may be established to focus solely on ethical challenges and/or dilemmas that social workers face. Becoming a member of a peer consultation group is also a valuable way for you to establish professional networks. However, it is important for you to remember that you need to be deliberate when setting up or joining a peer consultation group, because you want to ensure that you are joining with members whose opinions you value and trust, who have demonstrated their practice wisdom and expertise, and who have an open attitude about learning. This group needs to have a give-and-take attitude, where the responsibilities are equally shared and each member takes a turn facilitating the process. The stages of forming this type of group usually mirror the stages involved when establishing client-focused groups, and developing group cohesion takes work and time. This type of group can also play a valued role should a client situation get called into question or when a client makes a formal complaint. The fact that the social worker involved received supervision and/or peer consultation can help support the actions that were taken in the case.

Your receipt of supervision can mirror many of the processes of social work services. For example, you will need to allow time early in the process of supervision to establish rapport with the supervisor, much like you do with your clients. It is also important that you discuss—and preferably write—very specific objectives and goals for the supervision process. The objectives and goals can be revisited and revised over time, but the general idea is to ensure you have a road map that explicates the direction of the supervision process. Furthermore, having a set of objectives and goals can help you monitor outcomes of the supervision process—much like the process of measuring outcomes with your clients. Your resume and e-portfolio can provide an important backdrop in bringing clarity to what you want to accomplish.

We strongly recommend that your supervision sessions organized around an agenda that you develop collaboratively with your supervisor. The agenda should be set prior to the session and allow sufficient time to ensure that the content of the sessions balances the interests and needs of both you and your supervisor. An agenda is important because it can help ensure that each session addresses your short-term and long-term needs. And when agenda items are not sufficiently covered during the session, they can be added to the agenda of subsequent supervision sessions.

The use of an agenda, of course, assumes that your supervisor is open to setting an agenda. Some people may consider an agenda a limiting factor in the flexibility of the supervision session. While this may be true to a certain degree, it is hardly a trade-off to ensuring that time is appropriated for everything that needs to be accomplished during the session. An agenda should be developed with enough time prior to the session that each party can adequately prepare.

When establishing an agenda, it is important to balance the amount of time devoted to specific issues that arise in the practice context with the need to clarify and develop your current and future identities. We suggest that you establish an agenda framework that gives each supervision session significant time to devote to items that promote lifelong learning. The reflective learning activity below contains various ideas for agenda items oriented around the concept of lifelong learning.

REFLECTIVE LEARNING ACTIVITY

Read the following agenda items to consider how they may help advance your knowledge, skills, and experience. Then try to think of other agenda items that could also move you closer to your future identity. Share your ideas with other students to build a comprehensive list.

1. Comprehensive review of your resume and e-portfolio: As previously stated, your resume and e-portfolio provide a public definition of your current identity. It is important to receive critical feedback to help identify various gaps in your knowledge and skills. Your supervisor can help you acquire various experiences within the organization to address these gaps.

2. Discussion of your future identity: Spend time discussing your ideas of your future identity with your supervisor. Seek critical feedback on this future identity and the various experiences that are necessary to achieving it.

3. Broadening your professional network: Discuss with your supervisor the various networking relationships you should develop that will be of benefit to your immediate and future needs as a social worker.

(Continued)

(Continued)

4. Continuing education opportunities: Review potential continuing education opportunities that will be of value to both your immediate and future needs as a social worker. Depending on your state's licensing laws, you may also be required to complete a certain number of hours of continuing education in order to maintain your license. You can focus these on subjects that will assist you in meeting your learning goals.

5. Review of cases: Share how you have handled particular cases or problems in your practice. Review decisions that you thought were both successful and unsuccessful. Case discussions are a tool that encourage open reflection and can help you uncover things you did well (or not so well), understand why what you did was important, and think about what you can do with what you learned in future situations. Case reviews also provide you and your supervisor with an opportunity to identify ethical challenges and/or dilemmas that may need further discussion/exploration. Ask your supervisor to think aloud about how he or she might have handled these cases to better understand the thought processes involved in expert decision making.

Mentorship

At this point, it is important to differentiate *supervision* from *mentorship*. While we consider supervision to be a primary mechanism for providing important learning opportunities to advance your core social work skills, a mentor serves a slightly different yet overlapping function. Foremost, you are not required to have a mentor to practice social work, but nearly all social work positions require some type of supervision. Similar to a supervisor's role, a mentor's role is one of education, guidance, and support, but the scope of the role is different—that is, the supervisor provides guidance on issues related to your current job or practice, whereas a mentor often helps with career planning, taking into account both your personal and professional life. In this sense, the mentor helps with the long-term navigation of your career and work-life balance.

Because mentors are typically not connected to your current organization or position, you have significantly more control in selecting a mentor. You are not required to have a mentor, and you are certainly not limited to having only one. Ideally, a mentor should be able to cover the full realm of professional issues that you face while having the capacity to help you think through their impact on your personal life. In certain circumstances, you may choose to have more than one mentor, although you need to ensure that sufficient time is devoted to the development and maintenance of the professional relationship.

The relationship with a mentor must be built on open communication and mutual respect. It is advisable to take time when selecting a mentor, getting to know not only her or his professional expertise but also her or his style of communication, history of mentorship relationships, and availability of time. When establishing a mentor relationship, goals for the relationship should be established. As with supervision goals, they should allow for outcomes to be monitored and discussed at regular intervals. Because this relationship extends beyond the organization or workplace, the relationship can often be more personal. The mentorship meetings can also be less formal, taking place outside of the workplace. Even though the meetings are informal, it is important to remain clear about the goals and purpose of the relationship.

Remaining Current With the Research

We live in an age of information, and the majority of our research is delivered electronically. In fact, so much research is being produced that it can feel overwhelming to try and remain current with everything there is to know. Furthermore, remaining current with the research after you graduate is complicated by limited access to key information sources. Nevertheless, it is difficult to be fully engaged in the process of lifelong learning without a commitment to remaining current with the best available and most relevant research. Doing so requires strong skills to effectively and efficiently identify the research that can inform your current practice. Furthermore, an awareness of the latest research and social work innovations can also help shape your future identity.

As a social work student, you likely have access to a wide range of journals and databases that are critical to your professional development. The reality is that many of these resources will not be available to you after you graduate. This is a problem, but it is one that can be overcome with a few different strategies involving technology. In this section, we focus on two particular strategies that we think are essential for remaining current with the literature—as a student and as a professional social worker. These strategies involve the use of open access journals and really simple syndication (RSS).

Open Access Journals

Professional journals are expensive, which is the reason why social service agencies that employ social workers do not maintain regular subscriptions to a range of journals that are relevant to the services they provide. Fortunately, the field of social work is seeing a growing number of open access journals. Open access journals are free of charge and free of most copyright and licensing restrictions (Suber, 2012). This means that a significant amount of professional literature is currently available outside of the traditional subscriptions—and the availability of this professional literature is constantly increasing. Open access journals are funded using a different business model than traditional subscription-based journals. Readers who are interested in learning more about this business model can find excellent information on Wikipedia, which is also considered a form of open access information.

Provided in the companion website to this book, you will find a list of links to open access journals in social work and related disciplines. Of course, similar to subscription-based journals, you will need to be a good consumer of research in open access journals. Nonetheless, they represent a key resource as part of a broader lifelong learning strategy. We encourage you to spend some time with this list of journals and review the contents of the journals to determine what journals you may consider following over time. You can use these journals as a primary avenue for accessing professional social work literature.

It should be noted that open access journals are part of a broader philosophy and movement to make information more available to the general public. Thus, federal agencies that provide funding for social work and related research are also requiring researchers to make research available through open access mechanisms. For example, all research that is funded by the National Institutes of Health (NIH), which is a major funding source for many areas of social work research, must be made available in an open access mechanism within one year of publication in an open access journal. Provided in the companion website is a videocast demonstrating how to obtain this research, as these studies are likely to be published in traditional subscription-based journals.

REFLECTIVE LEARNING ACTIVITY

1. Review the companion website to find a list of open access journals. Peruse the journals that appear most relevant to your own training needs and interests as well as the needs of the agency where you are doing your internship. Try to identify at least three journals that you can follow regularly over time. Plan on sharing one of these journals with your supervisor by adding it to your supervision agenda. Show your supervisor how you accessed the journal and why you think this particular journal is relevant to your practice.

2. Conduct an Internet search to locate other open access journals that are not found on the companion website. Add these journals to the list of journals that you plan to follow over time.

Really Simple Syndication (RSS)

While open access journals are a source of information, RSS is a tool for accessing information. It can be used to access information from subscription-based journals, open access journals, and other information sources relevant to social work practice, although the total amount of information that you can retrieve using this tool will ultimately be determined based on whether the information source is subscription-based or open. RSS is used to pull information from various websites that regularly update the information that is available. The easiest way to conceptualize RSS is in the form of a single electronic magazine or newspaper that you create. It is customizable because it allows you to specify the information sources to be included in this electronic magazine, and you are free to add and exclude information sources as you like. The information is continually updated when new information becomes available—and it is done automatically. Thus, it can be highly efficient and effective in providing you with new information. Provided below are further details on using RSS technology. In the companion website, you will find specific demonstrations on setting up and using an RSS reader.

Overview of RSS Readers

To use RSS, you will need a reader, also referred to as an *aggregator*. Readers can be installed on personal computers and mobile devices. We recommend the use of freely available readers (e.g., Feedly) rather than fee-based readers, although this is ultimately a personal decision that will be determined by resources, skills, and usage. An RSS reader will pull new information automatically for you from the various sites that syndicate information using RSS technologies. This is very different from the typical method of visiting each site of interest or having information sent to your e-mail. While the use of e-mail alerts is certainly a way of being notified when new information is available, the problem with this strategy is that the e-mail alerts can easily be buried among all the other notifications you receive. More importantly, the RSS reader helps you organize the new information when you want it, and it is stored in a place that will not get mixed up with your other communications.

Obtaining and Using RSS Readers

If you are not already familiar with RSS, this discussion of RSS may seem a bit complicated, but the required skill level is no different from that of e-mail. So let's focus on the essentials in order to make it practical for you. Your first step is to obtain an RSS reader. You may already have immediate access to an RSS reader if you use a common e-mail system such as Google or Yahoo. You can do a simple Internet search for free RSS readers or refer to the companion website for other options. Again, it is strongly recommended that you begin with one of the many available free readers.

Once you have acquired a reader, you need to begin populating it with sources of syndicated content. The syndicated content we will focus on in this chapter is used to inform social work practice. If the journals are *gated*—require a paid subscription to access—you typically can obtain only the journal abstracts on your reader. However, even though you cannot obtain the entire article, a well-written abstract from a quality journal can provide you with essential information about the study and the relevant findings. With open access journals, the RSS feeds can provide you with the abstract and typically a link to the full text of the article.

Now you have to identify the syndicated content on a website. Before doing so, it is important to emphasize that not all websites or professional journals have syndicated content, and if they do, the format and the amount of syndicated information is likely to differ across your target sources. The standard indicator of RSS on any given website is an orange square icon that has a circle in the bottom left corner and two arches above the circle (see Figure 12.1). If an icon is not listed, then you may see a text link for RSS, RSS feed, or XML link. You then click on the icon or text link, which lets you add the

Figure 12.1 Really Simple Syndication (RSS) Icon

feed to your reader. The companion website provides videocasts that show a few technical steps to adding, deleting, and reading RSS feeds.

At this point, we encourage you to familiarize yourself with this technology. With any technology, you will go through a process of adoption. For the adoption process to be most successful—that is, for it to become a regular part of your work routine—it is important that you work with the technology on a regular basis and try to solve problems early in the process. We hope that you come to a point with this technology that you not only rely on it as a way to efficiently and effectively retrieve useful information but that you also regularly update the syndicated content, selecting new content to best meet your needs and excluding content that you find irrelevant. You should also look at the other features that your selected reader may offer, including tagging and starring articles that you find of interest.

REFLECTIVE LEARNING ACTIVITY

1. Go to the companion website and complete the RSS training and then set up an RSS reader.

2. Check whether RSS feeds are available for the online journals you identified in the earlier reflective learning activity. Subscribe to those journals that offer the RSS feed.

3. Identify other subscription-based journals that are relevant to your area of practice and subscribe to the RSS feeds if available.

4. Identify other information sources relevant to your area of practice and subscribe to the RSS feeds if available.

Licensure

Social workers are commonly employed in positions that require the individual to have a current social work license. The rules and regulations can vary significantly across states, so it is beyond the scope of this chapter to provide a full description of the licensure you may be required to obtain. It is strongly recommended that you begin looking at issues of licensure before you graduate with your social work degree. You will want to sort through what type of licensure you need to obtain as well as the process for obtaining the license. It is likely that you will be required to take a national exam that is administered by the Association of Social Work Boards (ASWB). Again, it is important that you determine the exact requirements for the state in which you will be working, because licensure requirements differ across states. The best way to locate this information is to find the website of the social work licensing board of the specific state in which you will be working as opposed to a blog or website of another organization or person. In other words, you want to review the specific rules for your state. With respect to licensure, it is essential that you have a file that contains all of your critical documents, especially any continuing education information that may be required. Although the administrative process can be tedious, you will be able to navigate the system more effectively and efficiently by having all of your documents organized.

With respect to examinations, students (and graduates) are faced with the issue of having to prepare for the licensure examination. No clear rules or guidelines exist with respect to how much one ought to study or whether taking a licensure preparation course is warranted. At minimum, you should become familiar with the structure of the exam (e.g., how it is administered, time limit, number of questions, question types, score needed to pass, content areas). Persons who take the exam without any advance knowledge of the structure almost always do poorly. Those who have delayed taking the exam following graduation will likely need to invest more time in licensure preparation materials or possibly a course compared to a recent graduate, given that their academic knowledge isn't nearly as fresh. Also, be sure that you consider test accommodations if you have a disability that might negatively impact your score or if English is your second language. Each state has its own rules and regulations regarding test accommodations, so it is important that all requests are made through the respective state board of social work as opposed to the ASWB.

Continuing Education

Continuing education is an obvious and required part of ongoing professional development in social work as well as a critical ingredient in lifelong learning. Like all learning opportunities, continuing education courses, workshops, and lectures should be selected with care, especially because of the variability in their quality. Given the numerous opportunities that are available, it is important to be deliberate and strategic in your selection. Provided below are a number of suggestions that you should consider:

1. Does the learning opportunity address a specific learning need that is part of your short- or long-term learning goals?

2. What are the qualifications of the instructor and the background that qualifies him or her as an expert on the topic?

3. To what extent is the training grounded in the best available evidence?

4. Will the training apply toward any type of licensure or certification you are seeking?

When considering training opportunities, be sure to give attention to opportunities that are delivered in a traditional in-person format as well as those that are provided online. In fact, numerous free high-quality training opportunities are provided online (refer to the companion website for links to such trainings).

Professional Social Networks

Virtually every aspect of social work relies on some type of network relations. Thus, it is important that you don't underestimate the value of networks in the practice context or in your own process of lifelong learning. In fact, network relations are among the most important factors in opening new career opportunities. Consider the classic study "The Strength of Weak Ties" (Granovetter, 1973). Granovetter studied the effects of weak and strong ties within an individual's social network. *Weak ties* refer to those relationships that were at least at an acquaintance level but were absent of a strong personal connection, such as a close friendship. *Strong ties* refer to those relationships that involved a strong personal connection.

A key finding of this research was that jobs were more likely secured through weak ties than strong ties—a finding that still holds true today. This finding is explained by the fact that our closest friends tend to also be friends with each other, thereby producing a rather circumscribed set of network connections. Our weak ties tend to be disconnected with each other but actually extend the overall reach of our network.

The influence of network ties extends beyond employment purposes. For example, the adoption of innovations and evidence-based practices involves influential opinion leaders within social networks. Social networks are also the primary mechanism for the sharing of resources. And the benefits of diversity can only be realized by having connections with many different people of varying backgrounds. From this perspective, your social networks are important to both your current and future identity as a social worker in a variety of ways. While there are obvious benefits of establishing and maintaining strong network ties, do not underestimate the importance of developing and maintaining a large number of weaker ties within your network.

REFLECTIVE LEARNING ACTIVITY

Review the following ideas for developing professional network ties. Consider how they could be of benefit to you as a student in addition to when you are a practicing social worker. Expand the list and share your ideas with other students to develop a comprehensive list.

1. Reach out to other agencies that provide services related to your current area of social work.

2. Establish a professional social media presence.

3. Explore with your supervisor and mentor the various relationships you may establish through their networks.

4. When attending trainings, conferences, or other functions that bring together professionals in your area, appropriate time to meeting others and letting them know who you are and the work you do.

CONCLUSION

The purpose of this chapter is to orient you to the concept of lifelong learning—the process of self-directed and individualized learning over the life span. You will encounter a vast array of educational opportunities following graduation. We encourage you to be active and strategic in your decision making in order to maximize the gains for both your career and your clients. We use the concepts of your current and future identity as a way to guide your selection of opportunities. This involves bringing clarity to your current knowledge and skill set as well as projecting yourself into the future to think about your desired life as a social worker. By having a clear idea of where you currently are and where you want to be, you are better positioned to select the opportunities that will bridge this gap. We encourage you to think broadly about lifelong educational opportunities. Some of the key lifelong learning strategies we suggest include the use of supervision and mentorship, remaining current with the best available evidence, broadening your social network, and carefully selecting continuing education classes.

REFERENCES

Granovetter, M. S. (1973). The strength of weak ties. *American Journal of Sociology, 78*(6), 1360–1380.

Suber, P. (2012). *Open access overview*. Retrieved January 17, 2013 from http://bit.ly/oa-overview

Index

ABCDE Multiple Perspectives Framework, 66–68
ABC model, 154–155, 158, 161
  cognitive behavioral therapy and, 161–167
  extinction, 167
  functional analysis and, 171
  punishment, 166–167
  reinforcement, 163–166
ABCT Association for Behavioral and Cognitive Therapies, 173
AB design, 222–223
abstracts/abstraction, 51, 156
accomplishment questions, 86
acculturation, 207–208
acquisition of skills, 40, 42
acting, 183–184
action, 92–94
  plan of, 48–49, 84
  taking, 118
activation, 87
active intervention, 144–145
active listening, 88
active problem solving, 185–186
actual reinforcer, 163
Adams, R., 24
adaptable intervention, 144
administrative records, 232
advocacy, 3
affirmation, 91–92
Affordable Health Care Act, 198, 200, 220
Agency for Healthcare Research and Quality (AHRQ), 37
aggregator, 247
Alegría, M., 25–26, 87
Alle-Corliss, L., 214
Alle-Corliss, R., 214
alliance building, 96
American Psychiatric Association, 41, 122
Andrews, G., 153

answerable questions, 46–47
antecedent, 151, 155, 161
APA Presidential Task Force on Evidence-Based Practice, 37
appraisal/appraising, 48–49
assessment, 40–41, 199, 228
  bio-psycho-social-spiritual perspective on, 104, 110–112, 120
  comprehensive, 132–133
  cultural, 122–123
  defined, 102–110
  Diagnostic and Statistical Manual of Mental Disorders and, 122–123
  mandated reporting responsibilities for, 119–122
  multidimensional functioning and, 105–108
  of options, 66–67
  problem-based approach to, 104
  purposes of, 102
  resiliency approach to, 104, 108–110
  role of, 102
  screening tools for, 112–119
  strengths-focused approach to, 104, 108–110
  suicide risk, 112, 117–119
  systemic approach to, 108–110
  trauma, 119–122
Association of Social Work Boards (ASWB), 71, 249
attainable goals, 141
attentive listening, 88
automatic thoughts, 151–152
autonomy, 61, 63
available evidence, 47–48
avoidant approach, 183

balance, 111–112
Baldwin, S. A., 210
Barnett, J., 72
Barter, K., 132

Barth, R. P., 30
baseline, 161
Beauchamp, T. I., 61
Beck, A. T., 228
Beck Depression Inventory, 223, 228–229
Beevers, C. G., 157–158
behavior, 161–162
    adjusting, 160
    cognitive behavioral therapy, aspects of,
        160–161
    defined, 161
    goals of, 141
    representative, 227–228
    unethical, 74–75
behavioral counts, 227–228
behavioral theory, 161
being mindful of the process, 66–67
beliefs, 151, 155, 161
    core, 152–153
    structure of, 151–153
beneficence, 61, 63
best available evidence, 48
best research evidence, 37–39
biases, 40, 156, 229
Bickman, L., 132
bio-psycho-social-spiritual assessment/
        perspective, 104, 120
bio-psycho-social-spiritual history summary,
        110–112
Bisson, J., 39
blame, 156
Blogger, 72
body-mind-spirit social work, 111–112
Bogardis, J., 171
Bond, G. R., 48
Borduin, C., 193–194
boundaries of professional, 60
brainstorming for solutions, 185–186
Brendel, D. H., 72
Brendel, R. W., 72
Breton, M., 38
Brown, G. K., 228
Bufford, R. K., 72
Burnette, B., 140

CAGE questionnaire, 224
Canino, G., 25–26
care management approaches, 198–200
care manager, 198
care navigator, 198

Carroll, K. M., 168–169
case management approaches, 198–200
case manager, 198
causal chain, 135–136
Centers for Disease Control (CDC), 37
Chan, C. L. W., 104, 108, 110–111
Chang, K. B. T., 72
change goals, 134–142, 224. See also Goals
change planning/plans. See also Goals
    collaborative development of, 131–132
    core principles of, 129–134
    defined, 129
    flexible, 133
    informed by comprehensive assessment,
        132–133
    intervention and, 142–145
    program-driven, 130–131
    tailored, 130–131
    understood and personally meaningful to
        client, 133–134
    written, 145–146
changing families, 205
Childress, J. F., 61
Chorpita, B., 31
Churchill, R., & Wessely, S., 39
Clarke, S., 132
classical conditioning, 161
Client-Oriented Practical Evidence Search
        (COPES), 29–31
clinical hypotheses, 171
clinical/practice expertise, 38–44
    assessment and, 40–41
    decisions and, 40–46
    diagnosis and, 40–41
    diversity and, 40, 43
    interpersonal expertise and, 40, 42
    intervention planning and, 40–41
    research evidence and, 40, 42–43
    resources and, 40, 43
    self-reflection and, 40, 42
    service planning and, 40–41
    skill acquisition and, 40, 42
Cochrane Collaboration, 51
cognitions, 151, 158
Cognitive and Behavior Practice, 173
cognitive behavioral therapy (CBT), 149–150
    ABC model and, 161–167
    behavioral aspects of, 160–161
    belief structure and, 151–153
    cognitive aspect of, 151–153

cognitive restructuring and, 153–160
functional analysis of, 170–171
as integrative framework, 168
ongoing professional development and, 173
practice of, 168–169
skills training and, 171–172
structural features of, 169–172
Cognitive Behaviour Therapist, The, 173
Cognitive Behaviour Therapy, 173
cognitive errors, 156, 172
cognitive restructuring, 153–160.
    See also Thinking/thoughts
of behavior, 160
defined, 153
of interpretations, 153–158
co-leadership, 215
collaborative approach, 131–132
collaborative development, 131–132
collaborative helping map, 83–84
collaborative partnership, 80, 82
collectivity, 23
common factors, 30–31
common practice elements, 30–31
community domains, 26–27
compassion, 61, 63
competence, 60–62
complex intervention, 143
complex reflections, 88–89
comprehensive assessment, 132–133
concept, 7–8
confidentiality, 69–70
Confidentiality of Alcohol and Drug Abuse Patient Records, 70
confirmation bias, 40, 156, 229
conflict of interest, 60
conscientiousness, 61, 63
consequences, 151, 155, 161, 163
constructed scales, 229–230
constructive approach, 183
consultation, 66–67
consumers as experts, 80, 82
contemplation, 92–94
continuing education, 249–250
continuous reinforcement, 165
core beliefs, 152–153
core principles of change planning/plans, 129–134
Council on Social Work Education (CSWE), 17

Council on Social Work Education Educational Policy and Accreditation Standards (CSWE–EPAS), 4–5, 24, 52
couples, working with, 210–211
Cournoyer, B. R., 42
Cowger, C. D., 132
critical thinking, 4–5
critical values, 61–63
Cross, K. F., 140
Crowe, T., 132
CRUfAD Clinic, 191
cultural assessment tools, 122–123
Cultural Formulation Interview (CFI), 123
Cunningham, P., 193–194
current professional identity, 238–239

Daguio, E. R., 60
Daleiden, E., 31
data, 230–233
Deane, S., 132
DeBonis, J., 94
decisions
    defined, 8
    documentation of process for, 66–67
    ethical making, 66–68
    making, 40–46
    rationale for, 8, 40, 43–44
description questions, 86
development
    collaborative, 131–132
    of groups, 211–215
    ongoing professional, 173
    of professional identity, 240
Devereaux, P., 44
diagnosis, 40–41, 123
Diagnostic and Statistical Manual of Mental Disorders (DSM-5), 41, 103, 122–123
dialogue reflections, 91–92
Diamond, G. M., 210
dichotomous ratings, 225
dichotomous thinking, 156
DiClemente, C. C., 92
difference questions, 86
dignity of the person, 61–62
discernment, 61, 63
discrepancies, 90–91
Dishion, T. J., 136
disputation of cognitions, 158
distal goals, 135–136
distortions, 156, 172

diversity, 40, 43
documentation of decision process, 66–67
double-sided reflections, 89
DuFour, R., 140
duration, 161–162
duty to warn, 69–70
dynamic flow, 111–112
Dysfunctional Attitude Scale (DAS), 157–158
D'Zurilla, T. J., 172, 182–183

easy goals, 139
ecological context, 45–46, 207–208
ecological systems perspective, 20–24
eco-map, 112–115
educational goals, 141
educational workshop, 189–190
effectiveness, 185–186, 219
emotional well-being, 109
empathic responses, 89
empathy, 88–89, 90–91
empirical research, 220
empowerment, 24–25, 87, 205
encounters, poor clinical, 26–27
engagement, 199
engagement and relationship-building skills
    alliance building and, 96
    approaches that impact, 85–86
    emphasizing collaboration to improve
        follow-through, 87–92
    pathways to, 82–84
    Stages of Change Framework and, 92–95
    values guiding, 80–82
environments
    context of, 26–27
    families, interaction in, 206
    work, 20–24
e-portfolio, 238–239
equifinality, 20
Escudero, V., 210
ethical decision making, 66–68
ethical dilemmas, 61
ethical principles, 58–63
ethical responsibilities, 63–66
ethics, 4
Ethics in Social Work Practice statement,
    18–19
evaluation, 199, 200
evidence
    appraising, 48
    available, 47–48

best available, 48
best research, 37–39
decisions based on, 50–51
research, 40, 42–43
evidence-based intervention, 143–144
evidence-based practice (EBP), 4
    best research evidence and, 37–39
    clinical/practice expertise and, 39–44
    defined, 37–44
    to evidence-informed practice, 52
    individual and family values/preferences,
        38, 44
    in social work profession, 44–52
    steps in applying, 46–50
    transdisciplinary model of, 45–46
evidence-informed (EI) practice, 52
    ecological context for, 45–46
    perspectives of, 29–31
experts/expertise
    clinical/practice, 38–44
    consumers as, 80, 82
    families as, 80, 82
    interpersonal, 40, 42
extinction, 167

Facebook, 71–74
Falicov, C. J., 206–207
families
    changing, 205
    conceptualization of, 205
    defined, 205
    empowerment of, 205
    environments, interaction in, 206
    as experts, 80, 82
    life cycle of, 207–208
    network map for, 114–115
    organization of, 207–208
    relationships with members of, 208–209
    skills need when working with, 205
    social work's mission in working with,
        205–206
    work models of, 209–210
Family Educational Rights and Privacy Act
    (FERPA), 70
Family Psychoeducation: Training Frontline Staff
    (SAMHSA), 80
family values/preferences, 38, 44
Fields, S., 132
Finn, J., 18
fit factor mapping tool, 195–197

fixed-interval reinforcement, 165–166
fixed-ratio schedule, 165
flexible change planning/plans, 133
Flickr, 72
focal values, 61–63
Fonagy, P., 37
Ford, J., 120
formation, 211–213
fortune telling, 156
Frahm, K. A., 129
Frankel, A., 198
Franklin, C., 85
frequency, 161–162
Friedlander, M. L., 210
Fristad, M., 191
functional analysis, 170–171
functioning and wellness screening tools,
    112–119
   eco-map, 112–115
   genogram, 112–114
   social network map, 112, 114–117
   suicide risk assessment tool, 112, 117–119
future professional identity, 239

Gambrill, E., 69–70, 80, 102–103
Garvin, C. D., 205, 211
gated journals, 247
Gelman, S., 198
generalist social work practice, 1–3
generalizable intervention, 143
generalizable knowledge, 7–8
generalizable skills, 7–8
generalizablility, 7–8, 139
generalized anxiety disorder (GAD), 191
genogram, 112–114
Germain, C., 22
Gibbs, L., 29
Gingerich, W., 85
Gitterman, A., 22
Glasziou, P., 29
global focus, 3–4
goals
   attainable, 141
   behavioral, 141
   distal, 135–136
   easy, 139
   educational, 141
   generalizablility of, 139
   impairing, 139
   importance to client, 138

   intermediary, 134–136, 146
   measurable, 140–141
   outcomes of, 136–137
   processes of, 136–137
   proximal, 135–136
   questions on, 86
   relevant, 141
   safety, 137–138
   selection of, 137–139
   specification of, 139–142
   time bound, 141–142
   ultimate, 134–136, 146
Goldberg Arnold, J., 191
Google, 72, 217
Google Reader, 247
Goscha, R. J., 109
Graham, J. R., 132
Granovetter, M. S., 250
Greene, G. J., 83
groups
   development of, 211–215
   leading, 211–215
   skills needed when working
     with, 211
Guseh, J. S., 72
Guyatt, G., 44

Halford, W. K., 210
Hall, P., 224
Handelsman, J. B., 132
Haynes, R. B., 29, 37, 44
Health and Psychosocial Instruments, 229
Health Insurance Portability and
   Accountability Act (HIPAA), 70
Heatherington, L., 210
Heller, N., 22
Henggeler, S., 193–194
Hepworth, D., 21, 88–89, 99
hope, 80, 82
hopelessness, 118–119
Houston-Vega, M. K., 60
Hudson, R., 24–25
human relationships, 61–62
Hyer, K., 129

iatrogenic effects, 38, 136
impairing goals, 139
impulsive approach, 183
individual and/or family/small group system,
   20–24

individual factors context, 26–27
individual values/preferences, 38, 44
inferences, 233
informed consent, 60, 69–70
Institute of Medicine, 37
instruments, 228
integrity, 61–63
intended reinforcer, 163
intermediary goals, 134–136, 146
intermittent reinforcement, 165–166
International Association of Social Work with
    Groups, Inc. (IASWG), 211
International Federation of Social Workers
    (IFSW), 16, 18–19, 59
International Statistical Classification of
    Diseases and Related Health Problems
    (ICD-10), 103, 122–123
interpersonal expertise, 40, 42
interpretations, 153–158
intervention, 146, 199
    active, 144–145
    adaptable, 144
    case/care management approaches to,
        198–200
    complex, 143
    evidence-based, 143–144
    generalizable, 143
    measurement following, 222
    Multiple-Family Psychoeducation Program
        for, 191–193
    multisystem approaches to, 193–197
    office-based, 169
    online psychoeducational modules
        for, 191
    outcome monitoring following, 222
    planning for, 40–41
    problem-solving approach to, 182–186
    psychoeducational approach to, 187–189
    research on, 48–49
    resource sensitive, 143
    selection of, 142–145
    simple, 143
    skill-focused, 142
    Substance Abuse and Mental Health Service
        Administration Evidence-Based Toolkit
        for, 189–190
inventories, 228

Jacobson, M., 18
joining, 189–190

Journal of Cognitive and Behavioral
    Psychotherapies, The, 173
justice, 61, 63

Karver, M. S., 132
Kelly, James, 138
Kessler, R. C., 130
Kimerling, R., 120
knowledge, 7–8, 30–31
Kroenke, K., 112

larger community systems, 20–24
Larsen, J., 21, 88–89, 99
latency, 161–162
Lazarus, A., 140
leading groups, 211–215
Lee, J., 24–25
Lee, M. Y., 83, 104, 108, 110–111
Leffler, J., 191
Lehavot, K., 72
Lehmann, P., 109
Leo, G. I., 171
Leung, P. P. Y., 104, 108, 110–111
level of functioning, 129
licensure, 248–249
life cycle of family, 207–208
lifelong learning
    concept of, 237–238
    continuing education and, 249–250
    defined, 237
    framework for, 237–238
    licensure and, 248–249
    mentorship and, 244–245
    process of, 237
    professional identity and, 238–240
    professional social networks and, 250–251
    research and, 245–248
    supervision and, 241–243
life model of social work practice perspective,
    20–24
lifetime questions, 224–225
LinkedIn, 72, 74
listening, 88, 90–91
Lukens, E. P., 187
Lynch, R. L., 140

Madsen, W., 83
magnification, 156
magnitude, 161–162
maintenance, 92–94

malpractice, 74–75

managed care coordinator, 198

mandated reporting responsibilities, 119–122

manualized evidence-supported treatments
(MESTs), 30–31

maturity, 211–213

Mayfield, D., 224

McCollum, E., 85

McCord, J., 136

McFarlane, W. R., 187

McLeod, G., 224

McMinn, M. R., 72

measures/measurement
accuracy of tools for, 224–225
behavioral counts for, 227–228
constructed scales for, 229–230
dichotomous ratings as, 225
following intervention, 222
of goals, 140–141
monitoring records and, 225–226
outcome, 224
process, 224
questions for, 234–235
repeated, 222–223
standardized, 228–229, 234–235
types of, 225–230

Medicaid, 129

Medicare, 129

mental health, 140

Mental Measures Yearbook, 229

mental status examination (MSE), 123

mentorship, 244–245

meta-analyses, 51

metaphors, 89

Meyer, B., 157–158

migration, 207–208

Miller, I. W., 157–158

Miller, W. R., 90

mind reading, 156

Mini-Mental State Examination
(MMSE), 123

minimization, 156

mission of social work profession, 17–18

monitoring records, 225–226

moral principles, 61–63

motivational enhancement therapy, 90–91

multidimensional ecosystemic comparative
approach map (MECAmap), 207–208

multidimensional functioning (MDF), 105–108

multifinality, 20

multiple family/caregiver group (MFG)
sessions, 189–190

Multiple-Family Psychoeducation Program
(MF-PEP), 191–193

multisystem approaches, 193–197

multisystemic therapy, 193–194

narrative, 146

NASW Technology Standards, 71

National Association of Cognitive-Behavioral
Therapists, 173

National Association of Social Workers
(NASW) Code of Ethics, 4, 17–18,
58–75, 138, 219
confidentiality and, 69–70
ethical decision making and, 66–68
ethical principles of, 58–63
informed consent and, 69–70
malpractice and, 74–75
privileged communication and, 70
professional use of self and, 75
purpose of, 58–63
self-determination and, 68–69
social media and, 71–74
social workers core values/concepts in,
58–63
standards of, 63–66
technology and, 71–74
unethical behavior and, 74–75

National Center for Trauma
Informed Care, 119

National Guidelines Clearinghouse, 51

National Institutes of Health (NIH), 37, 51,
235, 246

National Registry of Evidence Based Practices
and Programs (NREPP), 210

negative punisher, 166

negative reinforcer, 163–164

neighborhoods, 20–24

Nezu, A. M., 172, 182–183

Nezu, C. M., 182–183

Ng, S-M., 104, 108, 110–111

non-maleficence, 61, 63

Norcross, J. C., 92

Nuehring, E. M., 60

Nussbaum, A. M., 122–123

Oades, L., 132

OARS, 91–92

observation, 231–232

obstacles, 84
office-based intervention, 169
O'Hare, T., 105
Olatunji, B., 183
O'Neill, J., 140
ongoing professional development, 173
online psychoeducational modules, 191
open access journals, 50–51, 245–246
open-ended questions, 91–92
operant conditioning, 161
operationalizing, 227
options, 66–67
original research, 51
Otto, M., 183
Ouimette, P., 120
outcome. *See also* Outcome monitoring
  defined, 217
  evaluating, 49–50, 66–67
  of goals, 136–137
  measures of, 224
outcome monitoring. *See also* Measures/
   measurement
  benefits of, 219–220
  data for, 230–232
  inferences and, 233
  intervention and, 222
  overview of, 219–220
  principles of, 221–225
  as program evaluation, 221
  purpose of, 219
  quality of, 233
  research on, 220–221

Parental Kidnapping Prevention
  Act (PKPA), 70
parent leaders, 187
Patient Health Questionnaire (PHQ-9), 112
peer advocates, 187
personal choice, 80, 82
personal network map, 114–115
Pescosolido, B., 25–26
Pfizer, Inc., 112
physical well-being, 109
Pilkonis, P. A., 157–158
plain language summaries, 51
planning/plans. *See also* Change
   planning/plans
  for intervention, 40–41
  pre-group, 211–212
  service, 40–41

plan of action, 48–49, 84
policy directives, 30–31
Pollack, M., 183
poor clinical encounters, 26–27
positive punisher, 166
positive reinforcer, 163–164
post-traumatic stress disorder
  (PTSD), 120
Poulin, F., 136
Powers, D., 72
practice expertise, 38–40. *See also* Clinical/
  practice expertise
practice principles, 30–31
precontemplation, 92–94
pre-group planning, 211–212
preparation, 92–94
Primary Care Post Traumatic Stress Disorder
  Screen (PC-PTSD), 120
principal diagnosis, 123
Prins, A., 120
privacy, 60
privileged communication, 70
problem-based approach, 104
problems, 182, 185–186
problem solving, 182–186
  avoidant approach to, 183
  components of active, 185–186
  constructive approach to, 183
  impulsive approach to, 183
  objectives of, 183
  SOLVE model for, 183–184
  SSTA model of, 183
  structured, 172
problem statement, 146
process measures, 224
Prochaska, J. O., 92
professional boundaries, 60
professional identity, 238–240
professionalism, 60
professional social networks, 250–251
professional social work values, 58–63. *See also*
  National Association of Social Workers
  (NASW) Code of Ethics
professional use of self, 75
program-driven change planning/plans,
  130–131
program evaluation, 221
proximal goals, 135–136
psychoeducational approach, 187–189
psychological well-being, 109

PubMed, 51, 235
punisher, 166
punishment, 166–167

quality of outcome monitoring, 233
quantity, 233
questions/questionnaire
    accomplishment, 86
    answerable, 46–47
    CAGE, 224
    description, 86
    difference, 86
    goal, 86
    lifetime, 224–225
    measures/measurement, 234–235
    open-ended, 91–92
    right, 87–88
    scaling, 86
    socratic, 158–160
    standardized, 157–158

Rapp, C. A., 109
reactive tools, 171
Readiness to Change Ruler, 95
really simple syndication (RSS), 246–248
Reamer, F., 61, 67, 74
records
    administrative, 232
    monitoring, 225–226
    thought, 154–157
reflection, 88–89
    complex, 88–89
    dialogue, 91–92
    double-sided, 89
    simple, 88
reflective listening, 90–91
reinforcement
    ABC model, 163–166
    continuous, 165
    fixed-interval, 165–166
    intermittent, 165–166
    schedules of, 164–166
    variable interval, 166
reinforcer, 163–164
reinforcing stimulus, 163
relapse, 92–94
relationships. *See also* Engagement and
    relationship-building skills
    human, 61–62
    with members of families, 208–209

relevant goals, 141
reliability, 229
repeated measures/measurement, 222–223
representative behaviors, 227–228
research
    empirical, 220
    evidence on, 40, 42–43
    on intervention, 48–49
    lifelong learning, 245–248
    original, 51
    on outcome monitoring, 220–221
    scientific, 220
Research on Social Work Practice, 229
resiliency approach, 104, 108–110
resistance, rolling with, 90–91
resources
    to promote evidence-based decisions,
        50–51
    seeking and utilizing available, 40, 43
    sensitive intervention, 143
respect, 80, 82
response costs, 166
restricted pathways, 26–27
revision/revising, 172, 211–213
Richardson, S., 29
Richardson, W. S., 37
right question approach, 87–88
Rivas, R., 213
Roberts-DeGennaro, M., 198
Rogers, K., 120
rolling with resistance, 90–91
Rollnick, S., 90
Rooney, G., 21, 88–89, 99
Rooney, R., 21, 88–89, 99
Rose, S., 39
Rosenberg, W., 37
Roth, A., 37
Rounsaville, B. J., 169
Rowland, M., 193–194

Sackett, D. L., 37
safety goals, 137–138
St Vincent's Hospital, 191
satiation, 165
Satterfield, J. M., 45
scaling questions, 86
schedules, 164–166
Schoenwald, S., 193–194
schools, 20–24
Schuller, R., 171

scientific research, 220

screening tools for assessment, 112–119.
See also Functioning and wellness
screening tools

Seabury, B. A., 205, 211

Seabury, B. H., 205, 211

selective abstraction, 156

self-centering, 156

self-determination, 60, 68–69

self-efficacy, 90–91

self-reflection, 40, 42

self-reports, 230–231, 235

service, 61–62

    effectiveness of, 219

    planning, 40–41

Sexton, T. L., 137

Shadish, W. R., 210

Simmons, C. A., 109

Simon, N., 183

simple intervention, 143

simple reflections, 88

Simpson, D. D., 137

skill-focused intervention, 142

skills. See also Engagement and relationship-
building skills

    acquisition of, 40, 42

    empathy, 88–89

    families, need when working with, 205

    generalizable, 7–8

    groups, needed when working with, 211

    social, 172

    training, 171–172

slowing down, 183–184

SMART approach, 135, 139–142, 146.
See also Goals

Snyder, D. K., 210

Sobell, L. C., 171

Sobell, M. B., 171

social justice, 3, 61–62

social justice lens, 18–19

social media, 71–74

social network map, 112, 114–117

social network sectors, 26–27

social phobia, 36

social skills training, 172

social well-being, 109

Social Work, 229

social work abstracts, 51

social workers core values/concepts,
58–63

social work ethics, 4

Social Work Policy Institute, 37

social work profession/practice

    defined, 16–17

    evidence-based practice, 44–52

    generalist, 1–3

    mission of, 17–18, 205–206

    principles of, 16–17

    purpose of, 17

    social justice lens in, 18–19

    specialist, 2–3

    theoretical perspectives of, 20–32

    value guideposts for, 80–81

Social Work Research, 229

sociocultural perspective, 25–28

socratic questions, 158–160

solution-focused brief therapy (SFBT), 85

solutions

    brainstorming, 185–186

    defined, 182–183

    effectiveness of, 185–186

    evaluating, 185–186

    implementing, 185–186

    selecting, 185–186

SOLVE model, 183–184

specialist social work practice, 2–3

specific goals, 139–142

specific practice knowledge, 30–31

Spitzer, R. L., 112

SSTA model, 183

Stages of Change Framework, 92–95

standardization, 228

standardized measures/measurement,
228–229, 234–235

standardized questionnaires, 157–158

Standards for Technology and Social Work
Practice (ASWB), 71

Stanley, M. J., 42

statement of problem, 146

Steer, R. A., 228

stopping, 183–184

Straus, E., 29

Strauss, S. E., 37

"Strength of Weak Ties, The," 250

strengths-based approach, 104

strengths-focused approach, 108–110

stress management, 172

Strom-Gottfried, K., 21, 61, 66,
88–89, 99

Strong, D. R., 157–158

strong ties, 250
structured problem solving, 172
Suber, P., 245
subjective well-being, 109
Substance Abuse and Mental Health Services
    Administration (SAMHSA), 210
    Evidence-Based Toolkit, 189–190
substance use disorders (SUDs), 171, 173
Suicide Assessment Five-Step Evaluation and
    Triage (SAFE-T) tool, 118
suicide risk assessment tool, 112, 117–119
summarization, 91–92
Sung, S., 183
supervision, 241–243
support, 84
system, 26–27
systematic reviews, 51
systemic approach, 108–110

tailored change planning/plans, 130–131
taking action, 118
Tarasoff v. Regents of the University of California
    (1976), 69–70, 117
Taylor, L., 72
technology, 8–9, 71–74
termination, 211–213
texting, 72
theoretical perspectives, 20–31
    ecological systems, 20–24
    empowerment, 24–25
    evidence-informed practice, 29–31
    integrating, 31–32
    life model of social work practice,
        20–24
    of social work profession, 20–32
    socioculture, 25–28
theory, 4, 7–8, 161
therapy
    motivational enhancement, 90–91
    multisystemic, 193–194
    solution-focused brief, 85
thinking/thoughts, 183–184
    automatic, 151–152
    critical, 4–5
    dichotomous, 156
    identifying, 153–158
    inaccurate, 160
    objectively looking at, 158–159
    records of, 154–157
    unrealistic, 160

THIS WAY UP Clinic, 191
Thomas, K. S., 129
ties, 250
time bound goals, 141–142
tools
    accuracy of, 224–225
    cultural assessment, 122–123
    fit factor mapping, 195–197
    functioning and wellness screening, 112–119
    reactive, 171
    for screening, 112–119
    suicide risk assessment, 112, 117–119
Toseland, R., 213
transdisciplinary model, 45–46
trauma, 119–122
Trauma Events Screening Inventory (TESI),
    120–121
treatment, 50–51
    planning/plan for, 127, 145 (*See also* Change
        planning/plans)
Trepper, T. S., 85
trustworthiness, 61, 63
Tryon, G. S., 131
Tumblr, 72
Twitter, 72–73

ultimate goals, 134–136, 146
unethical behavior, 74–75
Uniform Child Custody Jurisdiction Act
    (UCCJA), 70
Uniform Child Custody Jurisdiction and
    Enforcement Act (UCCJEA), 70
U.S. National Library of Medicine, 51, 235

validity, 229
values
    critical, 61–63
    directives for, 30–31
    family, 38, 44
    focal, 61–63
    guideposts on, 80–81
    guiding engagement and relationship-
        building skills, 80–82
    individual, 38, 44
    professional social work, 58–63 (*See also*
        National Association of Social Workers
        (NASW) Code of Ethics)
    social workers core, 58–63
variable interval reinforcement, 166
variable ratio, 165

vision, 84
Vongxaiburana, E., 129

weak ties, 250
Weissman, A. N., 157
Weisz, J., 31
well-being, 109. *See also* Functioning and
    wellness screening tools
Wessely, S., 39
Whiston, S. C., 137

Williams, J. B., 112
Williams, S., 25–26
Winograd, G., 131
work environments, 20–24
working with couples, 210–211
work models of families, 209–210
worst, assuming the, 156
worth of the person, 61–62
written change planning/plans,
    145–146

About the Authors

Mary C. Ruffolo, PhD, LMSW, is a professor with the University of Michigan's School of Social Work. She teaches classes on topics related to assessment and interventions with children, adolescents, adults, families, and small groups. Dr. Ruffolo's research emphasizes the development, evaluation, and sustainability of evidence-based or evidence-informed practices in public behavioral health settings as well as in integrated health environments.

Brian E. Perron, PhD, is an associate professor with the University of Michigan's School of Social Work. He teaches classes on topics related to diagnosis and treatment of mental health and substance use disorders. Dr. Perron is also actively involved in research related to these topics, with an emphasis on clinical assessment, measurement, evidence-based practices, and predictive modeling.

Elizabeth Harbeck Voshel, LMSW, ACSW, is an associate clinical professor and director of field instruction with the University of Michigan's School of Social Work. She has been a leader in the School's integrative learning effort and teaches a capstone seminar. Elizabeth has presented nationally and internationally on field instruction curriculum and social work ethics and previously was employed for 22 years by the U.S. Department of Veterans Affairs.

⑤SAGE research**methods**

The essential online tool for researchers from the world's leading methods publisher

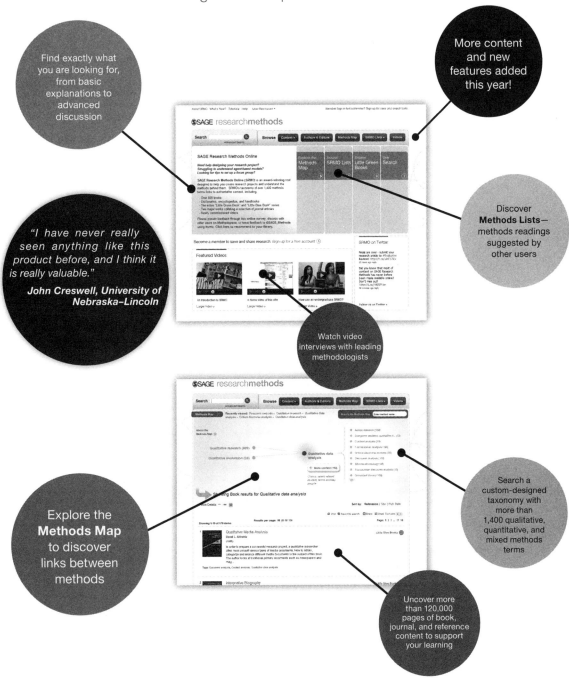

Find exactly what you are looking for, from basic explanations to advanced discussion

More content and new features added this year!

"*I have never really seen anything like this product before, and I think it is really valuable.*"

John Creswell, University of Nebraska–Lincoln

Discover **Methods Lists**— methods readings suggested by other users

Watch video interviews with leading methodologists

Explore the **Methods Map** to discover links between methods

Search a custom-designed taxonomy with more than 1,400 qualitative, quantitative, and mixed methods terms

Uncover more than 120,000 pages of book, journal, and reference content to support your learning

Find out more at
www.sageresearchmethods.com